语言思维与核心语法
LANGUAGE THINKING AND CORE GRAMMAR

沈朗浪 编著

浙江工商大学出版社
ZHEJIANG GONGSHANG UNIVERSITY PRESS
·杭州·

图书在版编目(CIP)数据

语言思维与核心语法 / 沈朗浪编著. —杭州:浙江工商大学出版社,2021.1
ISBN 978-7-5178-4301-6

Ⅰ. ①语… Ⅱ. ①沈… Ⅲ. ①英语—语法—中学—教学参考资料 Ⅳ. ①G634.413

中国版本图书馆 CIP 数据核字(2021)第012721号

语言思维与核心语法
YUYAN SIWEI YU HEXIN YUFA
沈朗浪 编著

责任编辑	张莉娅	
封面设计	沈　婷	
责任印制	包建辉	
出版发行	浙江工商大学出版社	
	(杭州市教工路198号　邮政编码310012)	
	(E-mail:zjgsupress@163.com)	
	(网址:http://www.zjgsupress.com)	
	电话:0571-88904980,88831806(传真)	
排　　版	杭州朝曦图文设计有限公司	
印　　刷	杭州高腾印务有限公司	
开　　本	787mm×1092mm　1/16	
印　　张	13.75	
字　　数	307千	
版印次	2021年1月第1版　2021年1月第1次印刷	
书　　号	ISBN 978-7-5178-4301-6	
定　　价	65.00元	

前　言

　　随着中国在义务教育阶段对英语教材的不断完善,语言学习的广度和深度得到了极大的提升。与此同时,教育工作者与越来越多受过高等教育的家长们,在学生和孩子的学习过程中,都在试图针对不同学习者的特点,为其找寻理解英语和提升学习质量的有效途径,以便其掌握语言,并在不同的语境中,能准确并顺畅地使用英语。

　　我们已经清醒地认识到,教育手段应该是多元化的,没有哪一种方法是可以做到对所有学生同时有效的,或者说是在语言教学方式中排名第一位的,笔者也深知并认同这一点。但是,我们也应该归纳总结语言学习的共性,尝试找寻一种能学好语言、相对有效并可推广的通用方法,这种学习模式不仅可以在语言能力突出的学生身上看到,同时也一直为先进的教育工作者所采用。作为老师,我们是否可以深入探讨并持续深化这一学习方法,结合具体教学工作,传授予学生,让其在未来脱离老师后还拥有自我教学和深化学习的能力呢? 作为学生,我们是否可以结合自身的领悟能力,反复摸索和实践该方式,将之培养成自己的学习习惯,在自学中强化与深化,引导自我不断提升和完善呢?

　　《中国英语能力等级量表》(China Standards of English,简称CSE)由教育部、国家语言文字工作委员会正式发布,已于2018年6月1日起正式实施。这是我国首个面向中国学习者的英语能力标准。《中国英语能力等级量表》分为九个等级。一、二级大致对应小学水平,三级对应初中,四级对应高中,五、六级对应大学,七级对应英语专业,八、九级对应高端外语人才。每个等级在听力、口语、阅读、写作、翻译、知识策略等方面,都有不同的要求。

　　本书以《中国英语能力等级量表》为指导思想,以三、四级语言能力为起点,通过学习和理解,要求读者达到六级语法能力和表述能力,并以七级语言能力为目标。三、四级语言能力要求学生能理解一般日常生活中和社交场合中常见话题的简单语言材料,获取特定或关键信息,抓住主题和主要内容,清楚他人的意图和态度,表达准确、清晰、连贯;五级要求学生能理解不同场合中一般性语言材料,把握主旨,抓住重点,明晰事实、观点与细节,领悟他人的意图和态度,能够在较为熟悉的场合就学习、工作等话题进行交流、讨论、协商,表明观点和态度,表达准确、连贯、得体;六级要求学生能理解多种话题(包括一般性专业话题)的语言材料,把握要点及其逻辑关系,分析、判断、评价材料中的观点、态度和隐含的意义,能在熟悉的学术或工作中参与多种话题的讨论,有效传递信息,比较和评析不同的意见,发表见解,表达连贯、得体、顺畅,符合相关文体规范和语体要求。七级要求学生能理解多种话题的语言材料,包括自己所学专业领域的学术性材料,准确把握主旨和要义,客观审视、评析材料的内容,理解深层含义,能就多种相关学术和社会话题进行深入交流和讨论,有效地进行描述、说明和解释、论证和评析,表达规范、清晰、得体、顺畅。

我们可以看到,语言等级达到六级时,符合文体规范和语体要求的重要性开始显现,对语法运用能力的要求提升到了一个全新的高度,要求能运用多种句式结构表达思想,能理解和掌握复杂句法结构的意义。在语言组构能力上,六级要求学生能理解语篇中复杂结构的表意功能,能运用常见的语法结构组织信息,层次清楚,能使用有效的衔接手段,提高表达的连贯性。因而六级能力标准将词法、句法的准确领悟和精确使用提到了一个显著的高度,语法的理解与否,以及能否准确使用,决定着语句的质量和表达的效果。本书要求读者在学习和掌握重点难点语法与 SDP 句型解构模式后,通过对语篇句型的解构,深度理解语法内在逻辑和运用场景,精确组构英语句型,在将语言能力提升至六级的同时,追求更具专业性、更为全面的七级语言水平。

通过探寻当前西方语言教学过程中的改变和《中国英语能力等级量表》对英语能力的详细要求,我们可以清晰捕捉到当前教育学家和语言学家对于英语语法重要性的重新探讨和认识。笔者通过结合自身在翻译学习中的理论基础和翻译实践中的心得体会,提出 SDP 句型解构模式,并尝试将该语法学习的方式更加清晰地介绍给大家,让持有相同观念的教师在教育过程中更加笃定,让认可该方法的学生更有恒心地坚持并执行,收获扎实的基本功。笔者希望重新唤醒大家对语法重要性的正确认知,戒骄戒躁,脚踏实地,并能格物致知,探究其规律,让语言运用的精确性犹如呼吸般自在。笔者相信,慢也是一种力量。

在我们深入探寻语法解构模式和重点难点语法总结归纳的过程中,由于笔者水平有限,难免产生错误纰漏,望广大读者批评指正。

目　录

第四章　语篇解构 / 128

第一章　语言思维

Section 1　语法的重要性

近些年,越来越多的老师和家长已然认识到语法的重要性和语法学习的宝贵性,西方国家在教学过程中也相较以往更加强调语法基础教学,试图在教学过程中增加词法和句法的分析讲解,让学生打下良好的语言基础。假如没有语法体系作为支撑,学生将在复杂句型的分析和高级句法的理解上,以及正式场景的表达运用上如履薄冰,犹如当前很多老师在学生口语对话中发现的那样,在没有系统学习国际音标的情况下,学生的口语发音很难不受影响。

在孩子低龄时期,语言学习常以培养兴趣、调动其积极性为主,让其融入英语氛围,沉浸于语言环境中积极探索与发现。而在中学阶段,探索语言规律,建立语言思维刻不容缓;教师若担忧语法的枯燥从而在教学中避讳语法解析,反而会耽误了学生在语言理解上的深度,阻碍其未来在语言钻研深度上的造诣。我们需积极探索,思考如何结合其他教育方法和自身优点,让学生逐步转变思维并注重语法规律,注重语言逻辑的训练,避免其对语法一知半解,遇到理解上的困难便时常解释"这是固定搭配"。

有些教师和家长可能会有不同意见,他们认为可以通过海量的听读,或者多读多背的方式,尽可能模拟西方国家的语言环境,通过语感训练,培养优良的运用能力。这个出发点是好的,但是这里涉及这样一个问题:西方孩子的英语环境犹如我们的中文环境,是一种母语语境,从小会有大量的传承、训练、校对和感知,同时这个过程会被不断加强和提升,因此其语言运用能力和语法逻辑能潜移默化地在多种场景下得到培养,但即使在此环境中,西方国家如今认为青少年的语法知识体系和语言使用的规范性也需要重新进行客观评估和认识。

我们再来谈一谈什么是真正的语感。要学好任何一门语言,我们可以鼓励学习者多读多背,但不是死记硬背。多读多背的核心是提高学习频率,在遗忘之前反复增加印象,增加学习材料的曝光率,提高大脑中的思考频率,增强记忆能力,达到熟能生巧、融会贯通,从而拥有对语言的感知力和把控能力,这就是所谓的语感。语感是一种感觉,但其实是一种反复自我体验后的体会心得,是一份经验的累积,这份经验让自己看到新的语言内容时能快速融入并逐句成体系地分析。因此笔者认为,语感不仅是一种感觉,更是一份经验,语感养成的背后是大量的思维训练,语言思维能力的培养需要语法的正确融合,因为语法是从语言中提炼出的规律,脱离了语言规律,学好英语、将英语运用得当是几乎不可能的。

笔者倡导中学阶段是语法学习的重要人生阶段。中学阶段(CSE 三、四级)的学生往往已经有了良好的思考能力和认知能力,同时该阶段的学生具备优异的记忆能力,处于逻辑思维得到升华的重要阶段。中学阶段的学生已经对英语有了一定的认知和理解基础,我们需着重思考如何结合自身优点,如何烘托课堂氛围,如何在调动学生思考能力的前提下,增加以语法为导向的句型解构分析,深度拆解词法句法原理,有效增加句型解构分析的频率。随着句型的不断改变,语法的不断积累,学生熟能生巧后运用语言的自信,才是其真正的信心来源。准确使用语言后产生的自信心催化其更深入探索语言规律的自信心,才是学生语言学习的核心自信,这是一种良性循环,也是语言精确使用、反复优化的开始。语法能力的提升有助于学生对语言准确性的把握程度,并可为日后更高层次的语言追求提供理论支持和学术支持。

Section 2 SDP句型解构模式

笔者提出的SDP句型解构模式,是自己所倡导并实践多年的语法教学和自我学习模式。它早已存在于无数中学与大学的授课过程中,笔者结合自身翻译与教学实践经验,现对该方法进行归纳总结并做简练表述,从而与各位深入探究其效用。

SDP(Sentence Deconstruction Pattern)句型解构模式,以分析解构语篇句型中的重点语法为导向,深度学习关键词法、句法,清晰句型结构,探究并归纳语法规律,从而使自己的思维逻辑与语法逻辑相契合,在语言运用表达过程中更加精准,并为高阶语言学习提供基础支撑。语言是语法的载体,英语的单位是句子,通过对句型结构和句法的准确分析,同时辅以高频的句型解构实践,可以解构分析并逐步累积重点语法板块知识,并且随着不同语法板块之间的搭配协作,从而加深对语法内在逻辑的理解并掌握各种语法的运用规律,达到语言表达过程中的精确应用。

句型解构模式并非对文章的每个句型做过度细致的语法分析,而是结合其他教学手段和学习方法,有意识地增加对句型中重点语法的思考和分析,结合学生理解和接受程度,由浅入深,锻炼逻辑思维和理解能力,以达到学以致用。笔者希望分享该方法的有效性,让教师坚定语法的重要性,结合自身特色,在教学中更有信心地利用该朴素的学习法则;让学生能够发掘自学潜力,了解语言规律,在学习中提升英语学术素养,做到基础扎实,运用顺畅。

同时,利用句型解构模式学习语法具有重要的实际意义。我们中大多数人在大学生涯,或走上社会岗位后,若没有选择英语相关专业或岗位,实际上会逐渐把英语置于相对次要的位置。这也是一个对语言慢慢生疏的阶段,若有朝一日他们有运用英语的需求,或是有重拾这门语言的冲动,那么曾经语法体系的完善,语法基础的扎实,将是他们快速回忆、适应、融入这门语言和最终实现自我学习提升的宝贵钥匙。

并且我们也能时常接触到一些朋友,他们有的生活在海外,有的在国内工作中需使用英语,通过多年的锻炼和经验积累,他们已有强大的感知力和深度的思辨力,能做到口语流利,交流自如。但在下笔写一封正式的英语邮件、一封正式的邀请信或者外贸的询盘时,心里便会知道自己写的句子有衔接等语法问题,虽未严重影响工作结果,但若能将语法精准运用,他们会求之不得。这是一类工作能力和思维能力都极为优秀的人群,若他们能在繁忙的工作之余,抽出部分时间有规律地接受一些语法训练和学习一些语法分析,结合工作中对英语的运用,他们就有能力通过自学而对自我的语言运用过程加以优化,故语言的层次会因句型得到优化而提升不少。因此以句子为单位,对关键语法进行解构分析的学习过程,是学习和理解语法、巩固和运用语法的有效路径。

Section 3 英语特点与SDP句型解构模式

深入对比汉语和英语的语言形式,我们能够发现,汉语和英语在使用过程中,其语句的衔接方式是极为不同的,这也是两门语言在形态上的主要差异之一。汉语是一门以意合为主的语言,而英语则是一门以形合为主的语言。

意合语言中,语句之间通过意义上下贯通衔接。我们在日常使用汉语时,只要稍加留意就能发现,汉语语句往往更注重内在语义的上下连贯,句子之间注重的是意义的契合,讲究语义的逻辑衔接,这是一种较为隐形的连接形式(Covert Coherence)。而且,汉语的语言文字没有明显的形态变化和丰富的词类区分,因此汉语使用过程中相对弱化了词法和句法的重要性,且汉语的词义极为丰富,字词的组合也相对自由。在意思的交流表达上,汉语的表达更注重且依赖语言环境,并非其语言本身的字句衔接形式,因此我们说中国是一个高语境文化的国家。我们更注重的是语境,而非语言本身的形式。

举个例子,汉语中的四字格是对意合形式的完美诠释,四字短语音律生动,言简意赅,是经过历史淬炼后的中文语义精华。如"不进则退",英文可译为"He who does not advance falls backward"或"Move forward, or you'll fall behind"。再如"物极必反",英文可译为"Once a certain limit is reached, a change in the opposite direction is inevitable"。汉语诠释了意合的言简意赅,注重语义,而英语诠释了形合的严谨衔接,更注重形式。

形合语言中语句之间遵循句法前后贯通连接。观察分析英语的语句就会看到,英语的句子内部以及句与句之间采用词法或句法手段相连,往往使用关系词或连接词等以便达到句子之间的衔接目的,有着严格且丰富的词类区分和句型结构,语言的使用对句法要求也更为严谨,对语言的形式更为讲究,这是一种较为显性的连接形式(Overt Coherence)。也就是说,英语更加注重语言结构的完整性与其形态上的严谨性,因此英语的语句在本质上决定了它对词法和句法的依赖性,语言表达的缜密程度也就离不开对语法的掌握程度,英语的精确表达是语义和语法结合的产物。

举个例子,"She was reading a book while I was watching TV."(她正在看书,我在看电视。),其中while是时间连词,意为"当……时",引导一个时间段;因此"我在看电视"是整个事情的时间背景,在此期间"她正在看书";同时was reading/was watching体现时态为过去进行时,是过去正在做的事情或一段时间内做的事情。因此英语语句的理解和表达,往往需要通过语句之间的衔接,理解英语语句需要通过分析句型以及其中的语法。再看此例,"If you don't like it, I'll not buy it."(如果你不喜欢,我就不买了。),其中if引导的从句是一个条件句,I'll not buy it是主句,前后语句在形式上紧密衔接。分析语法可以得出,这个if条件句是第一类if条件句,往往if条件句使用现在时,主句用将来时,第一类if条件句是非常有可能实现的一种假设情况。通过对两个简单的复合句分析,我们可以深感语法在英语运用中的地位。

总结以上汉语和英语在形态本质上的区别,我们可以深刻了解到,汉语更加注重语义和语境,需要通过语义和语境的分析体会,方能理解其表达的意思和逻辑,因此形散而神聚,或所谓的"以神御形"。语义的表达时常如中国古话所说的"只可意会,不可言传",因此汉语更加依赖意义进行表达,语法则处于相对次要的地位。英语的语句注重词句之间显性的连接,更重视连接的形式,往往通过主谓搭架,结构严谨,也就是所谓的"以形达意"。同时英语更注重句型结构的完整性,从句型结构的组成部分可以分析得出语义之间的内在关系。

现代语言学奠基人王力曾指出:"西洋语的结构好像连环,虽则环与环都联络起来,毕竟有联络的痕迹;中国语的结构好像无缝天衣,只是一块一块的硬凑,凑起来还不让它有痕迹。西洋语法是硬的,没有弹性的;中国语法是软的,富有弹性的。唯其是硬的,所以西洋语法有许多呆板的要求;唯其是软的,所以中国语法只以达意为主。"正如王先生进一步风趣的总结:"西洋语言是法治的,中国语言是人治的。"

是的,"西洋语法是硬的",学习英语最重要的基本功是深度学习语言结构和语法框架,积累语法知识。英语所要表达的含义,需准确安放在句型结构当中,从而拥有语法上的完整和语句上的严谨。结合英语形合特点与笔者下一篇所描述的翻译过程,我们便可清楚了解到,英译汉时,我们要先分析句子结构和形式,才能确定句子的功能和意义;而汉译英时,我们需要先分析句子的功能和意义,才能确定译文的结构和形式。

因此笔者认为,语法学习是根据形合语言特点,遵循英语语言本质的依势而行,以语言的单位——句子为基础的SDP句型解构模式,是深度理解语法逻辑,掌握并熟练运用语法进行精确重构,准确表达的有效实践,是一条通用并长期有效的学习法则。

Section 4　翻译过程与SDP句型解构模式

想要运用语言,首先需要学习该语言,如果将语言划分为一个个小的单位,对这些小单位加以研究并学习,分析、总结这些单位的规律,从而在需要使用语言时就可以正确组织并准确输出。那么,这个单位是什么?其实,语言的单位是句子,并非词,许多人往往误解这一点。我们在听、说、读、写过程中所使用的往往是句子的形式,句子表达完整的单位意思,而词则是翻译过程中的单位,翻译过程较为细化,需要精准到词的筛选和斟酌。

在如何以语言单位分析语句语法和累积经验之前,我们首先来看一看翻译的过程,因为翻译是语言运用的高级形式,而翻译的过程和笔者所倡导的SDP解构模式有异曲同工的契合点。翻译的过程涉及语言、文化、语境、审美、修辞等等多方面的综合能力。标准的

翻译过程,并非将原文(译入语)直接转换成译文(译出语),而是如下图所示:

```
        原文  ─────────────  译文
      (表层意义)              (表层意义)
        │  语                  ↑  语
     解 │  内               重 │  内
     构 │  转               构 │  转
        │  换                  │  换
        ↓                      │
      深层意义 ── 语际转换 ── 深层意义
```

图 1　翻译流程图

　　翻译的过程是理解和表达的过程,从语言学角度剖析,理解和表达的过程就是译者分析解构原文和整合重构译文的过程:第一步,Comprehension—Deconstruction;第二步,Representation—Reconstruction。

　　从翻译流程模型图中我们看到,原文不能直接转换成译文。第一次的语内转换是分析型的,译者通过分析解构原文含义,包括其背后的文化和语境等,确定其确切的含义;第二次语内转换是综合型的,译者在原文所表达的深层意义基础上,将其转换成以译文语言为基础的深层意义,并通过综合归纳比较,整合重构成最终的译文,并最大限度地保持与原文在形式和含义上的一致性。

　　从以上过程我们不难发现,最终译文的质量与对原文的分析解构过程息息相关。译者对原文深层意思把握的准确度,会直接影响重构过程中译文的准确性,而译者的语言功底,将会在重构时决定译文的质量。语言功底包含对语言的理解能力,展示了译者对语言的运用能力,译文语句的表达准确,离不开译者的语法功底作为支撑。若缺失语法这一基石,译文将漏洞百出,那么,严复先生对于翻译"信、达、雅"(忠实、通顺、文雅)的要求也将无从谈起,钱锺书先生对于翻译所提出的最高要求——"化境"标准更是无法企及。翻译涉及双语之间的交互,外语作为翻译的工作语言,好比工人手中的工具,译者如果没有坚实的语言功底,如丰富的英语词汇、熟练的词语搭配能力、准确的语篇解构能力以及译文重构所必需的语法素养等,是无法进行复杂的翻译实践的。

　　我们已然看到,解构能力和语法能力对于翻译而言十分重要,对原文的解构,决定着理解原文的深度,译者在重构过程中的语法能力,也决定着译文翻译的效果。翻译如此,语言学习亦是如此,英语学习中,对句型的解构和语法的积累,也决定着语法理解的深度和语言表达的效果。因此笔者所倡导的 SDP 句型解构模式,以实事求是的态度看待语法的重要性,正确摆正语法位置,通过解构句型,学习并积累语法,是提升语言能力的一条通用法则。

Section 5 说明

在进入第二章时态篇与第三章句法篇之前,有必要对本书做一个说明。本书定位为英语重点语法的深度解析,因此并非为一本语法大全。本书将重点针对语法中的难点篇章做解析,并结合具体例句进行呈现。归纳时态和句法的同时,在容易产生逻辑偏差的语法点上做编注,通过对语法的深度分析和运用举例,让读者建立语法思维、摸索难点语法规律。

时态和句法这两大方面是建立英语语言思维的重中之重。通过强化这两大语法板块,提升语言学习者的理解能力和掌握程度,便能为高阶段英语学习提供学术支撑。英语语句的使用通常离不开时态,好比我们离不开地心引力,语言的进步和提升,又离不开对句型种类与句子成分的学习和分析。因此,我们在这两章重点从学习语言思维最为关键的两大板块入手,深度探索语法含义和逻辑规律,体会语法的运用场景,提升时态和句法的理解深度。

语法是语言的组织规律,也是对语言规律的提炼,对语法规律的归纳总结能够加深对语言的理解并有效地建立语言思维,探索并遵循语言规律,从而才能在语言运用过程中逐步自我优化并越加精确,不断实现自我语言能力质的提升。

第二章 英语时态

表1 英语十六大时态

	一般	进行	完成	完成进行
现在	一般现在时 the Simple Present Tense	现在进行时 the Present Continuous Tense	现在完成时 the Present Perfect Tense	现在完成进行时 the Present Perfect Progressive Tense
过去	一般过去时 the Simple Past Tense	过去进行时 the Past Continuous Tense	过去完成时 the Past Perfect Tense	过去完成进行时 the Past Perfect Progressive Tense
将来	一般将来时 the Simple Future Tense	将来进行时 the Future Continuous Tense	将来完成时 the Future Perfect Tense	将来完成进行时 the Future Perfect Progressive Tense
过去将来	过去将来时 the Past Future Tense	过去将来进行时 the Past Future Continuous Tense	过去将来完成时 the Past Future Perfect Tense	过去将来完成进行时 the Past Future Perfect Progressive Tense

表2 英语十六大时态示例（以 study 为例）

	一般	进行	完成	完成进行
现在	study studies	am studying is studying are studying	have studied has studied	have been studying has been studying
过去	studied	was studying were studying	had studied	had been studying
将来	shall study will study	shall be studying will be studying	shall have studied will have studied	shall have been studying will have been studying
过去将来	should study would study	should be studying would be studying	should have studied would have studied	should have been studying would have been studying

▶ Part 1 一般时 ◀

Section 1 一般现在时(the Simple Present Tense)

在英语学习的初级阶段,语法通常较为基础,一般现在时往往是英语学习者最早接触的时态之一,但也正因如此,许多学生便会在潜意识里将一般现在时视为一个简单的入门时态。其实不然,正因为一般现在时是一个通用时态,所以其具有广泛的使用场景和重要的语法意义。空杯心态,有助于我们冲破思维定式,从而探索语法深度。

1 语法概念

一般现在时,表示经常性、习惯性、规律性的动作或现在存在的状态,或用来表示客观事实或普遍真理。

通俗地理解,就是描述一种平时所处的状态或平时的一些特征,这个动作或状态可能会经常发生,或具有一定的普遍规律。也就是说,一般现在时通常表达当下的一种情况或目前的一种常态。使用时需要注意的是,如果句中的谓语动词是实义动词,当主语为非第三人称单数时,谓语用动词原形即可;而当主语为第三人称单数时,谓语动词则用第三人称单数形式,也就是常说的"三单"或"单三"形式。比如:

①I go running everyday.

我每天都去跑步。(描述经常性、习惯性的动作,谓语用动词原形)

②He has a younger brother.

他有一个弟弟。(描述平时的状态,谓语用第三人称单数形式)

③The moon goes around the earth.

月球绕地球运行。(描述科学事实、客观的规律,谓语用第三人称单数形式)

2 语法基本运用

(1)一般现在时表示主语的特征、性格、职业、能力等,通常用来描述现在或现阶段的动作或所处的状态

①I'm a student from China.

我是一个来自中国的学生。

②She's an expert at music.

她擅长音乐。

③He works for a big firm.

他在一家大公司工作。

④Do you really love her?

你真的爱她吗？

⑤Are you busy now?

你现在忙吗？

⑥You look great.

你看起来很棒。

（2）一般现在时表示经常性、习惯性的动作或状态

该用法是一般现在时的重要用法之一，通常和 always、usually、often、sometimes、occasionally、never、rarely、every day、on Monday afternoons、once a month 等表示频率的副词或时间状语连用。

①I go to work at 8 o'clock everyday.

我每天8点去上班。

②He often smiles in the company.

他在公司里经常微笑。

③She visits her parents twice a week.

她每周去看望父母两次。

④He is always forgetful.

他总是很健忘。

⑤Children are usually keen on cake.

孩子们通常喜欢吃蛋糕。

注：即使不用表示频率的时间状语，一般现在时也能表示经常性、习惯性的含义。比如：

①He goes to work by subway.

他乘地铁上班。

②He doesn't speak clearly.

他说话不清楚。

③Do you drink?

你喝酒吗？

④I like drinking beer.

我喜欢喝啤酒。

（3）一般现在时表示客观事实或普遍真理

①Beijing is the capital of China.

北京是中国的首都。

②There are 24 hours in a day.

一天有24个小时。

③1 plus 3 makes 4.

1加3等于4。

④The sun rises in the east.

太阳从东方升起。

⑤Light travels faster than sound.

光比声音传播得快。

⑥Experiences broaden one's horizon.

经历开阔人的眼界。

（4）在含宾语从句的复合句中,如果从句所述内容是客观真理,主句即使是过去时,从句的谓语动词也用一般现在时

①The teacher said Japan is to the east of China.

老师说日本在中国的东面。

②He told me that Summer comes after Spring.

他告诉我春天过后就是夏天。

③The geography teacher taught us the earth turns from west to east.

地理老师曾教我们,地球自西向东转。

（5）表示"拥有、认知、情感"类的动词,通常属于静态动词,用一般现在时

①He owns a big house.

他有一个大房子。

②I don't remember him any more.

我不记得他了。

③My son likes oranges.

我儿子喜欢吃橙子。

注:表示存在和拥有(have、belong、own、exist)、心理状态(love、like、know、remember、forget、understand、want、hope、think、wonder)、感官感觉(see、hear、smell、taste、feel)等表示相对静止的动词,被称为静态动词(Static Verb)。这类动词往往描述平时的状态,通常不用进行时;而绝大部分动词皆可表示事物的运动状态,属于动态动词(Dynamic Verb),既可用于进行时,也可用于非进行时。

（6）一般现在时用在复合句的从句中,代替一般将来时,表示将来的动作

①If you invite him, I will not go with you.

如果你邀请他,我就不和你一起去了。(用于条件状语从句)

②Remember to lock the door when you leave home.

出门的时候,可别忘了锁门。(用于时间状语从句)

③I'll do exactly as she says next time.

下次我会完全按照她说的去做。(用于方式状语从句)

④She will finish her homework earlier than I do.

她会比我早完成作业。(用于比较状语从句)

⑤I'll tell you where you sleep tonight.

我会告诉你今晚睡在哪里。(用于宾语从句)

⑥There will be people who appreciate her.

会有人欣赏她的。(用于定语从句)

(7)一般现在时表示安排或计划好确定将要发生的动作

常用于 go、come、leave、arrive、start、begin、return、sail、fly、meet 等表示地点转移或动静状态过渡的动词。

①She leaves for the UK tomorrow.

她明天动身去英国。

②He comes back at 9 o'clock tonight.

他今晚9点回来。

③How long does she stay in this country?

她将在这个国家待多久?

④The visa expires in five days.

签证5天后到期。

⑤The trade talks take place next week.

贸易谈判将于下周举行。

注:除以上表示地点转移或状态变化的动词,其他动词也可表示一般将来时,描述即将出现的情况或事先已安排好的事情。比如:

①I make my announcement tomorrow.

我明天宣布我的决定。

②The meeting is at 8:30 tomorrow morning.

明天早上8点半开会。

③Do you have classes on weekends?

你周末有课吗?

④I hope she likes the gift.

我希望她会喜欢这个礼物。

（8）一般现在时用于 here/there 开头的句子，表示现在正在发生的动作

①Look! Here she comes.

　　快看！她来了。

②There comes the train.

　　火车来了。

③There she sits.

　　她正坐在那里。

（9）一般现在时用于表示过去的动作或状态，通常指离现在较近的过去

①What does she tell you?

　　她跟你说了什么？

②I hear that your brother has graduated.

　　我听说你哥哥毕业了。

③You hurt her feelings.

　　你伤了她的感情。

（10）戏剧旁白、电影介绍、文字说明和内容简介等通常用一般现在时

①Scene I (Jessie and Judy are at a grand New Year's ball.)

　　场景一（杰西和朱迪在一个盛大的新年舞会上。）

②The medicine may cause the following side effects.

　　该药物可能会导致以下副作用。

③ *Forrest Gump* is a film directed by Robert Zemigis, starring Tom Hanks, Robin White and others, and released in the United States on July 6th, 1994.

　　《阿甘正传》是由罗伯特·泽米吉斯执导的电影，由汤姆·汉克斯、罗宾·怀特等人主演，于1994年7月6日在美国上映。

④This novel describes the current living situation of black people in the United States.

　　这部小说描述了黑人在美国的生活现状。

（11）格言、谚语、名人名言等通常用一般现在时

①From small beginnings come great things.

　　伟大始于渺小。

②Life is but a span. Seize the day.

　　人生苦短，把握当下。

Section 2 一般过去时(the Simple Past Tense)

1 语法概念

一般过去时表示过去某一时间发生的动作或存在的状态,或表示过去习惯性、反复性的动作。

一般过去时通常由谓语动词的过去式体现,规律动词的过去式通常在动词原形后加-d或-ed,不规则动词的变化形式则通过其自身的语音,特别是元音的变化来实现,此类动词也被称为强势动词。强势动词通常是将古英语动词的不规则变化形式一直沿用至今,是一般过去时学习过程中需重点掌握的谓语动词形式。只有通过找寻其变化规律,并结合发音,才能更好地积累并巩固强势动词用法。

2 语法基本运用

(1)一般过去时,表示过去某个特定时间发生的动作或存在的状态

常与表示过去的时间状语连用,如 yesterday、just now、a few minutes ago、3 days ago、last night、the other day、once upon a time、then 等;也可用于表示现阶段的时间状语,描述说话之前发生的动作,如 this morning、today 等;也可与表示过去时间的从句连用。

①I graduated from college in 2011.

我于2011年大学毕业。

②My son was born 2 years ago.

我儿子两年前出生。

③What did the boss say to you just now?

刚才老板对你说了什么?

④I met her at the mall the other day.

前几天我在商场遇见她。

⑤I was late for work again today.

我今天上班又迟到了。

⑥She didn't speak much after she went abroad.

她出国后就不怎么说话了。

(2)一般过去时,表示过去习惯性或经常性发生的动作

常与 sometimes、always、never、usually、once a week、every Wednesday 等表示频率的时间状语连用。

①He always kept his promise and never ate his word.

他总是信守诺言,从不食言。

②He often showed up when I needed advice most.

　　他经常在我最需要建议的时候出现。

③She went to see his teacher occasionally after graduation.

　　毕业后,他偶尔去看望他的老师。

（3）若要强调过去的习惯或状态现在已经不存在时,需用 used to 表达

①I used to run marathons twice a year.

　　我过去常常一年跑两次马拉松。

②My grandfather used to buy me a beautiful cake on my birthday.

　　爷爷过去经常会在我生日时给我买一个漂亮的蛋糕。

③He used to eat a lot.

　　他过去吃得很多。

　　　注:used to 和 would 都可表示过去经常性、反复性、习惯性的动作,常可以互换。但 used to 通常强调过去的行为与现在的对比,该状态或动作现已终止;would 在该用法中表示单纯的过去习惯,有可能会再次发生,常与表示频率的副词连用。对比如下:

①When he was young, he would go fishing with his father.

　　在他年轻的时候,他常和父亲去钓鱼。

②When he was young, he used to go fishing with his father.

　　在他年轻的时候,他常和父亲去钓鱼。(强调现在不和父亲去钓鱼了)

①She would often go for a stroll in the park in the evening.

　　她过去常常在晚上到公园里散步。

②She used to go for a stroll in the park in the evening.

　　她过去常常在晚上到公园里散步。(强调现在不去公园散步了)

如需表示过去持续的状态或情况,通常用 used to,不用 would。比如:

①There used to be a big tree here.

　　这里过去有一棵大树。

②She used to own a great deal of money.

　　她过去有很多钱。

③He used to live with his grandparents.

　　他过去和他的祖父母住在一起。

④He is no longer what he used to be.

　　他已不再是过去的他了。

（4）一般过去时用于时间、条件状语从句等复合句的从句中，表示过去的将来会发生的动作

①He said he would inform us immediately if he heard any news about her.

　　他说如果听到任何有关她的消息，就会立即通知我们。

②He would inform us immediately as soon as he heard any news about her.

　　他一听到她的任何消息就会立即通知我们。

③He said he would inform us immediately when he heard any news about her.

　　他说他一听到有关她的消息就会立即通知我们。

（5）一般过去时，表示过去持续的动作或状态

该用法相比于过去短时间的动作或状态，其持续时间相对较长，通常没有具体的时间状语，可根据上下文判断。

①Where did you live when you were young?

　　你年轻时住在哪里？

②I grew up in the countryside with my grandparents.

　　我跟随爷爷奶奶在乡下长大。

③He felt different from others and was depressed for years.

　　他觉得自己和别人不一样，在好几年中都备感压抑。

④She spent her youth in England.

　　她的青春是在英国度过的。

（6）一般过去时，可以叙述过去接连发生的事件

通常没有表示过去的时间状语，而是根据上下文判断。

①He got up, brushed his teeth, washed his face, shaved his beard, put on his suit, and drove his car to work.

　　他起床后，刷牙、洗脸、刮胡子，然后穿上西装，开车上班去了。

②She went into the garden, watered the flowers, trimmed the branches, and then lay down on a chair, started to read a novel.

　　她走进花园，浇花、修剪树枝，然后躺在椅子上，开始读小说。

③He came up to me, sat down, said hello, and began to borrow money from me.

　　他走到我跟前，坐了下来，打了招呼，便开始向我借钱。

一般过去时对现在有无影响：

一般过去时描述的是过去的状态或过去的动作，通常这个动作或状态是过去发生的并已经结束的，只描述过去的一个事实。如果仅从概念看，一般过去时似乎与现在无关，对现在不造成影响，如需强调对现在的影响，我们会使用现在完成时。但假如有这样一个例子：今天我上班迟到了，老板问我为什么迟到，我对老板说："Sorry, I was drunk last night."很显然,今天上班迟到是由于"昨晚我喝醉了",昨天的事件和现在是存在联系并对现在造成影响的,那么我们又该如何正确理解所谓的"一般过去时对现在没有影响"呢?

正确的理解是,一个过去发生的动作,不论使用一般过去时或现在完成时,都可能对现在造成影响。选择一般过去时说明说话者只是纯粹地描述过去的事件,并不想强调对现在的影响;选择现在完成时则说明说话者想要强调或暗示一些其他含义。因而选择何种时态通常是说话人的主观意图,区别在于是否想要强调这个动作对现在的影响。比如:

①Did you read the book?(单纯询问是否读过)

②Have you read the book?(强调是否了解书的内容)

③I went to Shanghai with my friend.(陈述过去的一个事实)

④I have been to Shanghai with my friend.(强调有过该经历和体验)

动词时态的常用判断方式:

英语的时态是通过谓语动词的变化来体现的,通过谓语动词的形态变化,表达动作发生的时间(现在、过去、将来、过去将来)及所处的状态(一般、进行、完成、完成进行)。因此准确判断时态以及正确使用动词的变化形式在时态和句法学习中具有不可替代的重要意义。我们通常会借助习题,学习并强化动词和时态的使用,在具体审题、做题的过程中,可以根据句中的时间状语来确定其时态,称之为"依时定态",因为时间状语通常是判断时态的重要标志。但并非所有的句子都有清晰的时间,此时则需根据上下文语境分析判断时态,被称为"依境定态";最终根据时态的确定而准确变化谓语动词所需的形式,也被称为"依态定形"。

Section 3 一般将来时(the Simple Future Tense)

在英语学习中,我们往往会忽视一些基本语法的重要性,比如时刻都在运用的基本时态。我们需要更正以前的观念,即基础并非就能和简单画等号。正因为基础,往往该语法的运用会十分广泛,因而我们更需扩充对基础语法的认知维度,认识并掌握其不同深度的使用方法。

1 语法概念

一般将来时表示将来发生的动作或存在的状态,或将来某段时间内经常性的动作或状态。

说到一般将来时,我们许多人脑海中首先浮现的是will或be going to的用法,但将来时的表述方式远不止这些,与此同时,will与be going to的用法实际上也较为丰富,同时又存在多个区别。我们在以下探索一般将来时多种表达方式的同时,重点讲解并归纳will与be going to的用法和区别。

2 语法基本运用

（1）be going to 表示将来

表示按照主观意图,事先经过考虑,打算或决定将要做某事

①What are you going to do after work?

下班后你打算做什么?

②I'm going to have hot pot after work.

下班后我要去吃火锅。

③They are going to buy the wedding rings tomorrow.

他们明天要去买结婚戒指。

表示按计划、安排将要发生的事情

①The film is going to be shown next week.

这部电影将于下周上映。

②The World Expo is going to be held next month.

世博会将于下个月举行。

③The afternoon meeting is going to discuss the company's layoffs.

下午的会议将讨论公司的裁员问题。

表示有迹象将要发生的事,多指主观上有根据的判断和预测

①It looks like it's going to snow.

看起来要下雪了。

②The clouds are gathering. It's going to rain.

乌云密布,要下雨了。

③It is going to be difficult to find a job this year because of the impact of the pandemic.

由于疫情的影响,今年找工作将会很困难。

④I'm not feeling well. I think I'm going to be sick.

我感觉不舒服。我想我要生病了。

（2）will 表示将来

当主语是第一人称 I/we 时,常用 shall,否定式为 shan't;will 可用于所有人称,否定式为 won't。shall 较为正式且略显过时,在美式英语中已很少使用,但在英式英语中仍较为普遍。

预言将来会发生的事情,表示自己知道或认为会发生的事或请他人预言将来会发生的事

①I think she'll be a qualified teacher one day.

我认为她总有一天会成为一个合格的教师。

②He and I will be colleagues soon.

他和我马上会成为同事。

③I'll probably work late tonight.

我今晚可能会加班。

④When will you retire?

你什么时候退休？

⑤Where will you be this time next month?

下个月的这个时候你会在哪里？

预测将来发生的动作或状态,单纯表示将来的事实,不会以人的意志为转移

①I will be 35 years old next year.

明年我就35岁了。

②A running track will be built in the park.

公园里将建一条跑道。

③Next month will be the Spring Festival.

下个月就是春节了。

④There will be a big change in this city.

这个城市将会有很大的变化。

说话的当时突然决定去做某事,未经过事先考虑和安排,will作情态动词含有主观意志

①She has arrived, I'll pick her up at the station.

她已经到了,我去车站接她。

②It's raining hard, I'll take an umbrella.

雨下得很大,我拿把伞。

③I'll take care of the baby while you're away.

你不在时,我来照顾孩子。

表示意愿,如建议、请求、允诺、决心、提议、邀请、命令等情态意义

①Don't worry, I'll take you to the airport tomorrow.

别担心,我明天送你去机场。(表示允诺)

②Will/Would you give me a hand?

你能帮我一下吗?(表示请求)

③Shall/Will we have dinner together tomorrow evening?

我们明天晚上一起吃晚饭好吗?(表示提议)

④Will/Would you come and have dinner with us tomorrow?

你明天来和我们一起吃晚饭好吗?(表示邀请)

⑤You will assemble at the playground at 6 o'clock tomorrow morning.

你们明天早上六点钟在操场集合。(表示命令)

⑥I won't agree with his ideas.

我不同意他的想法。(表示拒绝)

⑦I will do as best as I can.

我会尽我所能。(表示决心)

⑧If you'll take care of my dog, I'll be grateful.

如果你愿意照看我的狗,我会很感激的。(条件句中的will表示意愿)

注:shall常用于第一人称后,但也可用于第二、第三人称,强调说话者的允诺、警告、指责、命令、威胁等或在条约、规章中表示义务或规定等。比如:

①You shall be kicked out if you're not diligent enough.

如果你不够努力,就会被开除。(警告)

②You shall pay him back tomorrow.

你明天把钱还他。(命令)

③She shall get a pay raise next month.

下个月她将加薪。(允诺)

④He shall be punished soon.

他很快就会受到惩罚。(威胁)

⑤The specific process of use shall be in accordance with the instructions.

具体使用过程按说明书执行。(规定)

可以表达猜测的情态意义,意为"想必、大概、我猜测、我料想"

①This will be the book he's looking for.

这本可能是他正在找的书。

②Go and ask her. She will know.

去问问她。她也许知道。

③I think we'll be home by this time tomorrow.

我想明天这个时候我们就到家了。

④I suppose he'll have been off work now.

我想他现在已经下班了。

表示规律性、习惯性或典型性的动作或表示客观事实

①Life will have ups and downs.

人生总会有起起落落。

②She will smile at you when you say hello to her.

当你跟她打招呼时,她会对你微笑。

③Sometimes he will sit in his study all day.

有时他会整天坐在书房里。

④Man will die without air.

没有空气人就会死。

有时可表示能力

①This cup will hold 500 milliliters of water.

这个杯子能盛500毫升水。

②Will the raft bear the weight of us?

这个木筏能承受我们的重量吗?

③Will it work?

这样能行吗?

④That will do if you can't rent a better car.

如果你租不到更好的车,那辆也行吧。

在正式的书面语(如官方消息、气象预报等)中通常用 will

①It will rain tomorrow in Hangzhou with the temperature from 18 to 22 degrees Celsius.

杭州明天有雨,气温18℃到22℃。

②The United States will formally impose sanctions on Iran starting next month.

美国将于下个月开始正式对伊朗实施制裁。

③China will advance reform and opening up in the financial sector.

中国将推进金融领域的改革开放。

(3)用一般现在时,表示事先安排或计划好确定将要发生的动作

参考一般现在时中此用法。

①When does the show begin?

演出什么时候开始?

②It's Friday tomorrow.

明天是星期五。

③The plane takes off at 5 o'clock.

飞机五点钟起飞。

④The crew set out tomorrow.

船员们明天出发。

(4)在复合句的从句中,通常用一般现在时,表示将来的安排

参考一般现在时中此用法。

①If you are in trouble, I will help you.

如果你有困难,我会帮助你。

②They will move into the city when their baby is born.

孩子出生后,他们将搬到城里去。

③After I finish writing, I'm going to travel.

书写完后,我要去旅行。

(5)用现在进行时,表示按计划或安排即将发生的动作

参考**现在进行时**中此用法。

①The bus is leaving soon.

公交车马上就要开了。

②They are meeting at the station tomorrow.

他们明天在车站见面。

③I'm having dinner with John on Monday.

我星期一要和约翰一起吃晚饭。

④What are you doing tomorrow afternoon?

你明天下午做什么?

(6)祈使句可表示将来的意义

①If he calls, please let me know.

如果他打电话来,请告诉我。

②Please wait for a while until he finishes his meeting.

请您等他开完会。

③Don't smoke when there are kids.

有孩子的时候不要吸烟。

(7)情态动词可表示将来的意义

①Can he recover next month?

他下个月能恢复吗?

②If he comes, you may ask him.

如果他来了,你可以问他。

③You must be surprised when you see his change.

看到他的变化时,你一定会很惊讶。

④You may see him tomorrow.

你明天能见到他。

（8）其他用于表示将来时的常用短语

be to do表示事先安排、准备要做某事,也可表示指责、义务、约定等

①You are to explain what's going on here.

　你必须解释这里发生了什么。

②As far as I can see, all of them are to blame.

　在我看来,他们都有责任。

be about to表示即将、立刻做某事

①We are about to go back home.

　我们马上要回家了。

②He is about to embark on his political career.

　他即将开始他的政治生涯。

be due to表示"定于……"开展某个事项

①The flight is due to arrive at 7 o'clock.

　飞机预计7点到达。

②The library is due to open on September 5th.

　图书馆定于9月5日开放。

be going to与**will**的用法区别:

（1）be going to常表示近期即将发生的事情,will可表示未来相对较远时间发生的事情

①She is going to write a book soon.

　她打算近期写一本书。(时间较近)

②She will write a book in the future.

　她将来要写一本书。(时间较远)

（2）be going to和will都可表示说话人的意图,但be going to表示经过事先计划或考虑的动作或安排,will表示在说话时临时想到的意图或临时做出的决定

①I'm going to pick her up at the airport tomorrow.

　我打算明天去机场接她。(事先经过考虑的决定)

②I'll pick her up at the airport tomorrow.

　我明天会去机场接她。(事先未经考虑的决定)

（3）be going to含有"准备、计划、考虑、决定"等主观意图,而will可用来单纯叙述未来客观的情况

①I'm going to visit our teacher.

我打算去拜访我们的老师。(主观的打算)

②I will visit our teacher.

我将要去拜访我们的老师。(客观的事实)

（4）be going to 表示主观上判断将会发生的事情，will表示客观上势必会发生的事情。因此表达绝对确定的事情时，通常用will；强调主观的推测时，用be going to

①I broke his glasses, he's going to be furious.

我打破了他的眼镜，他会生气的。(主观上的推测)

②I broke his glasses, he will be furious.

我打破了他的眼镜，他会生气的。(客观上的预测)

（5）在复合句中，条件句中可用be going to，主句中则多用will

①If you feel sad, I will come and accompany you.

如果你感到难过，我会来陪你。(will用于主句)

②You'd better not touch the watch if you are not going to buy it.

如果你不打算买这块表，最好不要碰它。(be going to用于从句)

③If you are going to figure this out, I will help you.

如果你想弄清楚这件事情，我会帮你。(be going to用于从句，will用于主句)

（6）will通常用于较正式的文体中，be going to多用于口语中

①I'm going to a concert tomorrow.

我明天要去听音乐会。(较为口语化)

②The concert will be held next month.

音乐会将在下个月举行。(较为书面化)

Section 4 过去将来时（the Past Future Tense）

1 语法概念

过去将来时表示从过去的某个时间看将来要发生的动作或存在的状态。

2 语法基本运用

（1）was/were going to 表示过去的将来

表示过去计划要发生的动作或可能将发生某事

①She said she was going to move to a new house after she got married.

她说结婚后要搬到新家去住。

②After he returned to his hometown, his house was going to be renovated.

回到家乡后,他的房子要整修一下。

③It looked as if it was going to rain.

看起来好像要下雨了。

表示说话者过去的意图,曾打算或准备做但没有做到的事情

①I thought I was going to forgive him, but I didn't.

我原以为自己会原谅他,但实际上没有。

②We were going to Guangzhou by high-speed train, but in the end we went by air instead.

我们原打算乘高铁去广州,但我们改坐飞机去了。

③I was going to tell you the truth when you left.

你走的时候我原本正打算告诉你真相。

(2)would表示过去的将来

主语是第一人称I/we时,可用should;would可用于所有人称。

表示过去的将来会发生的动作或出现的情况

①She told us that she would not study abroad.

她告诉我们她不会出国学习。

②Linda said there would be a concert that night.

琳达说那天晚上有一场音乐会。

③He was six that year. He would go to primary school soon.

那年他六岁,即将上小学。

④They asked me when I should leave for London.

他们问我什么时候动身去伦敦。

用于虚拟语气中,表示非真实的动作或状态

①If I were you, I would apologize to her.

如果我是你,我会向她道歉。(与现在事实相反)

②If she were to come tomorrow, I should/would tell her about it.

如果她明天来,我就把这件事告诉她。(与将来事实相反)

③I wish the housing price would come down.

我真希望房价能降下来。(与将来情况相反)

would可表示过去习惯性的动作

①When it was fine, he would often went fishing by the lake.

以前天气好的时候,他经常去湖边钓鱼。

②She would always stay up late on weekends.

她以前在周末的时候总是睡得很晚。

③We would play together all day when we were kids.

当我们还是孩子的时候,整天在一起玩。

注:would作为will的过去式,可以表示单纯的过去习惯,但不强调该习惯是否已结束。请参考一般将来时中will的此用法,以及一般过去时中used to与would的用法对比。

would和will一样,可以表达猜测的情态意义,意为"想必、大概、猜测、料想"

①Judging by her skin, she would not be old yet.

从她的皮肤看,她应该还不老。

②It would be midnight when I left the company.

我离开公司时可能已经半夜了。

③I thought you would have finished your work by now.

我原以为你现在可能完成工作了。

(3)一般过去时用于时间、条件状语从句等复合句的从句中,用来表示过去的将来会发生的动作

参考**一般过去时**中此用法。

①I would tell her the good news as soon as she got home.

她一到家我就告诉她这个好消息。

②Whenever we had a problem, she would come to help us.

每当我们有问题时,她都会来帮助我们。

③Every time if we asked him, he would answer patiently.

每次我们问他,他都会耐心地回答。

(4)用过去进行时,表示按计划或安排过去将要发生的动作

通常与表示位置转移的动词连用,如come、go、leave、arrive、start等。参考**过去进行时**中此用法。

①We didn't know how many guests were coming to the concert.

我们不知道有多少客人会来听音乐会。

②I wondered whether you were leaving for Beijing.

　　我想知道你是否要去北京。

③No one knew when she was arriving.

　　没有人知道她什么时候到。

（5）其他用于表示过去将来时的常用短语

was/were to表示过去经事先安排,准备做某事

①I was to finish the paper within a week.

　　我得在一周内完成这篇论文。

②She was to help you, but you gave her the cold shoulder.

　　她本想帮助你,但你却对她很冷漠。

was/were due to do表示过去将定于……做某事

①The ship was due to set sail at dawn.

　　这艘船定于黎明启航。

②The marketing plan was due to last for one month.

　　该营销计划将持续一个月。

was/were about to表示过去即将、立刻做某事

①He had a feeling yesterday that something bad was about to happen.

　　他昨天感觉马上会有不好的事情要发生。

②He was about to go to bed when the telephone rang.

　　他正要上床睡觉,这时电话铃响了。

was/were on the point of表示过去正要做某事

①I was on the point of going out when you came.

　　你来的时候我正要出去。

②They were on the point of giving up when the project manager encouraged them.

　　当项目经理鼓励他们的时候,他们原本正准备放弃。

注:be about to do/be on the point of doing通常不与表示将来的时间状语连用,但后面可以接when引导的从句。

▶Part 2 进行时◀

Section 1 现在进行时（the Present Continuous Tense）

1 语法概念

现在进行时表示现在正在进行的动作或现阶段正在进行的动作与状态,由"be动词+现在分词"构成。

当现在进行时表示现在正在进行的动作时,是一个时间点的概念,强调此时此刻正在发生的动作。如图所示:

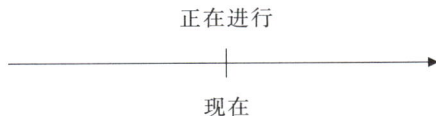

正在进行

现在

当现在进行时表示现阶段正在进行的动作时,是一个时间段的概念,强调目前一段时间内正在发生的事情,不一定指说话时正在发生。如图所示:

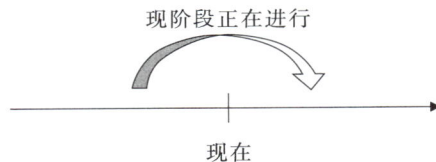

现阶段正在进行

现在

很多老师在教学过程中问学生"什么是现在进行时?",想必学生便会自信地回答:"现在正在进行的动作。"但随着学习阶段的推移,理解能力的提升,我们需要开始回顾并补充这些基本语法的其他主要用法,而现在进行时,是通常学生们容易低估的一个基本时态。通过以上对语法含义的分析,我们看到了现在进行时并非只是"现在正在进行的动作"这般简单,它也可以表示当前这段时间内的一个状态。比如:

①He is playing tennis with his friend now.

他现在正在和朋友打网球。

②Listen! She is singing a song.

听! 她正在唱歌。

③We are learning programming this semester.

我们这个学期正在学编程。

④We are working on a new project these days

这几天我们正在从事一个新项目。

注：①②描述的是现在正在发生的动作，强调动作现在正在进行中；③④描述的是当前一段时间内正在从事的事情，不一定指动作此时此刻正在发生。以上例句为现在进行时的两种基本用法，我们现在对该基本时态的主要用法做归纳。

2 语法基本运用

（1）现在进行时表示此刻正在发生的动作

常与表示现在的时间状语连用，如 now、right now、at the moment、just、still 等，或句中有暗示动作正在发生的词，如 look、listen 等。

①My mom is cleaning the living room now.

我妈妈正在打扫客厅。

②He is just talking to his friend.

他正在和朋友讲话。

③Listen! She is playing a tune on the piano.

听！她正在弹钢琴。

（2）现在进行时表示现阶段或当前一段时间正在进行的动作

常用的时间状语如 these days、at present、this month、recently 等。

①She's helping me with my geometry recently.

她最近在帮助我学几何。

②They are discussing how to transform the company these days.

他们这几天在探讨公司如何转型。

③The machine is being repaired at present.

这台机器当前正在被修理。

（3）现在进行时代替将来时，表示按计划或安排即将发生的动作

这类动词通常表示位置的转移，如 come、go、leave、arrive、fly、start、stay、sail 等。

①I'm leaving for London tomorrow.

我明天动身去伦敦。

②She is coming to see me.

她要来看我了。

③They are flying to Thailand for their holiday.

他们正飞往泰国去度假。

④He's arriving soon.

他马上要到了。

⑤Are you staying for dinner tonight?

你今晚会留下来吃饭吗？

注:如今在用现在进行时表将来含义时,动词范围已不再局限于表示位置转移的动词。比如:

①I'm taking a motorcycle test on Friday.

我星期五要参加摩托车考试。

②He is giving a speech after 2 hours.

他两小时后发表演讲。

③We are meeting tonight.

我们今晚见面。

④She is working all day tomorrow.

她明天要工作一整天。

⑤He's buying a new car soon.

他很快就要买一辆新车了。

(4)现在进行时表将来时,有时含有决心、拒绝或命令等语气

①I'm tired. I'm giving up.

我累了,我放弃了。

②I'm telling you again, I'm not going.

我再告诉你一遍,我不会去的。

③I'm not lending him money any more.

我不会再借给他钱了。

④You're not coming here again.

你不用再来这了。

(5)在复合句的从句中,可用现在进行时表示将来的意义

①If it is raining tomorrow morning, we won't go on an excursion.

如果明天早上下雨,我们就不去郊游了。(条件状语从句)

②Remember me to him while you are chatting.

你们聊天的时候,记得代我向他问好。(时间状语从句)

③When you are doing homework, please be careful.

你做作业的时候,请仔细一点。(时间状语从句)

④The director will come to our department to see how we are doing.

主任要来我们部门看看我们的工作情况。(宾语从句)

(6)现在进行时表示不断变化的状况,或当前事件的动向

这类动词通常表示动作的渐变,如 turn、get、become、grow 等。

①House prices are getting more and more expensive.

　　房价正变得越来越高。

②The leaves by the West Lake are turning green.

　　西湖边的树叶正在变绿。

③Do you feel that he is becoming more selfish than before?

　　你感觉到他比以前更自私了吗?

④Do you notice that he is growing fatter and fatter?

　　你注意到他越来越胖了吗?

(7)现在进行时表示反复出现或习惯性的动作

常与always、forever、constantly、continually等频度副词连用,通常带有某种感情色彩,如不满、称赞、惊讶、厌恶等。

①She is always helping others.

　　她总是乐于助人。(表达赞扬)

②He is constantly making mistakes.

　　他经常犯错误。(表达不满)

③He is forever lying to me.

　　他永远在对我撒谎。(表达厌恶)

④Why am I always losing keys?

　　为什么我总是丢钥匙?(表达自责)

⑤Why are you always interrupting me?

　　你为什么老是打断我讲话?(表达抱怨)

静态动词通常不使用进行时:

表示存在和拥有(have、belong、own、exist)、心理状态(love、like、know、remember、forget、understand、want、hope、think、wonder)、感官感觉(see、hear、smell、taste、feel)等静态动词,通常不使用进行时态。比如:

①I have a nice teacher.

　　我有个好老师。

②I think he'll be a good father.

　　我认为他会是一个好父亲。

③I wonder if he will help me this time.

　　我想知道他这一次是否会帮我。

④I saw a beautiful cloud in the sky.

　　我看到天上有朵美丽的云。

⑤I heard he resigned.

　　我听说他辞职了。

⑥I smell something burning.

我闻到什么东西烧焦了。

试比较以下例句：

①I'm having a good time.

我正玩得很开心。

②I'm having a meal.

我正在吃饭。

（两个例句中的have并非表示拥有，其用于词组中表示玩得开心、吃饭或开会等）

③I'm thinking of quitting my job.

我正在考虑辞职。

（此时think并非表示认为、确信，而是表示思考、打算）

④Are you seeing someone recently?

你最近在和什么人约会吗？

（此时see并非表示看见，而是表示约会）

⑤I'm seeing you tomorrow.

我明天见你。

（此时see并非表示看见，而是表示会见，代替一般将来时）

⑥I'm hoping that you will accept my invitation.

我希望你能接受我的邀请。

（相比于一般现在时更为委婉客气，语气相对不生硬）

⑦I'm wondering if he will help me this time.

我想知道他这一次是否会帮我。

（表现语气和感情色彩，更加委婉、客气或不肯定，参考**过去进行时**中此用法）

通过以上对比可见，静态动词通常描述的是一个状态，并非持续性动作，因此通常不使用进行时态；但当这类动词用于进行时态时，意味着动词的用法或表达的意思已发生改变，或由于其他特殊的语法所需，如表达感情和语气等。

"be动词+形容词"用于现在进行时：

对比以下一般现在时和现在进行时的例句：

①He is stupid. 他很蠢。（指通常的状态）

②He is being stupid. 他正在犯傻。（指此刻的表现）

③He is very arrogant. 他很自大。（指通常的状态）

④He is being arrogant now. 他现在很自大。（指暂时的行为）

注："be动词+being+形容词"结构，表示此时此刻的行为举止或暂时存在的状态，通常用来形容一个人短暂的或与平时有反差的行为。使用的形容词通常是动态形容词，如 angry、careful、careless、clever、foolish、stupid、kind、friendly、brave、rude、polite、 impolite 等,而表示静态的形容词,如 long、big、tall、beautiful、heavy、tired 等,则往往不能这样使用。

"系动词 be+介词短语"可表示正在进行的动作:

①He is at work now.

　他现在正在工作。

②The two countries are at war now.

　这两个国家现在正在打仗。

③She is in tears now.

　她正在哭。

④Look! The house is on fire!

　快看! 房子着火了!

⑤The news is on the air.

　新闻正在直播中。

⑥The bridge is under construction.

　这座桥正在建造中。

　　注:介词短语作表语时,可以用来表示正在进行的动作或存在的状态,有时还能起到一定的修辞作用,可以使语言变得更加生动形象。

Section 2 过去进行时(the Past Continuous Tense)

1 语法概念

　　过去进行时表示过去某一时间正在进行的动作或过去某段时间内正在发生或进行的动作,由"was/were+现在分词"构成。

　　当过去进行时表示过去某个时间正在进行的动作时,是一个时间点的概念,强调当时正在发生的动作。如图所示:

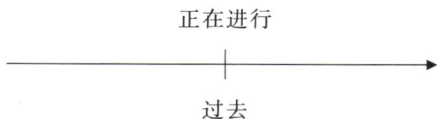

正在进行

←———————————|———————————→

过去

　　当过去进行时表示过去某段时间内正在进行的动作或状态时,是一个时间段的概念,强调过去的某段时间内正在发生的事情。如图所示:

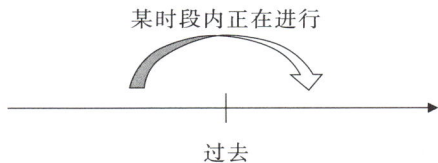

某时段内正在进行

过去

　　以上两点是过去进行时的主要语法含义,过去进行时和现在进行时的用法相似,均可表示某个时间点正在进行的动作,也可表示某段时间内正在进行的动作。但动作所处的时间不同,运用的场景和语法特点也会有所区别。接下来我们对过去进行时的主要用法做归纳。

2　语法基本运用

(1)过去进行时表示过去某个时刻正在进行的动作

常与表示过去的时间状语连用,如then、at that moment、6 o'clock yesterday等。

①What were you doing at 5 o'clock yesterday afternoon?

　昨天下午5点你在干吗?

②The moment I saw him yesterday, he was playing basketball.

　我昨天见到他时,他正在打篮球。

③I didn't see you passing by, I was answering the phone then.

　我没有看见你经过,我那时正在接电话。

④He was repairing his radio at this time yesterday.

　昨天这个时候他正在修收音机。

(2)过去进行时表示过去某段时间正在进行的动作或状态

常用的时间状语如all day、all morning、the whole week、from 8 to 10 o'clock、for+时间段等。

①She was preparing for the interview all morning.

　她整个早上一直都在为面试做准备。

②What were you doing yesterday? Why didn't you answer my phone?

　你昨天都在干吗? 为什么不接我电话?

③We were looking for a house to settle down for the past 3 days.

　过去3天我们一直在找房子安顿下来。

(3)过去进行时描述一件事情发生的时间背景

经常和一般过去时使用在同一个句子里。过去进行时表示过去正在进行的动作,一般过去时表示在此过程中另一个比较短暂的动作或事件的发生。从句中常用when、while、as、just as等连词:

①When I was washing the car, I found the key you left behind.

我在洗车的时候发现了你落下的钥匙。

（when 可引导时间段，动词为延续性动词，此句中两个动作有先后）

②I was leaving the house when the phone rang.

正当我要出门，电话铃响了。

（when 可引导时间点，动词为短暂性动词，此句中两个动作同时发生）

③I felt you were jealous while she was talking to me.

她跟我说话的时候，我觉得你在吃醋。

（while 只能引导时间段，作为时间背景，另一个动作在此过程中发生）

④Jacky Cheung was eating an apple on stage while he was giving a concert.

开演唱会的时候，张学友在台上吃着苹果。

（从句和主句的动作同时发生且都用过去进行时，往往用 while 引导）

⑤As I was reading, he fell asleep.

我在看书的时候，他睡着了。

（as 可引导时间段与时间点，强调主句和从句的动作同时发生）

（4）复合句中，表示动作同时进行时，主句和从句均可使用过去进行时，多用 while 引导

①While my mother was cooking, I was watching TV.

妈妈做饭的时候，我在看电视。

②Others were breathing in second-hand smoke while you were smoking just now.

你刚才在吸烟的时候，别人也在吸你的二手烟。

③While I was complimenting you in front of them, you were criticizing me.

我在他们面前夸你时，你却在批评我。

（5）过去进行时表示按计划或安排过去将要发生的动作

通常与表示位置转移的动词连用，如 come、go、leave、arrive、start 等。参考上一节**现在进行时**中的表将来用法。

①She asked me whether I was coming back for dinner.

她问我是否会回家吃晚饭。

②We were leaving for Chengdu, but it rained that morning.

我们原本准备去成都，但是那天早上下雨了。

③He told me that he was arriving soon.

他告诉我他很快就到。

（6）过去进行时表示过去反复出现或习惯性的动作

常与 always、constantly、continually、perpetually 等频度副词连用，带有感情色彩，表示不满、称赞、惊讶、厌恶等。

①He was constantly making the same mistake, which made me annoyed.

他老是犯同样的错误,这使我很恼火。

②We broke up because she was always asking me for money.

我们分手是因为她老是向我要钱。

（7）hope、wonder、think 等静态动词的过去进行时可用来表示现在的事情

语气相对于现在进行时和一般过去时更加委婉、客气,显得不生硬或唐突,有时又含有不确定的语气。

①I was wondering if you could lend me some money.

我想知道你是否可以借我一些钱。(语气委婉客气且不确定)

②I was thinking it might be better to invite him.

我在想可能邀请他一下会更好。(表达观点时更显委婉)

③What were you doing here?

你在这里干吗?(也可用于其他动词,此句中表达疑惑、意外之情)

静态动词通常不使用进行时:

表示存在和拥有（have、belong、own、exist）、心理状态（love、like、know、remember、forget、understand、want、hope、think、wonder）、感官感觉（see、hear、smell、taste、feel）等静态动词时,通常不使用进行时态。

注:该用法请参考上一节现在进行时中此用法,本节中不再展开叙述。

"be动词+形容词"用于过去进行时:

①He was stupid. 他很蠢。(指过去通常的状态)

②He was being stupid. 他刚才在犯傻。(指当时一时的表现)

注:该用法表示过去一时的表现或暂时的状态,请参考上一节现在进行时中此用法。

"was/were+doing sth."结构不一定是过去进行时,比如:

①Her job was designing clothes.

她的工作是设计服装。

②His suggestion was holding a meeting together tonight.

他的建议是今晚我们一起开一次会。

注:上述例句中"was/were+doing sth."并非过去进行时,其中 doing 作动名词,而非现在分词,动名词在句中作表语,构成系表结构。

Section 3 将来进行时(the Future Continuous Tense)

1 语法概念

将来进行时表示将来某一时刻或某一阶段内正在进行的动作或存在的状态,由"shall/will+be动词+现在分词"构成。该时态一般只用于持续性动词,不用于静态动词,也常用来表示礼貌的询问、请求或期待等语气。

2 语法基本运用

(1)将来进行时表示将来某一时刻正在进行的动作

①I shall be cleaning my room at 8 tomorrow morning.
　明天早上8点我将会打扫我的房间。

②We'll be having a meeting at 5 o'clock this afternoon.
　今天下午5点我们将在开会。

③She will be running at 6 o'clock tomorrow morning.
　明天早上6点她将会去跑步。

(2)将来进行时表示将来某一段时间内正在进行的动作

①Sam will be living in this town in the next two months.
　在接下来的两个月里,山姆将住在这个镇上。

②We will be having a meeting from 8 to 10 tomorrow morning.
　明天上午8点到10点我们将在开会。

③I'll be preparing for my speech all day tomorrow.
　明天一整天我都将在准备我的演讲。

④She will be writing a novel for the next three days.
　她接下来三天都将在写小说。

(3)将来进行时表示计划好的事情或预计要发生的事情,简单陈述将来事实

①I shall be seeing you in Shanghai next month.
　下个月我将在上海和你见面。

②The train will be leaving soon.
　火车马上就要开了。

③She will be waiting for you at home after work.
　她下班后将在家里等你。

④I hope you will be coming on time.

我希望你能准时来。

⑤The life of the peasants in our country will be getting better and better.

我们国家农民的生活将会越来越好。

(4)将来进行时表示亲切或委婉的语气,通常用于疑问句

①Shall we be seeing each other again?

我们还会再见面吗?

②When will you be coming to our city again?

您什么时候再来我们城市?

③What shall we be doing next?

我们接下来要做什么?

(5)在时间、条件状语从句中,一般用现在进行时代替将来进行时

①Be careful when you are driving my car.

你在开我车的时候要小心一点。

②If they are having a meeting when you arrive, please wait in the conference room.

如果你到达时他们正在开会,请在会议室等候。

③I won't bother him if he is working.

如果他在工作,我就不打扰他了。

一般将来时与将来进行时的区别:

区别1:一般将来时表示将来发生的动作或情况,将来进行时则强调这个动作的持续性。试比较以下3组例句:

组1:I will write an article tomorrow.(描述将来的情况)

I will be writing an article all morning tomorrow.(强调动作的持续性)

组2:We will have an exam this afternoon.(描述将来的情况)

We will be having an exam for two hours this afternoon.(强调动作的持续性)

组3:I'll work in Shanghai next year.(描述将来的情况)

I'll be working in Shanghai next year.(强调动作的持续性)

区别2:当将来进行时表示预计要发生的事情,陈述一个将来的事实时,和一般将来时所表述的含义是一致的。但两者存在细微的差别,一般将来时中的will常带有意愿、意图等情态意义,而将来进行时只是单纯陈述即将发生的动作,不用于表示"意志",不带有情态意义。将来进行时的语气也更为委婉,因此在疑问句和口语中也是较为常用的一个时态。试比较以下4组例句:

组1:China will play an important role in the world.(表达意愿)

China will be playing an important role in the world.(只陈述将来事实)

组2:I will mend your bike for you.(表示允诺)

I will be mending your bike for you.(只陈述将来事实)

组3:Will you meet him again soon?(询问计划)

Will you be meeting him again soon?(语气更委婉)

组4:Where will you spend your holiday?(询问打算)

Where will you be spending your holiday?(语气更客气)

Section 4 过去将来进行时(the Past Future Continuous Tense)

1 语法概念

过去将来进行时表示对于过去某一时间而言,将来某一时刻或某一段时间正在进行的动作,由"should/would+be+现在分词"构成。

2 语法基本运用

(1)过去将来进行时表示在过去的将来某一时刻或某段时间正在进行的动作

它主要用于宾语从句中,如间接引语中,从句与主句保持时态上的一致。

①He asked me what I should be doing at 11 o'clock the following day.

他问我第二天11点钟将做什么。(用于宾语从句中,作间接引语)

②She said she would be teaching me math all morning the next day.

她说第二天整个早上她都会教我数学。(用于宾语从句中,作间接引语)

③The principal informed us we would be cleaning our classroom in the next 2 hours.

校长通知我们在接下来的两个小时里要打扫教室。(用于宾语从句中)

(2)过去将来进行时表示在过去的某一时间之后按计划或预计将发生的事情

①I didn't know when she would be coming again.

我不知道她什么时候会再来。(用于宾语从句中)

②I thought you would be missing me.

我原以为你会想念我的。(用于宾语从句中)

③He said he would be seeing me off on the 7 o'clock flight.

他说他将送我乘7点钟的飞机。(用于宾语从句中,作间接引语)

④He asked me what I would be doing on the weekend.

他问我周末将做什么。(用于宾语从句中,作间接引语)

注:该用法和将来进行时一样,纯粹表示计划中的事情,不表达意愿或打算,只简单陈述过去将来的某个事实。通常用于宾语从句中,多用于间接引语中。

（3）过去将来进行时也常用于其他从句中

①He told me he was not able to come because he would be working overtime that night.

他告诉我他来不了了,因为那天晚上他要加班。(用于状语从句中)

②The new job he would be taking was to sell houses.

他将要接受的新工作是卖房子。(用于定语从句中)

③It was a surprise for us that he would be coming.

他会来对我们来说真的是个惊喜。(用于主语从句中)

④His fear was that his parents would be spoiling the child.

他担心他的父母会把他的孩子宠坏。(用于表语从句中)

（4）过去将来进行时用于独立句型中

①The crowd cheered; the spacecraft would be flying to Mars.

人群欢呼起来,宇宙飞船将飞往火星。

②I was very excited; we would be leaving for London the following day.

我很兴奋,第二天我们就要动身去伦敦了。

③This policy would be inspiring young people to devote themselves to science.

这项政策将激励年轻人投身于科学。

④Gary found a job, then he would be looking for a place to live.

盖理找到了工作,他将找个住的地方。

⑤He was down in spirits; he would be leaving his alma mater next month.

他情绪很低落,下个月他就要离开母校了。

（5）过去将来进行时用于虚拟语气中。

①If you listened to me, you would be working in a better company.

如果你那时听了我的话,你就会在一家更好的公司工作。

②I wouldn't be living with him if I were you.

如果我是你,我不会和他住在一起。

③If I were you, I would be taking the opportunity.

如果我是你,我会抓住这个机会。

④Without a car, we would be walking to work.

没有汽车的话,我们就得走路去上班。(含蓄虚拟语气)

⑤But for his help, we would be still working in the firm now.

如果没有他的帮助,我们现在仍在公司里上班。(含蓄虚拟语气)

⑥If you had taken my advice, you would not be living in regret.

如果你当时听了我的劝告,就不会活在遗憾中了。(错综虚拟语气)

⑦If he had informed me earlier, we would not be coming here now.

如果他早点通知我,我们现在就不会来了。(错综虚拟语气)

注:上述例句④⑤中所假设的条件并非通过if条件句表达出来,因此被称为含蓄条件句,条件从句通常会隐藏在上下文一定的短语中,例句中的条件通过介词短语来表示。在例句⑥⑦中,if条件句是对过去的虚拟,故用过去完成时,而主句则是对现在的虚拟,故用 would do/would be doing 的形式,这类主从句中时间不一致的条件句被称为错综时间条件句。含蓄条件句和错综时间条件句将在 **Part 5 语法相关补充**中再做介绍。

▶ **Part 3　完成时** ◀

Section *1*　现在完成时(the Present Perfect Tense)

在我们正式解析现在完成时之前,请先做一些思考:现在完成时的定位和功能是什么? 为什么我们需要现在完成时? 事实上,现在完成时属于重点时态,是开启 8 个难点时态的钥匙(4 个完成时和 4 个完成进行时),因此,我们应正视其特殊价值。

笔者曾询问学生:"一般过去时跟现在有关系吗?"学生答:"没有关系,因为是过去了。"笔者继续问:"我吃过饭了,5 点吃的。你觉得跟现在有关系吗?"学生开始思索:"好像是有关系的……5 点吃了,已经吃过了,说明现在不用吃了。"

学生的话答对了一半,的确,在英语的语法逻辑中,一般过去时与现在的动作通常不存在联系,不强调对现在的影响,因此"5 点吃的"只是讲述过去的一个事实,对应的是一般过去时;而"我吃过饭了"则说明了一个结果,对现在有了影响,因此"我吃过饭了"对应现在完成时,与现在存在联系。接下来,我们开始解析现在完成时。

1　语法概念

现在完成时表示过去发生或已完成的动作<u>对现在造成的影响或结果</u>,或表示过去的动作或状态<u>持续到现在</u>,有可能持续下去,由"助动词 have/has + 过去分词"构成。

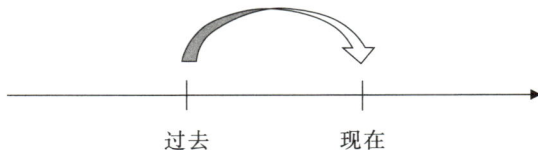

过去　　　　　　　现在

一般时通常是一个时间点的概念,完成时是一个时间段的概念。一般过去时在语法逻辑上不强调与现在的联系,只限于表示过去的动作本身。而过去发生的动作要对现在有影响,就需要用现在完成时来实现,说明动作已经有了结果,从而把过去与现在进行了衔接。同时,值得注意的是,现在完成时这个时态一旦生疏或学习得不扎实,就容易产生片面理解,因为除了表示影响和结果的已完成用法,现在完成时还可以表达持续功能,即未完成用法。比如:

①We have lived here since 2010.

我们从2010年开始住在这里。

②I have been to the US twice.

我去过美国两次。

③Lin has just finished her homework.

林已经完成了作业。

注:②③描述的是过去发生而现在已经结束,是与现在有关的事物或状态,强调对现在的影响和结果;①描述的是从过去某时到现在为止这一段时间中发生的情况,动作持续到现在。总而言之,现在完成时表现的是从过去到现在的事情。

2 语法基本运用

(1)现在完成时,表示过去发生或已经完成的动作对现在造成的影响或结果

①Joan has spent all of her money.

琼已经花光了她的钱。

(动作已完成,对现在有影响,含义是:她现在已经没有钱了。)

②Linda has just come.

琳达已经到了。

(动作已完成,是一个结果,含义是:Linda现在在这儿了。)

③I have been to London before.

我以前去过伦敦。

(动作已完成,已经有了经验,含义是:我对伦敦有客观认识和体验。)

已完成用法的常用时间标志:

以 already、just 和 yet 为标志:

①I have already read this book.

我已经看过这本书了。

②He has just got her help.

他刚得到她的帮助。

③She hasn't come back yet.

她还没有回来。

以 now、today、recently 和 lately 为标志:

①He has finished homework now.

他现在已经完成作业了。

②What have you learned recently?

你最近学了什么？

以 so far、up till now 和 before 为标志：

①He has visited six museums so far.

到目前为止他参观过6个博物馆。

②She has been to London before.

她之前去过伦敦。

以频度副词 often、frequently 和 three times 等为标志：

①He has been to the United States three times.

他已经去过美国3次了。

②They have often believed the stories told by the explorer.

他们常常相信探险家讲的故事。（表经常性、重复性完成的动作）

③I have always regretted giving up my swimming lessons.

我总是后悔放弃了游泳课。（表经常性、重复性完成的动作）

以 ever 和 never 为标志：

①This is the best film I have ever seen.

这是我曾看过的最好的一部电影。

②He has never been to Beijing.

他从没有去过北京。

已完成用法归纳：

通过以上的举例可以发现，现在完成时既可以和表示"现在"的时间状语连用，如now、today、this week、so far、up till now 等，也可以和表示"过去"的时间状语连用，但这些时间状语只能笼统地表示过去的时间，如just、lately、recently、before、never、ever、always、already（肯定句中）、yet（否定句/疑问句）等，现在完成时一般不可以和过去的具体时间连用，如two days ago、yesterday、five minutes ago、last year 等。

现在完成时跨越过去和现在两个时间，过去与现在的关系十分密切，但现在完成时属于现在的时态，因而我们在运用时侧重点不在于过去发生的这个动作，也不在于动作发生的时间，而在于该动作对现在造成的影响或结果。

（2）现在完成时表示发生在过去某一时刻的动作或状态，持续到现在

①I have been a teacher for 15 years.

我做老师已经15年了。

②They have been married for 20 years.

他们已经结婚20年了。

③She's been ill since 2010.

她从2010年开始生病。

④We haven't seen each other for 20 years.

我们有20年没见了。

⑤She hasn't bought anything for half a month.

她已经半个月没买东西了。

⑥No one has spoken to him since then.

从那以后没有人跟他说过话。

未完成用法的常用时间标志：

for+时段：

①I have lived here for 10 years.

我已经在这里住了10年。

②We have known each other for a long time.

我们已经认识很长时间了。

since+过去的时间点：

①I have lived here since 2010.

我从2010年开始住在这里。

②I have worked here since 1995.

自从1995年我就在这里工作了。

since+时段+ago：

①I have lived here since 10 years ago.

我从10年前开始住在这里。

②He has been missing since several weeks ago.

他已经失踪几个星期了。

since+从句：

①I have lived here since I was a child.

我从小就住在这里。

②Things have changed since he left the company.

自从他离开公司以来,情况发生了变化。

It has been+时段+since+从句：

①It has been 10 years since I have lived here.

从我住这里开始到现在已有10年了。

②It's been such a long time since we met last time.

自从我们上次见面以来已经有很长时间了。

未完成用法归纳：

表持续的用法通常与表示时间段的时间状语连用,并且需要使用延续性动词,如

study、live、be、last、teach、wait等,该动作是否会持续下去,需根据上下文判断。

终止性动词用于完成时中,通常表示动作已完成,但上述表持续的例句④⑤⑥中 haven't seen/hasn't bought/No one has spoken用非持续性的动词表示动作的持续,其原因 是,否定的这个动作犹如一个状态,这种状态可以持续。

（3）现在完成时用于时间、条件状语从句中,表将来完成的动作

①I'll come and see you when I've finished my work.

我完成工作后就来看你。

②You can't drive your car until the fog has cleared.

在雾散去之前,你不能开车。

③You can watch TV if you have finished homework.

如果完成了作业,你可以看会儿电视。

④As soon as I have finish the project, I'll take you on a trip.

我一完成这个项目,就带你去旅行。

for与since容易产生下列思维误区:

for+时段常用于完成时,但也可用于其他时态。比较:

①I worked here for 20 years.

我在这工作了20年。（现在已经不在这工作了）

②I have worked here for 20 years.

我在这工作20年了。（现在还在这里工作）

since常用于完成时,但也可用于其他时态。比较:

①It's 10 years since I graduated from college.

我大学毕业至今已有10年了。（强调时间的长度）

②It has been 10 years since I graduated from college.

我大学毕业至今已经10年了。（表示状态的持续）

在有since的完成时中,也可表示非持续的动作或状态:

①Since I lived here, I have often talked with him.

自从我住在这里后,我经常和他交谈。（表经常性、重复性完成的动作）

②She has changed since graduation.

毕业后,她已经变了。（表结果）

③What have you done since yesterday?

从昨天到现在你都做了些什么?（表结果）

区分易混淆词组:has gone (to)/has been (to)/has been (in):

Have/Has gone (to):去了（现在不在现场）

My father has gone to Shanghai.

父亲已经去了上海。(现在在上海)

Have/Has been (to)：去过(现在已经不在那边)

My father has been to Shanghai.

父亲去过上海。(现在不在上海)

Have/has been in：待在某地(还在此地)

My father has been in Shanghai for two months.

父亲在上海待了两个月。(现在还在上海)

Section 2 过去完成时(the Past Perfect Tense)

1 语法概念

过去完成时表示在过去某一时间或动作之前已经发生或完成了的动作,即"过去的过去",由"助动词 had + 过去分词"构成。

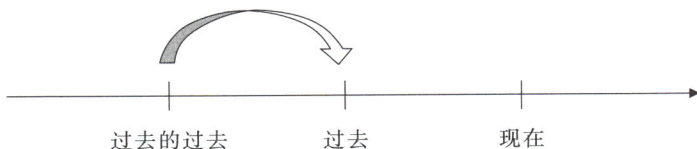

过去的过去　　　过去　　　现在

笔者曾问学生："1秒钟以前能用一般过去时吗?"学生回答："应该可以,因为是过去。"笔者继续问："1秒钟之前可以用过去完成时吗?"学生回答："应该不行,过去完成时是很以前的,因为比过去更过去。"学生的回答体现了很典型的思维误区,"过去的过去"并非遥远的过去,而是相比较一般过去时,更早一点而已,0.5秒以前可以是过去时,1秒以前相比较0.5秒以前则是"过去的过去",因此过去完成时在时间上只是一个相对区间。

0.5秒和1秒这个案例体现了过去完成时的一种重要用法,即对于过去的两个动作,动作在先可以用过去完成时,动作在后可用一般过去时。比如:

①She had read the the textbooks before she went to junior middle school.

她去读初中前,已经看过课本了。

②He had washed his hands before he ate dinner.

吃饭前他洗过手了。

③By the end of last year, they had been married for five years.

到去年年底,他们结婚已经5年了。

2 语法基本运用

(1)通过时间状语来判定

一般说来,各种时态都有特定的时间标志:

①**by + 过去的时间点**：

I had finished reading the novel by 10 o'clock last night.

昨晚10点前,我已经读完这本小说了。

②**by the end of + 过去的时间点**：

We had learned over 2 thousand words by the end of last term.

截止到上学期末,我们已经学了两千多个单词。

③**before + 过去的时间点**：

She had taught English for 3 years before she came back China.

回中国前,她已经教了3年英语。

（2）由“过去的过去”来判定

过去完成时表示“过去的过去”,是指在过去时中的两个动作有先后关系,动作先完成的可用过去完成时,动作在后的可用一般过去时。通常出现在宾语从句和状语从句中。

宾语从句中

当宾语从句的主句为一般过去时,从句的动作先于主句的动作时,从句可用过去完成时,且通常用在told、said、knew、heard、thought等动词后的宾语从句中。比如：

①She said that she had seen the film before.

她说她以前看过这部电影。

②He said he had bought a fancy car.

他说他买了一辆豪车。

状语从句中

在时间、条件、原因、方式等状语从句中,主、从句的动作发生有先后关系。动作在前的,用过去完成时;动作在后的,用一般过去时。比如：

①When I woke up, it had stopped raining.

当我醒来,雨已经停了。

②As soon as I had told him about it, he told someone else.

我一告诉他这件事,他就告诉了别人。

注意：before、after引导的时间状语从句中,由于before和after本身已表达了动作的先后关系,若主、从句表示的动作紧密相连,则主、从句常用一般过去时。比如：

①Where did you study before you came here?

来这之前,你在哪读书?

②After he closed the door, he left the classroom.

关了门之后,他离开了教室。

表示想法、意向的动词

如 hope、wish、expect、think、intend、mean、suppose、want、believe 等,用过去完成时可以表示过去未曾实现的希望、打算或意图,表达"原本……而实际未能……"的含义。比如:

①We had hoped that you would come, but you didn't.

　　我们本希望你会来,但你没有。

②She had thought she could get a good result in the exam, but she failed.

　　她原本以为能考好,结果并没有。

（3）根据上下文语境判定

①I met Iris in the street yesterday. We hadn't seen each other since she left hometown.

　　昨天在路上我遇到了艾瑞斯,自从她离开家乡后,我们就没有见过彼此。

②She called on her teacher last night, who had encouraged her during the last 3 years.

　　她昨天拜访了她的老师,他曾在过去的3年里给予了她莫大的鼓励。

（4）用于表示持续性

过去完成时,表示过去已经开始的某一动作或状态,一直延续到过去某一时间,而且动作尚未结束,仍然有继续下去的可能。

①By the end of last year, I had been a teacher for 5 years.

　　到去年年底,我做老师已经5年了。

②It had rained all the week before he left for Bangkok.

　　在他去曼谷前,已经下了一星期雨。

（5）用于特定句型中

hardly ... when...(几乎没来得及……就……/刚……就…)

I had hardly crossed the road when the accident happened.

我一穿过马路,事故就发生了。

no sooner ... than...（刚……就……）

We had no sooner taken off than we were told to land.

飞机一起飞,我们就被告知要着陆。

just ... when...（刚……就……）

I had just set out for Shanghai when I was asked to go back to the office.

我刚动身去上海,就被要求回办公室。

It was the first time ... that...（这是第一次……）

It was the first time that he had ever spoken to me in such a tone.

这是他第一次用这种语气跟我说话。

过去完成时可以用具体的过去时间：

在上一节中，我们归纳了现在完成时可以与一些笼统地表示"过去"的时间状语连用，而通常不与具体的过去时间连用，但在过去完成时中，可以用表示具体的过去时间。比如：

①I had seen them go out last night.

我昨晚看见他们出去了。

②We had finished the design drawing yesterday.

昨天我们已经完成了设计图纸。

③The suspect had escaped an hour ago.

嫌疑犯一小时前逃跑了。

④His family had gone to America in 1988.

他的家人在1988年去了美国。

过去完成时描述"过去的过去"：

现在完成时指的是动作在现在的以前完成，过去完成时指的则是动作在过去某个时间之前完成，这便是所谓的"过去的过去"。既然动作是发生在过去某个时间之前，那么在使用过去完成时的过程中，通常会有一个明确的过去时间做参考或可根据上下文体现这个过去的时间，因为过去完成时通常表示这个动作在先，该时态是一个相对的概念。

Section 3 将来完成时（the Future Perfect Tense）

1 语法概念

将来完成时主要表示在将来某个时刻之前已完成或一直持续的动作，由"shall/will have+过去分词"构成。

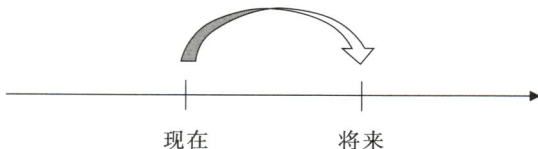

现在　　将来

2 语法基本运用

（1）将来完成时表示将来完成，描述在将来某个时间点之前会完成的动作

①I'm quite sure he will have changed his mind soon.

我很肯定他很快就会改变主意的。

②With the fast development of technology, many things will have changed by 2030.

随着科技的快速发展,到2030年,许多事情都将会改变。

③When we reach the station, the bus will probably have left.

等我们到车站,公交车可能已经离开了。

（2）将来完成时表示动作的持续,描述某种状况将一直持续到将来某一时间

①We will have been married for 10 years by this month next year.

到明年的这个月,我们将结婚满10年了。

②By tomorrow, I will have been a teacher for 5 years.

到明天,我做老师满5年了。

③By next month, we will have not seen each other for a year.

到下个月,我们将有1年没有见面了。

（3）将来完成时表示推测

①I'm sure he will have learnt the news.

我相信他已经得知了消息。

②There will have been a definite result before Sunday.

周日之前肯定会有结果。

③I believe you'll have been successful when you are 35.

我相信你35岁的时候已经成功了。

注:此时will作情态动词,表推测或猜想,翻译成"想必,大概",参考一般将来时中will的此用法;此处的will have done表示对过去的猜测,参考情态动词+have done结构。

Section 4 过去将来完成时（the Past Future Perfect Tense）

1 语法概念

过去将来完成时表示从过去的角度看将来某一时间,动作已完成,由"would have+过去分词"构成。除了时态功能外,还重点用于虚拟语气当中。

2 语法基本运用

（1）表示从过去某一时间点看将来某一时间会完成的动作

①I thought you would have known the truth by then.

我以为在那时你已经知道真相了。

②He promised me that he would have given me a lift early next morning.

他答应我第二天一早让我搭车。

③She said she would have bought a car in one month.

她说她将在一个月内买车。

（2）过去将来完成时的情态用法

①I would have thought she'd like the gift.

我看她会喜欢这个礼物。（表委婉语气）

②He would have planned a trip with you to celebrate your wedding anniversary.

他曾计划和你去旅行，以庆祝你们的结婚纪念日。（表过去想法）

③She would have refused your invitation owing to the past prejudice.

由于过去的成见，她可能会拒绝你的邀请。（表推测）

（3）过去将来完成时用于虚拟语气，表示与过去的事实相反

would have done 结构用于虚拟语气，是过去将来完成时的重要用法之一，常用于第三类 if 条件句中，被称为"非真实条件句"，表示与过去的事实相反。比如：

①If I had acquired Subjunctive Mood, I would have used the grammar in my composition.

如果我之前学过虚拟语气，我就会把该语法用在我的作文里了。

②I would have gone to a better college if I had worked harder.

如果我当时更努力读书的话，我就会去一所更好的大学。

③If I had been able to received better education, I would have been more successful.

如果当时我能接受更好的教育，我就会更加成功。

（if 条件句谈论想象中的情况，主句讲述想象的结果，但这种情况在过去实际没有发生，所以与过去的事实相反。if 条件句的主要用法，我们将在**常用 if 条件句归纳**中展开。）

上一节将来完成时中的 will 与本节过去将来完成时中的 would，都可作情态动词，表示推测。情态动词+have done 结构表推测的用法，我们将在**情态动词+have done 结构**的语法板块进行归纳，同时继续探究 would have done 结构的虚拟语气用法。

▶Part 4　完成进行时◀

Section 1　现在完成进行时（the Present Perfect Progressive Tense）

1　语法概念

现在完成进行时强调动作在某一段时间内一直在进行，通常动作在现在有了结果。

到现在为止,该动作可能已经停止,可能还将继续进行,需根据上下文确定。由"助动词have/has been+现在分词"构成。

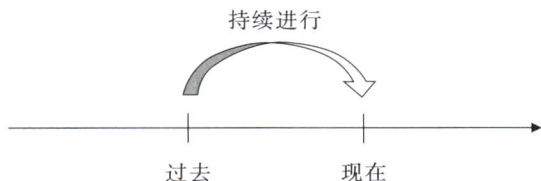

完成进行时和完成时一样,是一个时间段的概念,但完成进行时强调持续进行,因此常和表示时间段的时间状语连用。一般来说,完成时表示已完成的动作,完成进行时表示尚未完成的动作;完成时也可表示动作的持续,此时和完成进行时的含义一致,通常可以互换。但多数情况下,完成时表达动作的完成,而完成进行时强调动作的持续进行,因而从某种意义上讲,完成进行时是对完成时一种用法上的补充,赋予动词更多更灵活的表达功能。比如:

I have been thinking about life for a long time.

我思考人生很久了。

2 语法基本运用

(1)现在完成进行时表示过去开始的动作持续进行到现在,并且还将持续下去

①She has been teaching English for 5 years. She loves her career.

她教英语5年了,她热爱自己的事业。(动作将持续下去)

②We have been helping each other since we were 20.

我们从20岁起便一直互相帮助。(动作将持续下去)

③It has been raining for hours, we'd better cancel the trip.

雨已经下了几个小时了,我们最好取消旅行。(动作将持续下去)

(2)现在完成进行时表示过去开始的动作持续进行到现在,动作不再持续进行

①We have been waiting for you for 1 hour. We have to leave, or we'll be late for school.

我们等了你一个小时了,我们得走了,否则上学要迟到了。(动作将终止)

②I'm going to a new firm tomorrow, I've been working here for 10 years.

明天我要去一家新的公司,我已经在这儿工作了10年。(动作将终止)

③Why are you so exhausted? What have you been doing?

你怎么这么累?你刚才一直在干吗?(动作已终止)

归纳:语法基本运用(2)中,根据上下文我们得知动作将不再持续进行下去,但切勿与现在完成时用法混淆,现在完成时表达动作已完成时,侧重于对现在的影响和结果,虽然现在完成进行时也可暗示对现状的影响,但并非强调影响和结果,而是描述该动作从过去到现在的持续进行,也就是强调动作的本身,可以看作一个持续的进行时。并且在语气方

面,完成时通常只陈述一个事实,而完成进行时的感情色彩更为丰富。

（3）现在完成进行时表示从过去到现在的时间内经常重复的动作

①He has been calling me every night for the past month.

在过去的一个月里,他每天晚上都给我打电话。(动作反复进行)

②You've been talking about this ever since we knew each other.

自从我们认识之后,你就一直在说这件事。(动作反复进行)

③She has been writing to me all these years.

她这几年一直在给我写信。(动作反复进行)

现在完成进行时与现在完成时的比较：

现在完成进行时等同于现在完成时

I have worked in this school since 2000.(表持续)

= I have been working in this school since 2000.(表持续进行)

Mr. Smith has lived here for 5 years.(表持续)

= Mr. Smith has been living here for 5 years.(表持续进行)

注意:当动词可以表示持续性动作时,现在完成时可以和现在完成进行时替换,此时两者的时间标志相同。但现在完成进行时更强调动作的持续性,是现在完成时的强调形式。

现在完成进行时不同于现在完成时

We have already learnt this unit.(强调结果)

≠ We have been learning this unit.(表持续进行)

I have read the novel.(强调结果)

≠ I have been reading the novel.(表持续进行)

注意:当动词表示短暂性动作时,现在完成时表示动作已完成,不能与现在完成进行时相互替换,现在完成进行时通常使用持续性动词。

静态动词通常不使用现在完成进行时：

有些表达感官(hear、taste、smell、feel)、心理(believe、know、love、like、hate)、从属关系(belong to、contain、consist of)的静态动词,通常不使用现在完成进行时,因为此类动词通常描述一个状态,并非持续性动作,往往不使用进行时态,因而也不能使用完成进行时,但可以使用完成时。比如:

①This table has belonged to our family for a long time.

这张桌子已属于我们家很久了。

②I have known him since I was young.

我从小就认识他。

Section 2 　过去完成进行时(the Past Perfect Progressive Tense)

1 语法概念

过去完成进行时强调在过去更早的一段时间内持续进行的动作,且该动作到过去某一时刻有了结果,由"助动词had+been+现在分词"构成。动作是停止还是继续进行,需要视上下文而定。

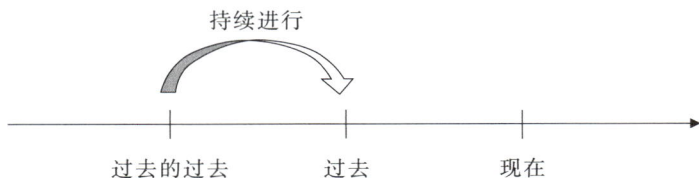

假如我们单独看进行时,该时态往往表示某个时间内动作正在进行,而完成进行时则侧重于较长时间的持续状态。因而可以这样理解,完成进行时实际上是一种强调动作持续发生或反复进行的进行时。过去完成进行时和现在完成进行时的用法基本相同,但因动作的时间不同,使用时也会产生细微差别,为了深化对完成进行时的理解,我们现在对过去完成进行时的主要用法加以归纳。

2 语法基本运用

(1)过去完成进行时表示过去某一时间之前持续进行的动作

①By the time he arrived, we had been waiting for him for half an hour.

到他来时,我们已经等了他半个小时。

②How long had it been raining after her departure?

她离开后雨下了多久?

③I had been living here for 10 years before I left for London.

我去伦敦前,在这里住了10年。

④Robin had been traveling alone for years when I first met him.

我第一次遇见罗宾时,他已经独自旅行好几年了。

归纳:过去完成进行时表示动作在过去某一时间之前已经开始,并延续到这一过去的时间,和过去完成时一样,通常会以一个过去的时间点为参照,表示到这个过去的时间点持续进行的某个动作。同时和现在完成进行时的概念一样,该动作是否还会延续下去需要通过上下文的语境来判断。过去完成进行时更强调动作在过去一段时间内的延续性，也就是侧重于动作本身，并非侧重于对过去的影响和结果。

（2）过去完成进行时表示过去经常重复的动作

①He had been borrowing money from me all those days.

那些日子里，他一直向我借钱。

②She had been mentioning you to me.

她之前多次跟我提起你。

③I was quite annoyed that he had been phoning me day and night.

他之前日日夜夜不断地打我电话，这令我十分苦恼。

（3）间接引语的句子中，当引述词是过去时，则将现在完成进行时改为过去完成进行时，以保持时态上的一致性。如在 told、asked、said、thought、supposed 等词之后：

①My teacher asked me what I had been doing.

我的老师问我一直都在做什么。

②He said he'd been looking for me.

他说他一直都在找我。

③I didn't understand why she had been standing in the rain for so long.

我不明白为什么她在雨中站了这么久。

（4）过去完成进行时的句子后接 when 从句，具有"突然"之意

①I had only been watching TV for a few minutes when my mom told me to go to bed.

我才看了几分钟电视，妈妈就叫我去睡觉了。

②We had been talking for a few minutes when he arrived.

我们只聊了几分钟，他就来了。

③We had been waiting for the bus for a little while when it came.

我们等公交车才一小会儿，它就来了。

过去完成进行时与过去完成时的比较：

过去完成进行时等同于过去完成时

I had worked for the firm for 5 years.（表持续）

= I had been working for the firm for 5 years.（表持续进行）

I had stayed here for years.（表持续）

= I had been staying here for years.（表持续进行）

过去完成进行时不同于过去完成时

I had read the book.（强调结果）

≠ I had been reading the book.（表持续进行）

I had cleaned the room.(强调结果)

≠ I had been cleaning the room.(表持续进行)

过去完成进行时通常不用于否定句中,比如:

组①:I hadn't been running for a long time.

      I hadn't run for a long time.(用过去完成时代替)

组②:I hadn't been speaking English for a long time.

      I hadn't spoken English for a long time.(用过去完成时代替)

Section 3 将来完成进行时(the Future Perfect Progressive Tense)

1 语法概念

将来完成进行时表示某个动作一直延续到将来的某一时间,这个动作是否会继续下去,需要视上下文的语境而定。该时态通常强调某种情况持续到说话人所提及的未来某个时间,由"shall/will have been+现在分词"构成。

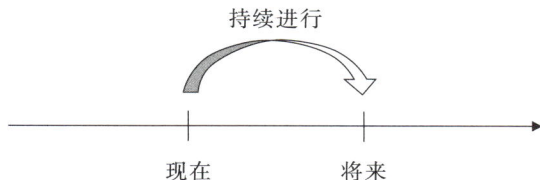

持续进行

现在　　将来

2 语法基本运用

(1)将来完成进行时表示现在到将来的某段时间内一直做某事

通常和表示将来某一时间的状语连用,如 by、before 等。

①By the end of next month, I'll have been teaching for 15 years.

  到下个月底,我教书将满15年了。

②I shall have been repairing the window for nearly 4 hours before sunset.

  到太阳下山,我修窗户将近4个小时了。

③We'll have been doing business together for 5 years by May 1st.

  到5月1日,我们一起做生意有5年了。

(2)将来完成进行时表示推测

此时will情态动词表推测,意为"想必,大概",参考**将来完成时**的表推测用法

①It's early summer now, it will have been raining in the south.

现在是初夏,想必南方一直在下雨。

②Dan isn't at home, he will have been going on a business trip.

丹不在家,他可能正在出差。

将来完成进行时与将来完成时的对比:

组①:He will have been running <u>for 3 hours</u> in 20 minutes.(表持续进行,动作连贯)

　　　He will have run <u>5 km</u> in 20 minutes.(表结果,动作被分割)

组②:He will have been traveling <u>for 2 months</u> by next week.(表持续进行,动作连贯)

　　　He will have traveled <u>to 20 cities</u> by next week.(表结果,动作被分割)

归纳:从以上两组对比可以看到,一旦把动作量化切割,相当于原本连贯的状态被分割成了片段,也就形成了以片段为单位的结果,则此时动作不再连贯,需用完成时。

Section 4 过去将来完成进行时(the Past Future Perfect Progressive Tense)

1 语法概念

过去将来完成进行时表示从过去某一时间开始的动作一直延续到过去将来某一时间,动作是否会持续下去,需要视上下文语境而定,由"should/would have been+现在分词"构成。过去将来某一时间,指的是站在过去的角度看将来的时间。

2 语法基本运用

(1)过去将来完成进行时常用于间接引语中

当引述词是过去时态,则宾语从句中的时态需要做相应改变。

①He told me they would have been working together for 10 years by the end of last year.

他跟我说到去年年底,他们将在一起工作满10年了。

②I heard by last quarter she would have been doing international trade for 5 years.

我听说到上个季度,她已经做国际贸易5年了。

③The criminal confessed that they would have been laundering money for 2 years by June.

罪犯坦白道,到6月份,他们洗钱已足足2年了。

(2)过去将来完成进行时表推测

情态动词would表推测或猜想,语气稍弱于will,参考**将来完成进行时**的表推测用法。

①He would have been wondering why she got so upset.

想必他一直很纳闷为什么她这么难过。

②Even though he was not there, she knew he would have been thinking of her.

尽管他不在,但她知道他应该会一直想念自己。

③It would have been snowing heavily in her city at the moment.

此刻在她的城市,可能已经在下大雪了。

(3)过去将来完成进行时用于虚拟语气,表示与过去的事实相反

过去将来完成进行时和过去将来完成时一样,都可用于第三类 if 条件句。

①If I hadn't eaten that much, I would have been running with him.

要是我那时没吃那么多,我就能和他一起跑步了。

②If I had won a lottery, I would have been traveling around the world.

如果当时我中了彩票,我就环游世界去了。

③I would have been lying in the hospital if I had driven along that wet road carelessly.

要是我在那段湿滑路面开车时开小差的话,我可能就要躺在医院里了。

注:if 条件句谈论想象中的情况,主句讲述想象的结果,该条件句讲述过去没有发生的事情,与过去的实际情况相反,因此是非真实条件句。

▶ Part 5　语法相关补充 ◀

Section 1　情态动词+have done 结构

(1)should/ought to have done 表示本该做而实际未做的事情,虚拟语气

①You should have told me earlier.

你本该早点告诉我的。(实际上没有告诉,含有责备意味)

②You should have invited her since you two are good friends.

你本该邀请她的,既然你们俩是好朋友。(实际上没有邀请,含有埋怨意味)

③He ought to have driven the car carefully.

他本应该小心开车的。(实际上没有谨慎驾驶,含有责怪和遗憾意味)

(2)needn't have done 表示本不必做某事而实际做了,虚拟语气

①You needn't have apologized for this.

你本不必为此而道歉。(实际上道歉了)

②Everyone is so kind that I needn't have been so anxious.

每个人都很好,我本不必这么焦虑的。(事实上之前很焦虑)

③You needn't have been so kind to him, since he was so ungrateful.

他这么忘恩负义,你本来就没必要对他那么好。(实际上对他很好)

（3）must have done 表示很有把握的推测,肯定做过某件事情

①We must have met somewhere before, I can still recognize you.

我们肯定在哪见过,我仍然能认得你。

②I feel you must have loved him before.

我觉得你曾爱过他。

③Your friend who is talking nonsense must have drunk.

你那个胡言乱语的朋友一定喝醉了。

（4）may/might have done 表示把握性较小的推测,可能发生了某事

①The film may have begun when we get to the cinema.

等我们到影院,电影可能已经开始放映了。

②I might have made a mistake in the exam.

我可能考试时犯了个错误。

③She might have been angry with me since she didn't answer my phone.

她没有接我的电话,可能在生我的气。

（5）might have done 也可表示原本某事有可能发生而实际未发生,虚拟语气

①A lot of people died who might have been saved.

许多人死了,他们原本是可能被救活的。(实际上没有被救活)

②He might have been killed if the police hadn't arrived in time.

如果警察没有及时赶到,他可能已经遇害了。(实际上警察救了他)

③But for the delay of flight, I might have been shopping in Dubai.

要不是航班延误,我可能已经在迪拜购物了。(实际上没能在迪拜购物)

（6）can/could have done 表示推测,可能做过某事

①He can't have stolen your money, he has gone home at that time.

他不可能偷你的钱,他那时已经回家了。

②Don't call her. She can have fallen asleep.

别给她打电话。她可能已经睡着了。

③It could have rained last night, the ground's wet.

昨晚可能下雨了,地是湿的。

（7）could have done 也可表示本来能够做某事而实际未做,虚拟语气

①You could have passed the exam, why were you so careless?

你本可以通过考试的,为什么这么粗心呢?(实际上没有通过考试)

②You could have been with her, she also had a crush on you.

你原本可以和她在一起,她对你也有好感。(实际上没有在一起)

③I could have made a profit, but I missed the boat.

我本可以赚一笔,但错过了机会。(实际上未赚到钱)

（8）would have done 对过去事情的假设,表示本来将会做某事而实际未做,虚拟语气

①I would have told you the whole story, but you were not here with me.

我原本会告诉你整件事情,但你不在我身边。(实际上没有告诉)

②I wouldn't have achieved so much without your help.

没有你的帮助,我不会取得这么多成就。(实际上取得了成就)

③I didn't know you were coming otherwise I would have picked you up at the station.

我不知道你要来,否则我会去车站接你。(实际上没有去接)

④I would not have succeeded but for your help.

要是没有你的帮助,我将不会成功。(实际上得到了帮助)

Section 2 常用if条件句归纳

假设类型	从句谓语时态	主句谓语时态
对现在的假设	一般现在时	will/can/may/must+动词原形
例:If it rains, we will stay at home. 　　如果下雨,我们将待在家里。 　　(真实条件句,很有可能实现)		
与现在事实相反	一般过去时	would/should/could/might+动词原形
例:If I were you, I wouldn't marry him. 　　如果我是你,我不会嫁给他。 　　(虚拟语气,非真实条件句,与现在事实相反)		
与过去事实相反	过去完成时	would/should/could/might have+过去分词
例:If I had been in your position, I would have given up. 　　如果我处在你的位置上,我可能会放弃。 　　(虚拟语气,非真实条件句,与过去事实相反)		

假设类型	从句谓语时态	主句谓语时态
与将来事实相反	一般过去时	would/should+动词原形
	例：If there were a fine day tomorrow, we would go fishing. 　　如果明天天气晴朗，我们就去钓鱼。 　　（虚拟语气，非真实条件句，与将来事实相反）	
	were to	would/should+动词原形
	例：If she were to tell me what happened, I would help her. 　　如果她告诉我发生了什么，我会帮她。 　　（虚拟语气，非真实条件句，与将来事实相反）	
	should	would/should+动词原形
	例：If he should come tomorrow, I should treat him to dinner. 　　如果他明天来，我将请他吃饭。 　　（虚拟语气，非真实条件句，与将来事实相反）	

虚拟语气条件句中，如果从句部分含有 were、should 或 had，if 可以省略，把 were、should 或 had 置于句首并采用倒装语序。比如：

①If I were you, I wouldn't do this.

= Were I you, I wouldn't do this.

如果我是你，我不会这么做。

②If she should come back home, we would celebrate her birthday.

= Should she come back home, we would celebrate her birthday.

如果她回家，我们会给她过生日。

③If he had heard the news, he would have been mad.

= Had he heard the news, he would have been mad.

如果他听到消息，他会疯的。

除以上所述的四类 if 条件句，还有一类常用的 if 条件句，被称为错综条件句。下一节，我们将对错综时间条件句语法做介绍。

Section 3 错综时间条件句

通常情况下，主句和从句的时间是一致的。要么主句和从句所讨论的情况都属于现在，要么主句和从句所谈论的情况都属于过去或将来，常用的这几类 if 条件句的用法，请参考上一节的**常用 if 条件句归纳**。

但有时，条件句中所表示的动作和主句中所表示的动作两者发生的时间并非一致，此时虚拟语气的形式不再规律，动词的时态应该根据具体情况做相应调整，这类句子被称为错综时间条件句或混合条件句。请看下列例句和分析：

①If she were available today, we would have invited her yesterday.

如果她今天有空,我们昨天就邀请她了。

(从句与现在事实相反,主句与过去事实相反)

②I would have let you go hiking with your colleagues if you were in better health.

如果你身体好一些,我就会让你和你的同事去远足。

(从句与现在事实相反,主句与过去事实相反)

③If I had followed the doctor's advice, I would be much better now.

如果我当时听了医生的建议,我现在会好得多。

(从句与过去事实相反,主句与现在事实相反)

④If I had studied hard in college, I would be working in a better company now.

如果我在大学时努力学习,我现在就会在一家更好的公司工作了。

(从句与过去事实相反,主句与现在事实相反)

⑤If you were to come tomorrow, we would not have gone to Nanjing.

如果你明天来,我们就不会去南京了。

(从句与将来事实相反,主句与过去事实相反)

⑥Should you come tomorrow, I would book a table in this fancy restaurant today.

如果你明天来的话,我今天就会在这家高级餐厅订个位置。

(从句与将来事实相反,主句与现在事实相反)

　　注:在错综虚拟语气中,主句和从句的时间不再像其他几类的if从句那般规律,应根据各自语境所表示的时间而对主从句中的谓语形式进行相应的调整,并非对时态进行随意拼接,而是需要在巩固吸收几类规律的if条件句用法后,清醒并准确地在使用错综条件句时选择动词所对应的时态。

Section 4 虚拟语气(Subjunctive Mood)

　　虚拟语气是极为重要的难点语法之一,是一种特殊的谓语动词形式,用来表示说话人所说的话并非事实,而是表示一种主观愿望、假设、怀疑、建议或推测等。

　　虚拟语气通常用于条件句中,是否使用虚拟语气,首先需要判断条件句是真实条件句还是非真实条件句。假设的条件能够实现的是真实条件句,不能使用虚拟语气;假设的条件不能实现的则是非真实条件句,要用虚拟语气。虚拟语气的条件句通常有三种情况:①与现在事实相反的情况;②与过去事实相反的情况;③将来实现概率极小的情况。

非真实条件句		
假设类型	从句谓语时态	主句谓语时态
与现在事实相反	一般过去时	would/should/could/might+动词原形
例：If I were you, I wouldn't marry him. 　　如果我是你，我不会嫁给他。 　　(虚拟语气,非真实条件句,与现在事实相反)		
与过去事实相反	过去完成时	would/should/could/might have+过去分词
例：If I had been in your position, I would have given up. 　　如果我处在你的位置上，我可能会放弃。 　　(虚拟语气,非真实条件句,与过去事实相反)		
与将来事实相反	一般过去时	would/should+动词原形
	例：If there were a fine day tomorrow, we would go fishing. 　　如果明天天气晴朗，我们就去钓鱼。 　　(虚拟语气,非真实条件句,与将来事实相反)	
	were to	would/should+动词原形
	例：If she were to tell me what happened, I would help her. 　　如果她告诉我发生了什么，我会帮她。 　　(虚拟语气,非真实条件句,与将来事实相反)	
	should	would/should+动词原形
	例：If he should come tomorrow, I should treat him to dinner. 　　如果他明天来，我将请他吃饭。 　　(虚拟语气,非真实条件句,与将来事实相反)	

以上三类条件句，我们已在**常用 if 条件句归纳**中已做了介绍。但有时，虚拟条件句并非通过 if 从句来表示，而是通过介词短语（如 otherwise/without/or/but for 引导的短语）或联系上下文等方式来表示，被称为含蓄虚拟语气句。比如在**情态动词+have done**结构中已归纳的用法：

①I would have told you the whole story, but you were not here with me.
　我原本会告诉你整件事的经过，但你不在我身边。(实际上没有告诉)
②I wouldn't have achieved so much without your help.
　没有你的帮助，我不会有这么多成就。(实际上取得了成就)
③I didn't know you were coming otherwise I would have picked you up at the station.
　我不知道你要来，否则我会去车站接你。(实际上没有去接)
④I would not have succeeded but for your help.
　要是没有你的帮助，我将不会成功。(实际上得到了帮助)

其他虚拟语气用法

（1）在 suggest/advise/demand/require/insist/order/request 等表示建议、要求、命令等意志类动词后的宾语从句中，谓语动词常用 should+动词原形或将 should 省略：

续表

其他虚拟语气用法

①My doctor suggested that I should take a rest.
　医生建议我应该休息一下。
②The manager demands that we obey the company's decision.
　经理要求我们应该服从公司决议。
③She insisted that I should stay to lunch.
　她坚持我应该留下来吃饭。

（2）在 advice/agreement/decision/decree/insistence/determination 等表示建议、要求、命令的名词后的表语或同位语从句中，谓语动词常用 should+原形或将 should 省略：

①My doctor's suggestion is that I should take a rest.
　医生的建议是我应该休息一下。
②The manager's demand is that we obey the company's decision.
　经理的要求是我们应该服从公司决议。
③Her insistence is that I should stay to lunch.
　她坚持我应该留下来吃饭。

（3）wish 的宾语从句中，表示现在或将来的愿望，谓语动词常用一般过去时或过去将来时：

①I wish I were still young.
　我真希望仍然年轻。（表示现在的愿望）
②I wish I would/could be as successful as you.
　我希望能和你一样成功。（表示将来的愿望）
③I wish the housing price would/could come down.
　我真希望房价能降下来。（表示将来的愿望）

（4）wish/wished 后面 that 的宾语从句中，用 had done 或 would/could/might+have done，表示过去并未实现或不可能实现的愿望：

①I wished you had helped me.
　我曾希望你能帮我。（过去没有帮忙）
②I wish you had written to me.
　我希望你曾写信给我。（过去没有写信）
③I wish I would/could have gone to a good college.
　我多希望能去一所好的大学。（过去没有进入好学校）

（5）在 it's (about/ high/ first) time that 引导的定语从句中，动词用过去式。表示"该是做什么的时候了"：

①It's about time you went to bed.
　该是睡觉的时候了。
②It is high time we put an end to the argument.
　该结束我们这场争论了。
③It is the first time he has spoken to me in this way.
　这是他第一次这样和我讲话。（有序数词时，主句用 is，从句用 has/have done）
④It was the third time that she had complained about me.
　这是她第三次抱怨我。（有序数词时，主句用 was，从句用 had done）

（6）在 would rather/would sooner/would just as soon 后面的 that 从句中，通常用过去时，表示"宁愿……，宁可……"，是虚拟语气而并非事实：

其他虚拟语气用法
①I would rather you didn't tell me the truth. 　我宁愿你不告诉我实情。(与现在情况相反) ②She'd sooner she had gone to the party than stayed at home. 　她宁愿去参加聚会,也不愿待在家里。(与过去情况相反)
(7)在 if only 感叹句中,表示"要是……就好了……",谓语动词与wish宾语从句中的形式相同:
①If only he didn't drive so fast! 　要是他开慢一点就好了。(与现在事实相反) ②If only she had asked my advice. 　要是她问了我的建议就好了。(与过去事实相反) ③If only the rain would stop soon. 　要是雨能马上停止就好了。(与将来事实相反)
(8)在 as if/as though 引导的方式状语从句中,谓语动词与wish宾语从句中的虚拟形式相同:
①He told me the story as if he had been on the spot. 　他跟我讲述了这件事情,仿佛他当时就在现场。(与过去事实相反) ②She loves me as though I were her son. 　她爱我就好像我是她的儿子。(与现在事实相反)
(9)在 even if/though 引导的让步状语从句中,可用虚拟语气,主从句结构和if从句一致:
①Even though he didn't help me, he should not pretend to know nothing. 　即使他不肯帮我,也不应假装什么都不知道。(与现在事实相反) ②Even if I had been there, I would have felt overwhelmed. 　即使我在那里,我也会感到不知所措。(与过去事实相反)
(10)在 it is/was+形容词后的 that 主语从句中,谓语动词用should+动词原形,should可省略。如在advisable/anxious/compulsory/crucial/desirable/essential/impossible/important/natural/necessary/preferable/urgent/vital/appropriate/proper/possible 等词后:
①It is essential that you should go to work on time. 　准时上班是非常重要的。 ②It is necessary that we should start early. 　早点动身是很有必要的。 ③It is natural that he betray us. 　他会出卖我们是很自然的事情。
(11)在 lest/for fear that/in case 引导的目的状语从句中,谓语动词用should+动词原形,should可省略;在 so that/in order that 引导的目的状语从句中,谓语为情态动词+动词原形:
①They spoke in whispers lest they should be heard. 　他们低声交流,唯恐被他人听见。 ②I worked hard for fear that I would be fired by the firm. 　我拼命工作,生怕被公司开除。 ③We got up early in order that we should/could/may/might catch the early morning train. 　我们一早起床,为了能赶上清晨的火车。 ④I speak loudly so that he can hear me clearly. 　我大声地讲话以便他能听得清楚。

第三章　英语句法

▶ **Part 1　句子成分（Ingredients of Sentences）** ◀

英语的句子由词和短语构成,不同的句子成分在句子中发挥的作用不同。所谓的句子成分,指的是构成句子的各个部分,可分为主要成分和次要成分。主要成分有主语和谓语;次要成分有宾语、定语、状语、补语、表语和同位语。

Section 1　主语（Subject）

主语是句子叙述的主体,一般位于句首,但在倒装句、疑问句或 there be 结构等句型中,主语位于助动词、谓语或情态动词等后面。主语可由名词、代词、数词、动名词、分词、不定式、短语和主语从句等表示。比如:

①The flowers are growing well.

　　这些花长得很好。(名词作主语)

②She is a teacher.

　　她是一名教师。(代词作主语)

③One plus two is three.

　　一加二等于三。(数词作主语)

④Running is my favorite.

　　跑步是我的最爱。(动名词作主语)

⑤To trust him is hard.

　　要相信他很难。(不定式作主语)

⑥The rich should help the poor.

　　富人应该帮助穷人。(名词化的形容词作主语)

⑦What he said embarrassed me.

　　他所说的让我很尴尬。(从句作主语)

⑧Whether she likes the gift remains unknown.

　　她是否喜欢这份礼物是个未知数。(从句作主语)

⑨It is a pleasure to meet you.

　　见到你很高兴。(it 作形式主语,不定式作逻辑主语)

⑩It is unlikely that she will accept your invitation.

她不大可能接受你的邀请。(it作形式主语,从句作逻辑主语)

⑪Only then did I realize that he was lying.

　　直到那时我才意识到他在撒谎。(倒装句,主语位于助动词之后)

⑫There comes the train.

　　火车来了。(倒装句,主语位于谓语动词之后)

Section 2　谓语(Predicate)

　　谓语表示主语所做的动作、行为或表示主语的特征和状态。谓语由动词担任,一般放在主语之后,谓语都是动词,但动词不一定是谓语。比如:

①He reads before bed every day.

　　他每天睡前读书。(动词作谓语)

②The hunter looked for prey.

　　猎人寻找猎物。(动词短语作谓语)

③He doesn't talk much.

　　他话不多。(助动词+动词原形作复合谓语)

④I have read this book.

　　我读过这本书。(助动词+过去分词作复合谓语)

⑤She can speak English fluently.

　　她能说一口流利的英语。(情态动词+动词原形作复合谓语)

⑥I felt embarrassed.

　　我感到尴尬。(系动词+表语作复合谓语)

⑦I am a student.

　　我是一名学生。(系动词+表语作复合谓语)

Section 3　宾语(Object)

　　宾语表示动作的对象,是动作的承受者,一般放在及物动词或介词后面。宾语可由名词、代词、数词、名词化的形容词、动名词、不定式、短语和宾语从句等表示。比如:

①He plays tennis every morning.

　　他每天早上打网球。(名词作宾语)

②I believe her.

　　我相信她。(代词作宾语)

③Please give me one.

　　请给我一个。(数词作宾语)

④We should care about the disabled.

我们应该关心残疾人。(名词化的形容词作宾语)

⑤I like hiking on weekends.

我喜欢在周末徒步旅行。(动名词作宾语)

⑥I began to run two years ago.

我两年前开始跑步。(不定式作宾语)

⑦I don't know how to express myself.

我不知道该如何表达自己。(短语作宾语)

⑧I think he is sure to succeed.

我认为他一定会成功。(从句作宾语)

⑨I found her smiling at me.

我发现她在对我微笑。(宾语+宾语补足语作复合宾语)

⑩I find it uneasy to support the family.

我认为养家是不易的。(it作形式宾语,不定式作逻辑宾语)

Section 4 定语(Attribute)

定语用于修饰、限定名词或代词,描述名词或代词的品质和特征等情况。单词作定语时,通常放在所修饰的词前面,即前置定语;词组或从句作定语时,通常放在所修饰的词后面,即后置定语。定语可由形容词、名词、代词、数词、分词、副词、动名词、不定式、介词短语或相当于形容词的词、短语或从句来表示。比如:

①He is a smart boy.

他是一个聪明的男孩。(形容词作定语)

②There is an apple tree over there.

那有一棵苹果树。(名词作定语)

③Your proposal will not be accepted.

你的建议不会被接受。(代词作定语)

④We've hired ten new employees.

我们已经雇用了10名新员工。(数词作定语)

⑤China is still a developing country.

中国仍然是一个发展中国家。(现在分词作定语)

⑥Japan is already a developed country.

日本已经是一个发达国家。(过去分词作定语)

⑦The boy talking to the teacher is my friend.

正在和老师说话的那个男孩是我的朋友。(现在分词短语作定语)

⑧The car repaired several times is still broken.

这辆车修了好几次了,还是没修好。(过去分词短语作定语)

⑨You should follow <u>the manager's</u> advice.

你应该听从经理的建议。(名词所有格作定语)

⑩The man <u>outside</u> is my father.

外面的那个人是我父亲。(副词作定语)

⑪We all like this <u>reading</u> room.

我们都喜欢这个阅览室。(动名词作定语)

⑫The man <u>in black</u> is my teacher.

穿黑衣服的那个人是我的老师。(介词短语作定语)

⑬I have something important <u>to attend to</u>.

我有重要的事情要处理。(不定式作定语)

⑭I have just finished reading the book <u>I bought last week</u>.

我刚读完我上周买的那本书。(从句作定语)

⑮Does anyone <u>else</u> know about this?

还有其他人知道这件事吗?(复合不定代词的定语须后置)

Section 5 状语(Adverbial)

状语用于修饰动词、形容词、副词或整个句子,表示事情发生的时间、地点、原因、结果、目的、条件、伴随、程度、方式和让步等。状语可用副词、介词短语、分词、不定式或相当于副词的词、短语或从句来表示。比如:

①I saw him <u>yesterday</u>.

我昨天看见他了。(副词作状语)

②He runs <u>fast</u>.

他跑得快。(副词作状语)

③We go fishing <u>now and then</u>.

我们偶尔去钓鱼。(副词词组作状语)

④We'll have dinner <u>in a restaurant</u>.

我们将在一家餐馆吃晚饭。(介词短语作状语)

⑤I have been here <u>for seven years</u>.

我在这里已经7年了。(介词短语作状语)

⑥He studied hard <u>to get into a good school</u>.

他努力学习为了进入一所好学校。(不定式作状语)

⑦I'm sorry <u>to have kept you waiting</u>.

对不起,让你久等了。(不定式作状语)

⑧<u>Turning off the TV</u>, he went to bed at once.

关掉电视,他就上床睡觉了。(现在分词短语作状语)

⑨Given more time, I'm sure I'll do better.

给我更多的时间,我相信会做得更好。(过去分词短语作状语)

⑩We will go outside if it's not raining.

如果不下雨,我们就出去。(从句作状语)

⑪Although he failed, he was not disappointed.

虽然他失败了,但他没有失望。(从句作状语)

Section 6 补语(Complement)

如果构成主语或宾语的词语尚不完整,则需加入其他成分对主语或宾语进行补充说明,这个成分就是补语。补语的作用对象是主语和宾语,具有鲜明的定语性描写或限制性功能,但是又和定语不同,补语在语法上是不可或缺的,去掉补语的补充说明会导致句子意思的不完整。对主语的补充,被称为主语补足语;对宾语的补充,被称为宾语补足语,通常构成主谓宾补句型。补语可由名词、形容词、副词、不定式、分词、介词短语或从句来表示。比如:

①She is diligent.

她很勤奋。(形容词作主语补语,构成系表结构)

②He is a teacher.

他是一名教师。(名词作主语补语,构成系表结构)

③He was elected President.

他被选为总统。(名词作主语补语)

④He was asked to work overtime.

他被要求加班。(不定式,作主语补语)

⑤He was found dancing in the park.

他被发现在公园里跳舞。(分词短语,作主语补语)

⑥My father named me Tom.

我父亲给我起名叫汤姆。(名词,作宾语补语)

⑦I won't make her sad.

我不会让她伤心的。(形容词,作宾语补语)

⑧He forbade me to watch TV.

他禁止我看电视。(不定式,作宾语补语)

⑨I heard her sing in the room.

我听见她在房间里唱歌。(省略to的不定式,作宾语补语)

⑩Don't let them in now.

现在别让他们进来。(副词作宾语补语)

⑪He found me <u>sleeping</u> in the library.

　　他发现我在图书馆睡觉。(现在分词,作宾语补语)

⑫I found my bike <u>stolen</u>.

　　我发现自行车被偷了。(过去分词,作宾语补语)

⑬She regards me <u>as her own son</u>.

　　她把我当作自己的儿子。(as的短语,作宾语补语)

⑭I found the kitchen <u>in good order</u>.

　　我发现厨房井井有条。(介词短语,作宾语补语)

⑮We will make the company <u>what you want it to be</u>.

　　我们会把公司变成你所期望的样子。(从句,作宾语补语)

Section 7 表语(Predicative)

　　表语用于说明、描述主语的性质、特征、身份和状态,本质上属于主语补足语。表语位于连系动词之后,并和系动词一起构成句子的复合谓语。表语可由名词、形容词、副词、介词短语、动名词、不定式、分词或起名词和形容词作用的词、短语或从句来表示。比如:

①China is a big <u>country</u>.

　　中国是一个大国。(名词作表语)

②I'm sure it's <u>him</u>.

　　我敢肯定是他。(代词作表语)

③I was <u>the first</u> to leave.

　　我是最后一个到的。(数词作表语)

④I feel <u>good</u>.

　　我感觉很好。(形容词作表语)

⑤My specialty is <u>swimming</u>.

　　我的特长是游泳。(动名词作表语)

⑥Snakes are <u>frightening</u>.

　　蛇是可怕的。(现在分词作表语)

⑦I'm <u>disappointed</u> in you.

　　我对你很失望。(过去分词作表语)

⑧The project is <u>over</u>.

　　项目结束了。(副词作表语)

⑨The fire was <u>under control</u>.

　　火势已得到控制。(介词短语作表语)

⑩The way to learn spoken English is <u>to speak more</u>.

　　学习英语口语的方法就是要多说。(不定式作表语)

⑪The truth is <u>that she has never really left you</u>.

事实上，她从未真正离开过你。(从句作表语)

⑫It seems <u>as if she is still waiting for you</u>.

她好像还在等你。(从句作表语)

Section 8　同位语(Appositive)

同位语是对名词或代词进行解释说明的成分，与其修饰的名词或代词格式一致、地位相同，是名词或代词全部内容的体现。同位语一般紧跟在它所修饰的词之后，充当的语法成分与前面的词一致。同位语和补语的最大区别在于：补语不可缺少，而同位语是可以缺少的。同位语可用词、短语或句子来表示。比如：

①My brother, <u>Sam</u>, has been a successful writer.

我的弟弟山姆成了一位成功的作家。(名词作同位语，补充说明)

②Mr. Russell, <u>my grammar teacher</u>, was very strict with me.

我的语法老师罗素先生对我非常严格。(短语作同位语，补充说明)

③They <u>each</u> bought a watch.

他们每人都买了一块手表。(代词作同位语，补充说明)

④You <u>two</u> come with me.

你们俩跟我来。(数词作同位语，补充说明)

⑤Students, <u>new and old</u>, will come to the celebration.

新老同学们都将参加庆祝活动。(形容词作同位语，补充说明)

⑥The country <u>of Japan</u> lies to the east of China.

日本位于中国的东部。(介词of引导同位语，补充说明)

⑦The car has a length <u>of 4.7 meters</u>.

这辆车有4.7米长。(介词of引导同位语，补充说明)

⑧She loves art, especially <u>painting</u>.

她喜欢艺术，尤其是绘画。(动名词作同位语，同时表示部分句子含义)

⑨We <u>Chinese</u> are very diligent and pragmatic.

我们中国人非常勤劳和务实。(名词作同位语，同时表示部分句子含义)

⑩She was unaware of the fact <u>that he was ill</u>.

她不知道他生病的事实。(从句作同位语，连词that不能省略)

⑪We have no idea <u>when he will come</u>.

我们不知道他什么时候来。(从句作同位语)

⑫The problem <u>whether he will be our new manager</u> remains unknown.

他是否会成为我们的新经理，这个问题还不清楚。(if不能引导同位语从句)

▶Part 2 简单句(Simple Sentences)◀

1 简单句的概念

英语的简单句是指只含有一个主谓结构,句子中的各个成分都是由单词或短语构成的独立句子或分句。也就是只有一个主语(或并列主语)和一个谓语(或并列谓语)的句子。比如:

①I love English.

　　我爱英语。(一个主语,一个谓语)

②She and I are friends.

　　她和我是朋友。(并列主语,一个谓语)

③She came and helped me yesterday.

　　她昨天来帮我了。(一个主语,并列谓语)

④My wife and I raised and educated our son together.

　　我和妻子一起抚养和教育儿子。(并列主语,并列谓语)

2 简单句的分类

根据句子基本结构,简单句可分为5种句型。分别为:①主语+谓语;②主语+系动词+表语;③主语+谓语+宾语;④主语+谓语+间接宾语+直接宾语;⑤主语+谓语+宾语+宾语补足语。

S=Subject,指主语;V=Verb,指谓语;O=Object,指宾语;C=Complement,指补语;P=Predicative,指表语。

Section 1 主谓

　　S　　　+　　**V**(主语+谓语)

Birds　　　　　fly.

主语　不及物动词

该句型中,句子的谓语动词可以表达完整的意思,这类动词被称为不及物动词(vi.),后面不能直接跟宾语,若要接宾语,须先在动词后添加某个介词再引荐宾语。主谓结构的句型可以在谓语动词后不加任何成分,也可在谓语动词后面接介词短语、副词、分词短语、动词不定式、状语等。比如:

①She is singing.

　　她在唱歌。(不加成分)

②He has come.

他来了。(不加成分)

③The sun rises in the east.

太阳从东方升起。(后接介词短语)

④He smiles to me.

他对我微笑。(后接介词短语)

⑤Birds fly happily.

小鸟快乐地飞翔。(后接副词)

⑥He comes early and leaves late.

他来得早,走得晚。(后接副词)

⑦She'll come to visit us.

她会来看我们。(后接动词不定式)

⑧We usually go shopping on Sundays.

我们通常星期日去购物。(后接分词短语)

⑨She sat for two hours, reading carefully.

她坐了两个小时,认真地看着书。(后接介词短语与分词短语)

Section 2 主系表

S + V + P (主语+系动词+表语)

I am a teacher.

主语 连系动词 表语

连系动词(Linking Verb),不能单独表达完整的意思,须加上一个表语(亦称补语),构成一个复合谓语,才能表达完整的意思。也就是说,系动词是用来辅助主语的一类动词,把表语和主语连接在一起,系动词通常本身具有词义,但不能单独作谓语,其后必须接表语,构成系表结构,说明主语的身份、状况、类别、性质、品性、特征等。后面可接形容词、名词、副词、介词短语、动名词、不定式、分词以及表语从句等作表语。比如:

①She is a student.

她是个学生。(后接名词)

②The question seems difficult.

这个问题似乎很难。(后接形容词)

③The film is on.

电影上映了。(后接副词)

④Her job is to design clothes.

她的工作是设计服装。(后接不定式)

⑤His hobby is singing.

他的爱好是唱歌。（后接动名词）

⑥The fire was <u>under control</u>.

　　火势已得到控制。（后接介词短语）

⑦It looks <u>as if it's going to rain</u>.

　　看起来好像要下雨了。（后接表语从句）

⑧The true is <u>that he has never loved me</u>.

　　事实是他从未爱过我。（后接表语从句）

　　系动词主要分为：状态系动词（be）、感官系动词（smell、feel、look、taste、sound、seem）、变化系动词（become、get、turn、grow、go、come、fall）、持续系动词（remain、keep、continue、stay、lie、stand、rest）、表象系动词（look、seem、appear）、终止系动词（prove、turn out）。比如：

①He is always like that.

　　他总是那样。（状态系动词）

②The quilt feels soft.

　　被子摸起来很软。（感官系动词）

③He is growing taller.

　　他长高了。（变化系动词）

④Her face went pale.

　　她的脸色变得苍白。（变化系动词）

⑤My dream came true.

　　我的梦想实现了。（变化系动词）

⑥She stays single.

　　她一直单身。（持续系动词）

⑦He stood there petrified.

　　他呆呆地站在那里。（持续系动词）

⑧The snow lies thick.

　　雪积得很厚。（持续系动词）

⑨It seems broken.

　　东西好像坏了。（表象系动词）

⑩The theory proved correct.

　　这个理论被证明是正确的。（终止系动词）

⑪He turned out to be right.

　　结果证明他是对的。（终止系动词）

　　注：当be动词用于构成进行时态或被动语态时，则不是系动词，而属于助动词；动词用作系动词时，无被动语态，只表示某种状态。

Section 3 主谓宾

S + V + O（主语+谓语+宾语）

I bought a book.

主语　及物动词　宾语

该句型中,谓语动词具有实际含义,体现主语的动作,但不能表示完整的含义,须后接一个宾语才能表达完整含义,即动作承受者。这类动词被称为及物动词(*vt.*)。"及物"说明动词通常需带"物"来完成一个动作,也就是后面要加一个宾语。及物动词可以接名词、代词、动名词、动词不定式和宾语从句等作宾语。比如:

①She opened <u>the window</u>.

　她打开了窗户。(后接名词)

②The government is helping <u>the poor</u>.

　政府正在帮助穷人。(后接名词性的形容词)

③He helped <u>me</u> a lot.

　他帮了我很多忙。(后接代词)

④I like <u>reading</u>.

　我喜欢阅读。(后接动名词)

⑤I want <u>to stay at home</u>.

　我想待在家里。(后接不定式)

⑥I think <u>she'll like the present</u>.

　我想她会喜欢这个礼物的。(后接宾语从句)

注:区分动词是及物动词或不及物动词,是英语语法学习的核心之一。动词是词法学习的重中之重,因为谓语动词体现句子时态和语态,并且在句法学习中,不同的句型所使用的动词性质也是不同的,及物动词和不及物动词构成不同的英语句型。从语态的角度上讲,通常及物动词有被动语态,而不及物动词无被动语态,因为其动作没有对象。同时在实际运用中,许多实义动词,既可作及物动词,也可作不及物动词。比如:

组①:The cook tasted the soup.

　　　厨师尝了尝汤。(taste 作及物动词)

　　　The soup tasted bitter.

　　　汤尝起来很苦。(taste 作系动词、不及物动词)

组②:Can you feel the pain?

你能感觉到疼痛吗?(feel作及物动词)

I feel very painful.

我感觉很痛苦。(feel作系动词、不及物动词)

组③:We'll start running at five.

我们5点开始跑步。(start作及物动词)

We'll start at five.

我们5点出发。(start作不及物动词)

组④:When did you leave home yesterday?

你昨天什么时候离开家的?(leave作及物动词)

I left at 6 o'clock.

我六点钟离开的。(leave作不及物动词)

组⑤:Can you sing a song for me?

你能为我唱首歌吗?(sing作及物动词)

You sing really well.

你唱得真好。(sing作不及物动词)

Section 4 主谓宾宾

S + **V** + **IO** + **DO**(主语+谓语+间接宾语+直接宾语)

I　　give　　him　　a book.

主语　及物动词　间接宾语　直接宾语　(亦称双宾语)

此句型的谓语动词为及物动词,谓语后面接两个宾语以表达完整的意思,一个被称为间接宾语,即动作的间接承受者;一个被称为直接宾语,即动作的直接承受者,此类及物动词也被称为双宾语动词。间接宾语通常由代词或名词充当,往往指的是"人",直接宾语往往由名词充当,往往指的是"物"。比如:

①He sent me a letter.

他给我寄了一封信。

②My grandpa told me a story.

我爷爷给我讲了一个故事。

③She made her doll a dress.

她给她的娃娃做了一件衣服。

④My brother bought me a gift.

我哥哥给我买了一件礼物。

双宾语动词,通常具有"给予"的含义。若要将直接宾语至于间接宾语之前,则需要借助介词to/for来表达,to侧重于动作的方向,for侧重于动作的受益者。借助介词to实现宾语易位的双宾语动词,如give、teach、take、lend、pass、offer、bring、hand、sell、award、write、answer、throw、pay、promise、owe、return、mail等;借助介词for实现宾语易位的双宾语动词,如buy、book、cook、find、make、fetch、choose、get、order、pick、serve、sing、draw、leave、save等。比如:

①He sold me a car.

= He sold a car to me.

他把一辆车卖给了我。

②The dean awarded me the prize.

= The dean awarded the prize to me.

院长给我颁了奖。

③She sang us a song yesterday.

= She sang a song for us yesterday.

她昨天给我们唱了一首歌。

④Can you book us a table?

= Can you book a table for us?

你能帮我们订张桌子吗?

注:双宾语动词在使用被动语态时,须根据具体句型分析,通常有以下三种情形:

(1)可用间接宾语作主语,保留直接宾语,也可用直接宾语作主语,用介词to/for连接间接宾语,如buy、give、lend、pay、show、teach、tell、offer、leave、award等动词。比如:

主动:He told me a story.

被动:I was told a story.

被动:A story was told to me.

主动:He left me a fortune.

被动:I was left a fortune.

被动:A fortune was left to/for me.

(2)用直接宾语作被动语态的主语,用介词to/for连接间接宾语,如do、make、pass、sell、sing、write、send、bring等动词。比如:

主动:He passed me the mustard.

被动:The mustard was passed to me.

主动:She made me a sweater.

被动:A sweater was made for me.

（3）用间接宾语作被动语态的主语，保留直接宾语，如 answer、refuse、save、spare、deny、envy 等动词。比如：

主动：You saved me a lot of trouble.

被动：I was saved a lot of trouble.

主动：She denied me the permission.

被动：I was denied the permission.

Section 5 主谓宾补

S　＋　V　＋　O　＋　OC（主语+谓语+宾语+宾语补足语）

I　consider　him　a good man.

主语　谓语动词　宾语　补语　（亦称复合宾语）

该句型的谓语动词为及物动词，但接一个宾语并不能表达完整的意思，还须在宾语后面加一个补充成分来补充说明宾语的身份或状态等，从而使意思表达完整。宾语与宾语补足语结构也被称为复合宾语，通常在逻辑上有主谓关系或主表关系。作宾补成分的有名词、形容词、副词、动词不定式、分词、介词短语等。比如：

①Coffee keeps me awake.

　咖啡让我保持清醒。（形容词作宾补）

②The movie makes him a star.

　这部电影使他成为明星。（名词作宾补）

③I heard her singing.

　我听见她在唱歌。（现在分词作补语）

④I had the car repaired.

　我请人把车修好了。（过去分词作补语）

⑤I saw him out with his friend.

　我看见他和朋友出去了。（副词作宾补）

⑥His mother told him not to smoke.

　他妈妈告诉他不要吸烟。（动词不定式作宾语）

复合宾语中，宾语补足语的形式通常取决于谓语动词的用法。如在 want、tell、ask、order、allow、advise、beg 等动词后，宾补通常用带 to 的动词不定式；在 let、make、have、see、watch、notice 等动词后，宾补可用不带 to 的动词不定式；在 hear、see、notice、watch、observe、have、make 等动词后，宾补也可用分词。当动词不定式、动名词或从句作宾语时，我们通常在宾补前用 it 作形式宾语，将真正的宾语移至句末，达到平衡句子结构的目的，符合英语的"尾重原则"。比如：

①I found it difficult to persuade him.

我发现说服他很困难。(it代替不定式)

②They thought it right to make such a plan.

他们认为制订这样一个计划是正确的。(it代替不定式)

③My friend considers it unnecessary reciting so many words.

我朋友认为背这么多单词是没有必要的。(it代替动名词)

④I find it difficult educating my own child.

我发现教育自己的孩子很难。(it代替动名词)

⑤I don't think it possible that she would forgive you.

我认为她不可能原谅你。(it代替从句)

⑥He found it unbelievable that I can't ride a bicycle.

我不会骑自行车,对此他觉得难以置信。(it代替从句)

Section 6 There be 句型

There be句型由"there be+主语+状语"构成,用于表示某处存在某物或某人,并无所属关系。there为引导词,无实际意义,be为谓语动词,there be后面的名词为句子的真正主语,因此该句型本质上是倒装句型。

there be句型的主谓一致

there be结构中,be动词应和紧跟其后的主语保持数的一致,即"就近原则"。

①There is a flower under the tree.

树下有一朵花。

②There are some people rowing on the river.

河上有一些人在划船。

③There is a teacher and ten students in the classroom.

教室里有一位老师和十个学生。

④There are ten students and a teacher in the classroom.

教室里有十个学生和一位老师。

there be句型的时态变化

there be结构的时态通过be动词的变化而体现,可构成多种时态。

①There will be great changes next year.

明年会有很大的变化。

②There have been many new stores in our city.

我们城市新开了许多商店。

③There had been a serious quarrel between them before.

他们之间以前有过一次严重的争吵。

there be 句型的情态变化

there be 结构可与情态动词连用,表达丰富的情态意义。

①There <u>may</u> be an opportunity for you to get a promotion.

你可能会有升职的机会。

②There <u>must</u> have been a thief in the house last night.

昨晚房子里肯定来过小偷。

③There <u>used to</u> be many tall trees there.

那里过去有许多参天大树。

there be 句型谓语动词的活用

there be 结构中,be 动词可由 stand、lie、live、go、come、exist、remain 等动词替代,也可与 seem to、appear to、happen to 等词组连用。

①There stands a high mountain over there.

那边矗立着一座高山。

②There lies a clear stream in our village.

我们村子里有一条清澈的小溪。

③There once lived a wise man in the temple.

从前,寺庙里住着一位智者。

④There comes the bus.

公共汽车来了。

⑤There seems to be something wrong in our management.

我们的管理好像出了点问题。

⑥There happened to be a policeman nearby when the robbery took place.

抢劫发生时,碰巧附近有一个警察。

there be 句型的非谓语用法

there be 结构的非谓语形式通常有两种结构,即 there being 和 there to be。there being 结构通常用作状语、主语或宾语;there to be 结构通常用作宾语。

①There being no good projects, we should reduce our investment at present.

没有什么好的项目,我们目前应该减少投资。

②There being an airport has accelerated our city's development.

机场的建成加速了我们城市的发展。

③The company planned on there being a team building.

公司计划进行团队建设。

④I never dreamed of there being your solicitude.

我未曾想到会得到你的关怀。

⑤Our country doesn't want there to be poverty again.

我们的国家不希望再有贫困。

⑥We hope there to be another detailed discussion.

我们希望再进行一次详细的讨论。

⑦It's impossible for there to be more reinforcements coming here.

不可能再有增援部队前来了。

▶ Part 3　并列句（Compound Sentences）◀

并列句的概念

英语的并列句是指用并列连词连接的两个或两个以上简单句。各句的意义同等重要、紧密联系，且互相无从属关系、独立存在，因此是平行并列的关系，各简单句之间根据上下文按逻辑次序排列。

Section 1　表示同等关系的并列句

这类并列句通常用and、not only ... but also (as well)、neither ... nor、on (the) one hand ... on the other hand、for one thing ... for another、so、nor、neither等连词连接或用分号隔开。比如：

①He works here and he's doing well.

他在这里工作，而且干得不错。

②Not only did he fail the math test, but he failed English as well.

他不仅数学考试不及格，英语也没过。

③She neither wanted to go out, nor ate any food.

她既不想出门，也不想吃任何东西。

④On the one hand we should work hard, on the other hand we should care about our health.

一方面我们应该努力工作，另一方面我们应该注意身体。

⑤For one thing the bag is not nice, for another it is too expensive.

一方面这个包不漂亮，另一方面它太贵了。

⑥She likes playing the piano, so do I.

她喜欢弹钢琴，我也喜欢。

⑦He is no longer young, nor am I.

他不再年轻了,我也不年轻了。

⑧He is not satisfied with his job, neither am I.

他对他的工作不满意,我也不满意。

⑨I feel tired; I want to rest for a few days.

我感到累了,想休息几天。

Section 2 表示选择关系的并列句

这类并列句通常用or、or else、either ... or、otherwise、not ... but等连词来连接。比如:

①Hurry up, or you'll be late for work.

快点,否则你上班要迟到了。(or意为"否则")

②You can go for coffee, or you can go shopping.

你可以去喝咖啡,也可以去购物。(or意为"或者")

③He must be a genius, or else he must be mad.

他一定是个天才,要不就是疯了。(or else为词组)

④You can either do well or leave the company.

你要么好好干,要么离开公司。

⑤Traffic is smooth today, otherwise I'll miss the meeting.

今天交通很顺畅,否则我就赶不上会议了。

⑥It's not that they won't do it, but they can't do it well.

不是他们不愿意做,而是他们做不好。

Section 3 表示转折关系的并列句

这类并列句通常用but、while、yet、still、whereas、when、nevertheless、however、nonetheless等连词来连接。比如:

①She is not pretty, but she is very intelligent.

她不漂亮,但很聪明。

②She is thin, while her sister is fat.

她很瘦,而她姐姐很胖。

③It's late, yet there are still a few colleagues working.

已经很晚了,但是仍有几个同事在工作。

④I seem to be ill, still I have to work.

我好像病了,但我还得工作。

⑤Some people are satisfied with their income, whereas most are not.

有些人对他们的收入感到满意，然而大多数人并不满意。

⑥He says he knows art, when I think he's just faking it.

他说他懂艺术，但我认为他是装的。

⑦What he said was shocking; nevertheless, it was all true.

他说的话令人震惊，但都是真的。

⑧I trusted him so much; however, he lied to me.

我很信任他，然而他却对我撒谎了。

⑨The working conditions are not good; nonetheless I don't want to quit anyway.

工作条件不太好，但尽管如此，我还是不想辞职。

Section 4 表示因果关系的并列句

这类并列句通常用so、and so、for、therefore、thus、hence等连词来连接。比如：

①It was cold, so she wore a sweater.

天气很冷，所以她穿了一件毛衣。

②He is proficient in machinery, and so he can help you fix it.

他精通机械，所以他可以帮你修理。

③She has many friends, for she is kind.

她有很多朋友，因为她很善良。

④You're still young; therefore, you still have a chance.

你还年轻，所以你还有机会。

⑤He didn't practice hard; thus, he didn't pass the driving test.

他没有努力练习，因此他没有通过驾校考试。

⑥The company's facing problems; hence he decided to return to management.

公司面临问题，因此他决定重返管理层。

Section 5 并列句的省略

(1)主语省略的情况

如果前后两个简单句的主语相同，通常可以省略后面一个简单句的主语。比如：

①He grabbed his car keys and rushed out.

他抓起车钥匙，冲了出去。

②You can either study abroad or become a civil servant.

你可以出国留学，也可以当公务员。

③He saw the doctor, but did not believe the diagnostic report.

他去看了医生,但不相信诊断报告。

④He broke his foot, so didn't come to work.

他的脚摔断了,所以没来上班。

（2）谓语省略的情况

如果前后两个简单句的谓语相同,通常可以省略后面一个简单句的谓语。比如:

①She wanted to learn the piano, and she did.

她想学钢琴,她的确这么做了。

②You can watch TV after finishing your homework, otherwise you can't.

你可以在做完作业后看电视,否则不能。

③I visited the teacher, yet he didn't.

我拜访了老师,但他没有。

④He didn't read the new text, for he couldn't.

他没有读新课文,因为他不会。

（3）主谓省略的情况

主语和动词也可以同时省略,但此时句子变为简单句,不再是并列句。比如:

①She is very beautiful, and (she is very) considerate.

她很漂亮,也很体贴人。

②Do you want to drink tea, or (do you want to drink) coffee?

你想喝茶还是咖啡?

③The meal was cheap, but (it was) delicious.

这顿饭很便宜,但很好吃。

④He is extravagant in spending money, thus (he is) poor in the end.

他花钱大手大脚,因而最终穷困潦倒。

（4）相同成分的省略

简单句前后重复出现的成分,在不影响理解的基础上,通常可以省略。比如:

①She had dinner with me tonight and (she) will (have dinner with me) tomorrow.

她今晚和我一起吃了晚饭,明天也将和我一起吃晚饭。

②The door must have been repaired and the table (must have been) installed.

门肯定已经修好了,桌子也一定装好了。

③He entered for the contest, but I won't (enter for the contest) .

他报名参加了这个比赛,但我不会去参加。

▶ **Part 4 复合句(Complex Sentences)** ◀

1 复合句的概念

英语的复合句由一个独立分句(即主句)和一个或一个以上的从属分句(即从句)构成,又被称为主从复合句。与并列句不同,复合句的各个组成部分并非同等重要:主句为句子的主体部分,常可独立存在;从句不能独立存在,只能作为句子的一个成分,如主语、宾语、表语、同位语、定语和状语等。复合句通常用于书面语,是语言综合能力提升的核心之一。

复合句的构成方法主要有两种:①用连词或关系代词连接主句和从句,构成复合句;②用分词结构或动词不定式(即非谓语短语)代替从句,构成复合句的一部分。比如:

①I don't know (主句) whether he has received my letter (从句).

我不知道他是否收到了我的信。(whether引导的从句作宾语)

②I'll tell him to call you (主句) as soon as he gets home (从句).

他一到家我就叫他给你打电话。(as soon as引导的从句作状语)

③Entering the study (分词短语), he began to read a novel (主句).

他走进书房,开始读一本小说。(分词短语代替从句)

④To get into a good college (不定式), you have to work hard (主句).

要进入一所好大学,你必须努力学习。(不定式代替从句)

2 复合句的分类

复合句按句子结构可分为三种:名词性从句、形容词性从句和副词性从句。

名词性从句	主语从句
	宾语从句
	表语从句
	同位语从句
形容词性从句	定语从句
副词性从句	状语从句

(1)名词性从句

It is certain that China will succeed in making chips.

中国在制造芯片方面肯定会成功。(that引导主语从句)

（2）形容词性从句

The books which I recommend to you will help you understand science.

我推荐给你的书会帮助你理解科学。（which引导定语从句）

（3）副词性从句

Although scientific research is difficult, we have to explore this area actively.

虽然科学研究很难，但我们必须积极探索这一领域。（although引导状语从句）

Section 1 主语从句（Subject Clause）

1 主语从句的定义

主语从句指的是在复合句中作主句主语成分的从句，通常放在主句的谓语动词之前，或由形式主语it代替，而从句放在句末。

2 主语从句的形式

（1）主语从句可由从属连词引导

主语从句可由从属连词that、whether引导。比如：

①That he wants to study abroad can't be changed by anyone.

他想出国留学，这是任何人都改变不了的。

②That she completed the design on her own amazed our manager.

她独立完成了设计，这使我们的经理大为吃惊。

③Whether she will pass the test or not is uncertain.

她是否会通过考试还不确定。

④Whether you should leave your job needs to be considered carefully.

你是否应离职需要经过慎重考虑。

注：上述例句①②属于陈述型主语从句，that作为从句标志词，在主语从句中不作任何成分，无任何词义，但置于句首时不能省略，能起到明确从句身份的作用，若不加that，听者接收到前半段时易误以为是全句，而that则能提示从句的出现而避免使听者产生误解。

上述例句③④是由一般疑问句或选择疑问句转换而来的疑问型主语从句，从句采用半倒装结构，可起到明确从句身份的作用，whether可置于句首引导主语从句，if则不能。主语从句若采用疑问句语序，听者会以为是疑问句而产生误解，这也是名词性从句都须使用陈述语序的一个重要原因，在以下由连接代词和连接副词引导的主语从句中亦是如此。

（2）主语从句可由连接代词引导

主语从句可由连接代词who、whom、whose、whoever、what、whatever、which、whichever等引导。比如：

①Who we are to blame doesn't seem so important.

我们该责备谁似乎并不那么重要。

②Whom we should ask for help is a problem.

我们应该向谁求助是个难题。

③Whoever breaks the law should be punished.

无论是谁触犯法律都应该受到惩罚。

④What we need most now is efficiency.

我们现在最需要的是效率。

⑤Whatever I have done before is not so important now.

不管我以前做过什么，现在都不重要了。

⑥Whichever brand you like would be quite expensive for me.

无论你喜欢哪个牌子，对我来说都很贵。

（3）主语从句可由连接副词引导

主语从句可由连接副词when、where、how、why、whenever、wherever、however等来引导。比如：

①When they will left for London hasn't been decided yet.

他们什么时候去伦敦还没有决定。

②Where we hold the meeting has not been notified.

我们还没有接到通知在哪开会。

③How she learns English is of great significance to us.

她如何学习英语对我们很有借鉴意义。

④Why he kept silent is still a mystery.

他为什么保持沉默还是个谜。

⑤Whenever you start reading will never be too late.

无论何时开始阅读，都不会太晚。

⑥However difficult life is can't be the reason to stop her.

生活再困难也不能成为阻止她的理由。

（4）用it作形式主语

为了保持句子的平衡、美观，通常在句首从句的位置使用it作形式主语，而将主语从句移至句末。比如：

①It is a serious problem that young people have to pay their mortgages monthly.

　　年轻人必须每月支付房贷,这是一个严重的问题。

②It is uncertain whether he will come tonight.

　　他今晚是否会来还不确定。

③It is necessary for us that we should work hard.

　　努力工作对我们来说是必要的。

④It remains a mystery what caused the tragedy.

　　造成悲剧的原因仍然是个谜。

⑤It suddenly occurred to me that I had forgotten to pay back the money.

　　我突然想起我忘记还钱了。

⑥It is widely believed that our tomorrow will be better.

　　人们普遍相信我们的明天会更好。

⑦It is reported that China will expand reform and opening up.

　　据报道,中国将扩大改革开放。

主语从句小结:

1. 主语从句可由从属连词、连接代词和连接副词等引导;

2. 主语从句的连词位于句首时,不能省略;

3. 主语从句属于名词性从句,须用陈述语序,不能用疑问句语序;

4. 为保持句子平衡,通常用 it 作形式主语,置于句首代替从句;

5. 从句的时态可以与主句不同,不会受到主句时态的影响和限制;

6. 通常将从句视为整体,作为单数看待,但主句的谓语应根据实际做调整,有时态和数的变化。

Section 2 宾语从句(Object Clause)

1 宾语从句的定义

　　宾语从句指的是在复合句中作宾语的名词性从句,通常放在主句的谓语动词(及物动词)之后,也可放在介词和部分形容词之后作宾语。

2 宾语从句的形式

(1)及物动词后的宾语从句

由从属连词引导

①I find that he has a crush on you.

　　我发现他对你有意思。

②I wonder if you can give me a lift tomorrow.

不知道明天你能否让我搭一程。

③The judge didn't know whether he was willing to testify or not.

法官不知道他是否愿意作证。

④Please make sure whether he will be present tomorrow.

请确认一下他明天是否会出席。

⑤He found out that the medicine he took every day was fake.

他发现他每天吃的药是假的。

注：上述例句①中 that 作宾语从句的从属连词，只起连接主句和从句的作用，无词义，也不作任何成分，通常可省略；例句②③中 if/whether 不作句子成分，但有词义，表示"是否"的含义；例句④⑤中为用于动词短语后的宾语从句。

由连接代词引导

①I've forgotten what she told me yesterday.

我忘了她昨天告诉我的事了。

②Do you know who designed this bridge?

你知道这座桥是谁设计的吗？

③Can you tell me which skirt I should buy?

你能告诉我该买哪条裙子吗？

④Could you please tell me whom I should talk to?

你能告诉我该找谁吗？

由连接副词引导

①Can you explain where you went last night?

你能解释一下昨晚去了哪儿吗？

②I just don't understand why I'm so disliked.

我就是不明白为什么我这么不受待见。

③I didn't see how he did his magic trick.

我不知道他是怎么变的这个魔术。

④He hasn't decided when we will leave for Shanghai.

他还未决定我们什么时候动身去上海。

注：当主句谓语为 think、suppose、believe、imagine、consider、expect、guess 等词时，宾语从句中的否定通常体现在主句中，被称为"否定转移"。比如：

①I don't think it works.

我认为这没用。

②He doesn't believe that I can make it by myself.

他不相信我靠自己就能做到。

采用否定转移的宾语从句中,主语是第一人称时,其反义疑问句与宾语从句中的主谓一致,否则须与主句的主谓一致。比如:

①I don't think it works. Does it?

我认为这没用。不是吗?

②He doesn't believe that I can make it by myself. Does he?

他不相信我靠自己就能做到。是吗?

（2）介词后的宾语从句

①He was surprised at what I had told him.

他对我告诉他的事感到惊讶。

②It depends on how you look at it.

这要取决于你怎么看它。

③He's been thinking of how we can improve management.

他一直在考虑我们如何改进管理。

④They are talking about whether they should adjust their strategy.

他们正在讨论是否应该调整战略。

注:介词后面用whether引导宾语从句时,不能用if替代。

（3）部分形容词后的宾语从句

①I'm afraid that I haven't got the point.

恐怕我还没明白你的意思。

②I'm glad that you made it right in time.

我很高兴你及时改正了。

③I'm quite sure she is the one.

我很肯定她就是那个人。

④I'm sorry I bumped your car.

对不起,我撞了你的车。

⑤He was surprised that his family actually had so much money.

他很惊讶原来他家里这么有钱。

（4）非谓语动词后的宾语从句

①Seeing that she was sitting alone by the window, he went to her.

看到她独自坐在窗边，他走了过去。

②Not realizing what had happened, he kept on talking on the phone.

他并没有意识到发生了什么事，仍在打电话。

③Asked how old she was, she immediately became unhappy.

当被问及年龄时，她马上不开心了。

④After being told that he was fired by the company, he smashed the computer.

在被告知他被公司解雇后，他砸烂了电脑。

⑤To conclude what we have learned today, we should review our notes.

为总结今天所学的内容，我们应该复习一下笔记。

（5）用it作形式宾语

在"及物动词+宾语+宾语补足语"结构中，如果宾语是从句，通常在宾语的位置用it作形式宾语，而将从句放在句末，即"及物动词+it+宾语补足语+宾语从句"结构。比如：

①I think it necessary that we do exercise for an hour every day.

我认为我们每天锻炼一小时是必要的。

②We all consider it right that slippers should be banned in the company.

我们都认为公司禁止穿拖鞋是对的。

③We made it very clear that you should wear a badge to work.

我们说得很清楚，你应该带着胸卡去上班。

④I feel it a pity that you didn't come with us yesterday.

很遗憾你昨天没有和我们一起来。

（6）某些动词接宾语从句时，需在从句前添加it

①I hate it that you lied to me in such a serious way.

我很厌恶你居然如此一本正经地对我撒谎。

②Can you see to it that the contract will be altered today?

你能安排一下今天对合同进行修改吗？

③We took it that they would obey the agreement.

我们认为他们会遵守协议。

④Rumor has it that the prime minister will soon resign.

有传闻说首相很快就要辞职了。

宾语从句小结：

1. 宾语从句可作及物动词、介词或形容词的宾语；

2. 宾语从句可由从属连词、连接代词和连接副词等引导；

3. 宾语从句属于名词性从句，须用陈述语序，不能用疑问句语序；

4. 在复合宾语中，原宾语位置通常用 it 作形式宾语，宾语从句置于句末；

5. 宾语从句的时态较为灵活，应根据主句的时态，并结合实际情况做相应调整。

Section **3** 表语从句（Predicative Clause）

1 表语从句的定义

表语从句指的是在复合句中作主句的表语的名词性从句，放在系动词之后，对主语进行解释、说明，使其内容具体化。

2 表语从句的形式

（1）表语从句可由从属连词引导

①The fact is that she doesn't want anyone to know the secret.

事实是她不想让任何人知道这个秘密。

②It seems that you are not familiar with the project.

看来你对这个项目不熟悉。

③The reason is that I was drunk last night.

原因是我昨晚喝醉了。

④The question is whether we should inform them of the issue now.

问题在于我们是否应该现在就通知他们这件事。

> 注：that 引导表语从句时，不作句子成分，无任何词义，只起连接作用，但通常不能省略；whether 不担当句子成分，表达"是否"的含义，能引导表语从句，if 则不能。

（2）表语从句可由连接代词引导

①He is no longer what he used to be.

他不再是过去的他了。

②Her problem is which car she should choose.

她的问题是该选哪辆车。

③She remains who she is all these years.

这些年来她一直保持着本色。

④The trouble is who I should believe.

问题是我应该相信谁。

⑤The key is whose work was not finished in time.

关键是谁的工作没有及时完成。

（3）表语从句可由连接副词引导

①Next year is when he will start school.

明年将是他开始上学的时间。

②This is where he works.

这是他工作的地方。

③That's why he is not willing to work with you.

那就是他不愿意和你一起工作的原因。

④The problem is how we can contact him now.

问题是我们现在怎么联系到他。

（4）由其他连词引导的表语从句

表语从句也可由其他连词引导，如从属连词 as、just as、as if、as though 或连接副词 because 等。比如：

①He is not as he seems to be.

他并不像他看上去的那样。

②It's just as what you said.

正如你所说的那样。

③You look as though you slept badly last night.

看来你昨晚睡得不好。

④I felt as if I can't feel my feet.

我觉得我的脚好像没知觉了。

⑤That's because he has never believed you.

那是因为他从来没有相信过你。

（because 强调原因；why 强调结果）

（5）使用虚拟语气的表语从句

表语从句用于表示建议、劝告、命令等含义的名词后，谓语动词需用"should+动词原形"表示，should 可省略。如在 plan、advice、suggestion、order、proposal、idea 等词后。比如：

①My suggestion is that we should fire him.

我的建议是我们应该解雇他。

②Her proposal is that we visit our teacher before the Spring Festival.

她的建议是我们在春节前去拜访老师。

③His plan was that we should book a hotel before setting out.

他的计划是我们应在出发前预订好酒店。

④My idea is that we be prepared early on.

我的想法是我们要尽早做好准备。

表语从句小结：

1. 表语从句可由从属连词、连接代词和连接副词等引导；

2. 表语从句属于名词性从句，须用陈述语序；

3. 从句的时态可以与主句不一致，应根据实际情况而定；

4. 可接从句的连系动词除be动词外，有look、remain、seem、appear、prove、turn out等。

Section 4 同位语从句（Appositive Clause）

1 同位语从句的定义

同位语从句指的是在复合句中作同位语的从句，用来补充说明前面的名词或短语，阐释其实际内容，并与该名词性成分是同位关系，被解释说明的词和同位语在逻辑上为主表关系。

2 同位语从句的形式

（1）同位语从句的先行词较为固定，通常具有一定的内容含义

可以接同位语从句的名词通常有 idea、fact、news、hope、opinion、belief、plan、promise、question、problem、answer、doubt、thought、message、evidence、suggestion、information、knowledge、conclusion、order、truth、theory 等表示抽象概念的名词。比如：

①I have a hunch that something good is about to happen.

我有一种预感，有好事要发生。

②The little boy denied the fact that he had broken the vase.

那个小男孩否认他打破了花瓶的事实。

③He broke his promise that he would help me at any time.

他违背了之前说的任何时候都会帮我的诺言。

④The thought came to me that he was lying.

我突然想到他在说谎。

（2）同位语从句可由从属连词引导

①He has a belief that good men are rewarded.

他相信好人有好报。

②Words came that you had emigrated.

有消息说你移居国外了。

③The doubt remains whether the price of gold will fall.

　　黄金价格是否会下跌仍是一个疑问。

④She needs to solve the problem whether she should stay here or not.

　　是否应该留在这里，她必须解决这个问题。

　　注：that引导同位语从句时，不作句子成分，无任何词义，只起连接作用，但不能省略；whether不担当句子成分，表达"是否"的含义，能引导同位语从句，if则不能；同位语从句通常紧跟在先行词之后，如例句①④，但有时会被其他词隔开，如例句②③，从而避免头重脚轻，使句子更为均衡美观，被称为分隔式同位语从句。

（3）同位语从句可由连接代词引导

①I have no idea what he said just now.

　　我不知道他刚才说了什么。

②She has no idea which car would suit her.

　　她不知道哪辆车适合她。

③He still has a question whose advice he should take.

　　他仍然有一个问题，不知道该听谁的建议。

④The company hasn't solved the problem who leaked the trade secrets.

　　公司还没有解决是谁泄露了商业机密的问题。

（4）同位语从句可由连接副词引导

①I don't get the idea where she has been these days.

　　我不知道她这几天去哪儿了。

②We have no idea when he went to Japan.

　　我们不知道他什么时候去的日本。

③We'd better listen to his suggestion how we can run the firm properly.

　　我们最好听听他的建议，关于怎样才能把公司经营好。

④I have found the answer why she is she so cold to people.

　　我已经知道她为什么对人那么冷淡了。

（5）同位语从句可由其他词或词组引导

　　有时候从句可由表示同位关系的词或词组引导，补充说明其前面的名词或代词，如that is、i.e.、that is to say、for example、in other words、for instance、namely等。比如：

①She told me the good news yesterday, namely, she's getting married soon.

　　她昨天告诉我一个好消息，那就是，她很快就要结婚了。

②He has expressed his opinion, that is, there are no ghosts or gods.

他已经表达了他的观点，那就是，世上没有鬼神。

③ There is only one way of solving the problem, namely, we can only rely on ourselves.

解决这个问题只有一个办法，那就是我们只能依靠自己。

④Fruit is good for our health, for instance, apples own the capacity of antioxidant.

水果对我们的健康有好处，比如苹果就具有抗氧化的能力。

同位语从句与定语从句的主要区别：

（1）同位语从句与前面的名词为同位关系，解释说明其内容；定语从句与前面的名词为修饰与被修饰关系，限定名词范围或补充名词信息。比较：

①He told me the news that he had found a job.

他告诉了我他已找到工作的消息。

（同位语从句，从句补充说明 news 的内容）

②The news that he told me was great.

他告诉我的消息很棒。

（定语从句，从句对 news 起到修饰和限制作用）

（2）that 在同位语从句中作从属连词，在从句中不担当成分，只起连接作用；that 在定语从句中作关系代词，除连接作用外，还在从句中担当主语、宾语或表语成分。比较：

①Her advice that I should practice spoken English more often helped me a lot.

她建议我应该更频繁地练习英语口语，这对我帮助很大。

（that 在同位语从句中不作句子成分，只起连接作用）

②The advice that she gave me yesterday was very helpful.

她昨天给我的建议很有帮助。

（that 在定语从句中作宾语，在意义上指代先行词 advice）

（3）同位语从句可用 whether、what、how 等连词引导，而定语从句则不能。比如：

①She can't find the way how she can learn English well.

她找不到学好英语的方法。

（how 引导同位语从句）

②He has no idea what kind of life he wants.

他不知道自己想要什么样的生活。

（what 引导同位语从句）

（4）引导同位语从句时，when、where、why 被称为连接副词，也在从句中担当状语，但不能转换成"介词+关系代词"的形式；引导定语从句时，when、where、why 被称为关系副词，在从句中担当状语，可以转换成"介词+关系代词"的形式。比较：

①The teachers have no idea why he dropped out of school.

老师们不知道他为什么辍学。

（why 引导同位语从句,不能转换成"介词+关系代词"的形式）

②That's the reason why he dropped out of school.

那就是他辍学的原因。

（why 引导定语从句,可转换成 for which 的形式）

同位语从句小结:

1. 同位语的先行词多为抽象名词,从句对其加以解释说明,从而让读者知道具体含义;

2. 同位语从句通常不修饰具体名词和代词;

3. 同位语从句可由从属连词、连接代词和连接副词等引导;

4. 同位语从句属于名词性从句,须用陈述语序;

5. 从句可与先行词隔开,从而保持句子的平衡美观;

6. 注意区分同位语从句与定语从句的区别,对同时学好两种从句具有重要意义。

Section 5 定语从句（Attributive Clause）

1　定语从句的定义

定语从句指的是在复合句中起定语作用、修饰句子中的名词或代词的从句,被修饰的名词或代词被称为先行词,定语从句也被称为关系从句、形容词性从句。

定语从句一般位于先行词的后面,引导定语从句的关联词（引导词）被称为关系代词或关系副词,关联词不仅连接主句与从句,还用来指代先行词,并在定语从句中担当句子成分,关系代词在定语从句中可用作主语、宾语、表语和定语等,关系副词在定语从句中用作状语。关系代词有 which、that、as、who、whom、whose 等,关系副词有 when、where、why 等,通常 who、whom 只用于指人,which、as 只用于指物,whose、that 既可以指人,也可以指物。关系代词作定语从句的主语时,从句中谓语动词的人称和数须和先行词保持一致。

定语从句分为限制性定语从句和非限制性定语从句。限制性定语从句用来限定修饰主句中的某个名词或代词,不能省略,译成汉语时一般译成从句;非限制性定语从句用来说明整个主句或主句中的一部分内容,省略后不影响对主句的理解,通常用逗号将从句与主句隔开,译成汉语时一般译成一个并列句。

2　定语从句的形式

（1）由关系代词 who、whom、whose 引导的定语从句

①She was the one who accompanied me through those years.

她是陪我度过那段岁月的人。(who作从句的主语)

②The man whom they are looking for is the key witness.

他们要找的那个人是关键证人。(whom作从句的宾语,可以省略)

③I know a man whose father is an airport designer in China.

我认识一个人,他的父亲是中国的机场设计师。(whose作从句主语father的定语)

④I like those books whose paper is of high quality.

我喜欢那些高质量纸张的书。(whose作paper的定语,相当于the paper of which)

(2)由关系代词which引导的定语从句

①Hangzhou is a place which is one of the most livable cities.

杭州是最宜居城市之一。(which作从句的主语)

②She loves the gift which her father bought on her birthday.

她很喜欢她爸爸为她买的生日礼物。(which作从句的宾语,可以省略)

注:上述关系代词whom/which在定语从句中作介词的宾语时,从句通常由"介词+whom/which"引出,此时关系代词不可省略,也不能用that替代。比如:

①He was a wise man from whom we learned a great deal.

他是一位智者,我们从他那里学到了很多东西。

②The book about which we are talking is sure to sell well.

我们正在谈论的那本书肯定会很畅销。

当从句中的介词放在句尾时,关系代词whom/which则通常可以省略。比如:

①The man (whom) we are looking for is dangerous.

我们正在找的那个人是个危险人物。

②The city (which) I used to live in is very clean.

我以前住过的那个城市很干净。

也可以由"名词/代词等+介词+whom/which"引出定语从句。比如:

①Her father the brain of whom was injured in the accident has now recovered.

她父亲在事故中脑部受了伤,现在已经康复了。

②Many people died in the disaster, some of which could have been saved in time.

许多人在这场灾难中丧生,其中一些人本可以及时得救的。

---

(3)由关系代词that引导的定语从句

that可以指人,也可以指物,代替which/who/whom,在从句中作主语或宾语,作宾语时可以省略,但是that不能在介词后面作介词的宾语。比如:

①The person that is talking to the teacher is my mother.

正在和老师说话的那个人是我妈妈。(that作从句的主语,代替who)

②The car that I drove yesterday was borrowed.

我昨天开的那辆车是借的。(that作从句的宾语,代替which,可以省略)

③The man that you saw yesterday was very kind.

你昨天见到的那个人很好。(that作从句的宾语,代替whom,可以省略)

(4)由关系代词as引导的定语从句

as既可以单独引导定语从句,也可以与主句中的such或the same等连用,as可作从句的主语或宾语,但as作宾语时通常不能省略。比如:

①I really want to have such a computer as the one he is using.

我真想拥有这样一台电脑,正如他在使用的那台。

②We are faced with the same dilemma as we once were.

我们面临着和过去一样的困境。

③As he soon learned, the company was considering layoffs.

正如他马上了解的那样,公司正在考虑裁员。(as引导非限制性定语从句,位于句首)

④She had just cried, as we could tell from her eyes.

我们从她的眼睛可以看出来,她刚才哭了。(as引导非限制性定语从句,位于句末)

⑤Trump, as you know, was the President of the United States.

如你所知,特朗普曾是美国总统。(as引导非限制性定语从句,位于句中)

(5)由关系副词when、where、why引导的定语从句

①I still remember the day when she married me.

我仍然记得她嫁给我的那一天。(when作从句的时间状语,意为on which)

②I always miss the place where I was born.

我总是想念我出生的地方。(where作从句的地点状语,意为in which)

③Can you explain the reason why you didn't go home last night?

你能解释一下为什么昨晚没回家吗?(why作从句的原因状语,意为for which)

注:关系副词when、where、why通常可用that或"介词+which"替代。当先行词表示的是时间、地点或原因,且用引导词在从句中作状语时,通常用when、where、why;但当从句中缺少主语或宾语时,则须用that或which作从句的主语或宾语。比如:

①She works in a city that/which has many Internet companies.

她在一个有许多互联网公司的城市工作。(引导词作从句的主语,须用that/which)

②I've forgotten the time that/which she told me.

我忘了她告诉我的时间。(引导词作从句的宾语,须用that/which,可省略)

关系代词 that 与 which 的用法区别：

（1）关系代词 that/which 都指物时，通常可以互换，但也有诸多区别，以下几种为只能用 that，不能用 which 的情况：

先行词为 all、something、nothing、anything、everything、little、few、much 等不定代词时。比如：

①That's all that he told me.

这就是他告诉我的全部。

②He gave me everything that he had.

他把他的一切都给了我。

③Sorry, there is little that I'm able to do for you.

对不起，我为你做不了什么事情。

先行词被 all、any、little、few、much、some、every、each 等修饰时。比如：

①I've forgotten all the things that I wrote down yesterday.

我把昨天写的东西全忘了。

②We don't have much money that is used for this trip.

我们能用于这次旅行的钱已经不多了。

③We should search every place that this car might be hidden.

我们应该搜查每一个可能藏匿这辆车的地方。

先行词被形容词最高级或序数词修饰时。比如：

①This is the best book that I have ever read.

这是我读过的最好的一本书。

②He was the first man that reached the top of the Alps.

他是第一个登上阿尔卑斯山的人。

③The last thing that you should do is to regret.

你最不应该做的事就是后悔。

先行词被 the same、the very、the only、the just 等修饰时。比如：

①This is the very bag that I wanted to buy.

这正是我原本想买的包。

②This is the only grammar that I know.

这是我唯一知道的语法。

③This is the same place that she and I both want to go.

这就是我和她都想去的地方。

先行词为既指人又指物的词组时。比如：

①We talked about the people and things that we still remembered from college.

　　我们聊了大学时代的那些如今还记得的人和事。

②The people and cars that were hit on the road have got their compensation.

　　在路上被撞的人和车都已得到了赔偿。

当关系代词在定语从句中作表语时。比如：

①Nanjing is not the city that it was.

　　南京已不是过去的南京了。

②His inside is not like the outside that he seems to be.

　　他的内在并不像他看上去的那样。

需要避免重复时。比如：

①Which is the skirt that you wear yesterday?

　　你昨天穿的是哪条裙子？

②Which is the book that you recommended last month?

　　你上个月推荐的书是哪一本？

（2）以下几种为只能用which，不能用that的情况：

which可以引导非限制性定语从句，that则不能。比如：

①He turned a blind eye to my request for help, which made me sad.

　　他对我的求助视而不见，这使我很伤心。

②This film, which I have seen three times, is still very hard to understand.

　　这部电影我已经看了三遍了，仍然很难理解。

which可用在介词后，that则不能。比如：

①This is the city in which I used to live.

　　这是我曾经住过的城市。

②I still remember the day on which she left me.

　　我仍然记得她离开我的那天。

需要避免重复时。比如：

①I prefer that one which is more in line with my aesthetic.

　　我更喜欢那一个，那一个更符合我的审美。

②She liked that most which her daughter had given her.

　　她最喜欢女儿送她的那一件。

关系代词 as 与 which 的用法区别：

（1）在限制性定语从句中，当名词前有 such 或 the same 修饰时，关系代词用 as，不用 which。比如：

①Don't watch such a type of film as you're not interested in.

　　不要看你不感兴趣的那种电影。

②Don't do the same stupid things as he did.

　　不要和他做一样的蠢事。

（2）在非限制性定语从句中，as 和 which 都可以指代前面的整个主句。如需有"正如，像"的含义，并且既能放句首，也能放句后，则用 as；which 引导的从句只能放句后，无"正如"的含义。比如：

①They won the first prize, as we had expected.

　　他们得了一等奖，正如我们所料的那样。（从句放主句后，as 意为"正如"）

②As we had expected, they won the first prize.

　　如我们所料，他们得了一等奖。（从句放句首，as 意为"正如"）

③They won the first prize, which we hadn't expected.

　　他们得了一等奖，这是我们没有料到的。（which 引导的从句只能放主句后）

限制性与非限制性定语从句：

（1）在限制性定语从句中，从句对先行词起修饰限制作用，如果将从句去掉，主句的意思就不完整、不明确，从句与主句的关系十分密切，通常不用逗号分开，从句是先行词不可或缺的定语。比如：

①She is the person who I adore.

　　她是我爱慕的人。（从句修饰限制先行词，不能去掉）

②She threw away the necklace which I gave her yesterday.

　　她把我昨天送她的项链扔了。（从句修饰限制先行词，不能去掉）

（2）在非限制性定语从句中，从句对先行词只做附加说明，与主句的关系并非十分密切，主从句较为松散，从句与主句之间用逗号分开，相当于一个插入语，省略从句后的主句意思仍然完整。从句不能用 that/why 引导，关系代词作宾语时也不能省略。比如：

①Their marriage, which lasted ten years, proved to be a mistake.

　　他们维持了十年的婚姻被证明是一个错误。（从句用逗号隔开，不能用 that 引导）

②This record, which she bought yesterday, is a pirate copy.

　　她昨天买的这张唱片是盗版。（从句用逗号隔开，which 作从句宾语，但不能省略）

③As Brian pointed out, it is the easiest thing in the world to give up smoking.

　　正如布赖恩指出的，戒烟是世界上最容易的事情。（从句用逗号隔开，相当于插入语）

（3）限制性定语从句修饰限制先行词,非限制性定语从句既可以修饰先行词,也可以修饰部分句子或整个句子,因此两种定语从句有时会有不同的意思。比如:

组①：All the employees who have MBA certificates are likely to enter management.

所有取得MBA证书的员工都有可能进入管理层。

（限制性定语从句,限定了员工的范围,指的是那些有MBA证书的员工）

All the employees, who have MBA certificates, are likely to enter management.

所有员工都有可能进入管理层,他们都拥有MBA证书。

（非限制性定语从句,可翻译成一个并列句,指所有员工都拥有MBA证书）

组②：Her father who is a noted doctor is a friend of mine.

她那位是知名医生的父亲是我的一个朋友。

（限制性定语从句,有修饰和特指功能,容易理解为"其中的一个父亲"）

Her father, who is a noted doctor, is a friend of mine.

她父亲是一位有名的医生,是我的一个朋友。

（非限制性定语从句,附加说明她父亲的特征,不具备较强限制性）

Section 6 状语从句（Adverbial Clause）

1 状语从句的定义

状语从句指的是在复合句中担当状语成分,起副词作用的从句,用于修饰主句中的谓语动词、非谓语动词、形容词、副词、定语、状语甚至整个句子。状语从句通常由从属连词或词组引导,与主句连接,当从句放在句末时,通常前面不加逗号。

状语从句根据其意义和作用可分为时间、地点、原因、条件、让步、目的、结果、方式和比较状语从句等。

2 状语从句的形式

（1）时间状语从句

时间状语从句的常用从属连词有when、while、whenever、as、after、before、since、until、once、as soon as、the moment、no sooner ... than、hardly/scarcely/barely ... when等。比如:

①When I left the house, I found I didn't have my key with me.

当我出门时,发现钥匙没有带。

②They were reading while I was sleeping.

我睡觉时,他们在看书。

③She tripped and fell as she got on the bus.

她上公共汽车时绊了一跤。

④Before I knew her, she was engaged.

在我认识她之前,她已经订婚了。

⑤She has been in this city since she was born.

她从出生起就一直住在这个城市。

⑥He didn't wake up until the thief took his TV away.

直到小偷搬走了他的电视机,他才醒来。

⑦Once you get to know him, you will make friends with him.

一旦你了解他,你就想和他交朋友。

⑧The moment she woke up, she burst into tears.

她一醒来就大哭起来。

⑨No sooner had she left home than it began to rain.

她一离开家,天就开始下雨了。

注:从上述例句中我们可以看到:当状语从句在前,主句在后时,一般要用逗号隔开;若主句在前,从句在后,则通常不用逗号。

⑩I'll tell him the good news as soon as I see him.

我一见到他就告诉他这个好消息。

⑪I'll wait until he comes back.

我会一直等到他回来。

注:在时间状语从句中,从句通常用现在时代替将来时,表达将来的含义,主句则用将来时,即"主将从现";同理,需表达过去将来的含义时,从句中通常用过去时。

(2)地点状语从句

地点状语从句通常由连接副词where、wherever、anywhere、everywhere引导。比如:

①Where there is a will, there is a way.

有志者,事竟成。

②Please stay where you are.

请待在原地。

③Wherever you go, I'll go with you.

无论你去哪里,我都会陪着你。

④Journalists will follow her everywhere she goes.

她走到哪,记者就跟到哪。

（3）原因状语从句

原因状语从句通常由 because、for、as、since、now that、in that、seeing that、considering that等从属连词引导。比如：

①Because he was ill, he asked for leave today.

因为他病了,所以今天请假了。

②He may be ill, for he didn't come to work today.

他可能病了,因为他今天没来上班。

③As you're abroad, you don't know what's going on.

因为你在国外,所以不知道发生了什么。

④Since you are short of money, you should spend less this month.

既然你缺钱,这个月你就少花点。

⑤Now that you asked, I'll tell you the truth.

既然你问了,我就把真相告诉你。

⑥I feel lucky in that I have very good parents.

我感到幸运,因为我有非常好的父母。

⑦Seeing that you didn't finish the task, I let him take your place.

鉴于你没有完成任务,我让他代替了你。

⑧Considering you two are good friends, I shouldn't speak ill of him.

考虑到你们俩是好朋友,我不应该说他的坏话。

注:上述表达原因的语气中,because语气最重,表示直接的因果关系,通常用于回答why的问句,用于句首或放在主句后;for一般不用于句首,表示根据逻辑推理得出的原因;since与as都表示众所周知或客观的原因,since通常放在句首,as比since语气更弱。

（4）条件状语从句

条件状语从句通常由 if、unless、in case (that)、as (so) long as、on condition (that)、providing/provided (that)、assuming that、suppose/supposing (that)、in the event that、given that、only if等引导。比如：

①If you don't want to go, I'll tell him for you.

如果你不想去,我会替你告诉他。

②We can't enter unless we are allowed.

除非得到允许,否则我们不能进去。

③In case I forget, you should remind me at once.

万一我忘了,你应该马上提醒我。

（in case引导条件状语从句时,意为"如果,万一,假使"）

④As long as they are here, the enemy won't invade.

　　只要他们在这,敌人就不会入侵。

⑤I'll tell you the truth on condition that you keep it a secret.

　　我会告诉你真相,条件是你得保密。

⑥Providing/Provided that my salary is paid, I won't sue them.

　　假如工资付清的话,我就不告他们。

⑦Assuming that he is still here, he would be happy for us.

　　假如他还在的话,他会替我们高兴的。

⑧Suppose/Supposing that we don't have enough water, what should we do?

　　假如我们没有足够的水,我们该怎么办?

⑨Who will take care of you in the event that you break down?

　　万一你身体垮了,谁会来照顾你呢?

⑩Given that you are relatively young, we decided to train you.

　　考虑到你比较年轻,我们决定培养你。

⑪Only if enough evidence is provided can he be accused.

　　只有提供足够的证据,他才能被指控。

注:条件状语从句与时间状语从句一样,从句往往用现在时表示将来意义,而不直接使用将来时态,主句通常使用将来时。

(5)让步状语从句

让步状语从句通常由 though、although、even if/though、however、whoever、whatever、whichever、no matter how/who/what/which、while(尽管)等引导。比如:

①Although it was very cold, he kept on doing exercise.

　　尽管天气很冷,他还是坚持运动。

②Though he is busy every day, yet he tries to spend time with his child.

　　虽然他每天都很忙,但他还是设法抽时间陪他的孩子。

③Even if you are extremely rich, you still shouldn't splurge.

　　即使你非常富有,也不应该挥霍无度。

④However hard I explained, she still chose not to trust me.

　　不管我怎么解释,她还是选择不相信我。

⑤No matter who our opponent is, we will win.

　　不管我们的对手是谁,我们都会赢。

⑥While I'm willing to help, she won't accept it.

　　虽然我愿意帮忙,但她不接受。

注:从句中用了 though/although,则不能在主句中用 but,但可以接 yet 或 still。

⑦Young as she is, he is very sensible.

她虽然年轻,却很懂事。

⑧Adult as he is, he is still childish.

虽然他是个成人,但还很幼稚。

⑨Whether you like it or hate it, we're going to live with them.

不管你喜不喜欢,我们都要和他们住在一起。

⑩I will buy this bag, whether you support me or not.

不管你支持不支持,我都会买这个包。

注:让步状语从句还可以用 as 或 whether ... or 等引导,由 as 引导的从句,语气往往较为强烈,通常将被强调的词放在句首,采用部分倒装结构。whether ... or 除表示"是否"之外,还可以引导让步状语从句,意为"不管是否……"。

（6）目的状语从句

目的状语从句通常由 that、so that、in order that、lest、for fear that、in case 等从属连词引导,从句的谓语动词常和 can、could、may、might、should 等情态动词连用。比如:

①Let's sit in the front row that we can have a better view.

我们坐前排吧,这样可以看得清楚些。

②He gets up early every day so that he can watch the sunrise.

他每天早起是为了看日出。

③She kept on studying after work in order that she may have a better opportunity.

她下班后继续学习,这样她也许会有更好的机会。

④I apologized in advance lest he (should) blame me.

我事先道了歉,以免他责备我。

⑤I won't make a promise for fear that I (should) break your heart.

我不会做承诺,怕伤了你的心。

⑥They watched him closely in case he (should) run away.

他们密切注视着他,以防他逃跑。

（in case 引导目的状语从句时,意为"以免,以备,以防"）

（7）结果状语从句

结果状语从句通常由 so that、so ... that、such ... that、with the result that、to such a degree that、to the degree that、to such an extent that、to the extent that 等引导。比如:

①I spoke loudly so that everyone heard me.

我说得很响,因而大家都听到了。

②He was so tired that he fell asleep on the subway.

他太累了,在地铁上睡着了。

③He is such a humorous person that his colleagues all like him.

他是一个非常幽默的人,因此同事们都很喜欢他。

④The company values its employees, with the result that everyone is absolutely loyal.

公司很重视员工们,因此每个人都极其忠诚。

⑤He was tired to such a degree that he finally fainted.

他太累了,最终昏倒了。

⑥Chen Yinque was erudite to such an extent that he is called the professor of professors.

陈寅恪先生学识渊博,因此被称为"教授的教授"。

(8)方式状语从句

方式状语从句通常由 as、just as、(just) as ... so、in the way that、as if/though 等引导。比如:

①Please do as what he says.

请按他说的去做。

②He's thoughtful, just as a leader should be.

他考虑周全,正如一个领袖所应做到的那样。

③(Just) as a machine needs to run, so a man needs to exercise.

正如机器需要运转一样,人也需要锻炼。

④He talks to me in the way that a leader talks to his staff.

他对我说话的方式好比是领导对下属说话一样。

⑤She is staring at him as if she is angry.

她盯着他看,好像是生气了。

⑥He looks at me as if he were looking at a prisoner.

他看着我,好像在看一个犯人。(虚拟语气)

⑦He passed me as if he had never known me before.

他经过我身边,好像从未认识过我似的。(虚拟语气)

注:as if/though引导的方式状语从句,如果从句内容是真实的或很可能实现的,从句随主句用常规时态;如从句内容是不真实的或与事实相反的,从句时态则要用虚拟语气。

(9)比较状语从句

比较状语从句通常由 as ... as、not so (as) ... as、比较级+than、the ... the 等引导。比如:

①He worked as hard as he could.

　　他尽可能努力地工作。

②He is not so honest as we expected.

　　他不像我们预料的那样诚实。

③Chemistry is more complicated than you think.

　　化学比你想象的要复杂。

④The more you give, the more you get.

　　你付出的越多,得到的就越多。

状语从句中的省略:

在不影响表达和理解的基础上,状语从句通常可以采用省略的方式进行简化。可以应用省略的状语从句往往满足两个条件:①从句和主句的主语一致;②从句的谓语是(或相当于)系表结构。比如:

①While (he was) absent from the press conference, he went to play golf.

　　缺席新闻发布会期间,他打高尔夫去了。

②He still attended the meeting today although (he felt) seriously ill.

　　他虽然病得很重,但今天还是参加了会议。

③Whether (she is) rich or poor, she is happy every day.

　　无论富有还是贫穷,她每天都很快乐。

④As (he was) a boy, he used to go fishing with his father.

　　他小时候常和父亲一起去钓鱼。

⑤Be restrained unless (you are) bullied.

　　除非被欺负,否则克制一点。

此外,当从句的主语为it,谓语动词为be动词时,也通常可采用省略形式。比如:

①I'm going to propose to her next month if (it is) possible.

　　如果可能的话,我打算下个月向她求婚。

②If (it is) necessary, you can wake me up at midnight.

　　如果有必要,你可以在半夜叫醒我。

③You should arrive on time unless (it is) postponed.

　　除非会议延期,否则你应该准时到达。

注意不同从句的区分:

连词引导什么类型的从句,不仅要根据该连词来判断,还需要根据句子结构和句子含义来分辨。下列例句以 where 为例:

①Where he came from is a mystery.

　　他从哪里来是个谜。(引导主语从句)

②She doesn't know where I used to work.

　　她不知道我以前在哪工作。(引导宾语从句)

③This city is where he once lived.

　　这是他曾经生活的城市。(引导表语从句)

④I have no idea where he came from.

　　我不知道他从哪来。(引导同位语从句)

⑤She has forgotten the place where he put the car key.

　　她忘记把车钥匙放哪了。(引导定语从句)

⑥She can't work where colleagues are very cold.

　　她不能在同事很冷漠的地方工作。(引导地点状语从句)

Section 7 非谓语短语(Non-Predicate Phrase)

　　复合句通常由主句和从句构成,也可用动词不定式或分词结构代替从句,即非谓语短语在复合句中的应用。动词不定式和分词结构属于非限定性动词,是短语而非从句,但大多可以用从句的形式表现出来,因此可以被称为非限定性从句,构成复合句(非简单句)的一部分。

　　非谓语动词是一种动词形式,不能作句子的谓语,但可以担当句子的其他成分,非谓语动词主要包括动名词、不定式和分词(现在分词和过去分词)。通常非谓语短语在复合句中作状语的应用最为丰富。在以下的归纳中,我们将着重以分词和动词不定式结构作状语的应用为例,探究并加深对该语法点的理解。

　　(1)现在分词(Present Participle)

　　现在分词由动词原形加-ing构成,可分为一般式和完成时,及物动词的现在分词有主动语态和被动语态。一般式的现在分词表示的动作通常具有未完成或正在进行的意义,或表示与谓语动词的动作同时进行;完成式的现在分词则表示动作已完成。如下表所示:

现在分词	及物动词take		不及物动词go
	主动语态	被动语态	
一般式	taking	being taken	going
完成式	having taken	having been taken	having gone

①China is still a developing country.

　　中国仍然是一个发展中国家。(表未完成、正在进行的意义)

②Being praised for her beauty, she blushed.

　　一夸她漂亮,她脸就红了。(表示的动作与主句谓语动词同时发生)

③Having hung up the phone, she went on reading.

挂断电话后,她继续看书。(表示动作先完成)

④Having been given so many clothes, the beggar thanked him.

被给予了这么多衣服后,乞丐向他道谢。(表示动作先完成)

现在分词短语通常可代替某个状语从句,表示时间、原因、条件、结果或伴随等。比如:

①While living here, she told me about her experiences every day.

住在这里期间,她每天都告诉我她的经历。(作时间状语)

②Smoking here, you will be fined.

如果在这里吸烟,会被罚款。(作条件状语)

③Not having received his reply promptly, I called him up.

由于没有及时收到他的答复,我给他打了电话。(作原因状语)

④He shut me in, beating and swearing.

他把我关在屋里,又打又骂。(作方式状语,或表伴随状态)

⑤Though having spent all his money, he didn't want to go home.

尽管花光了所有钱,但他还是不想回家。(作让步状语)

⑥He failed to meet the client's needs, completely losing the opportunity.

他未能满足客户的需求,彻底失去了机会。(作结果状语)

(2)过去分词(Past Participle)

过去分词由动词原形加-ed构成,也有许多过去分词为不规则的变化形式。过去分词只有一种形式,一般表示被动或完成的动作,及物动词的过去分词通常表示被动意义,不及物动词的过去分词通常表示主动并完成的意义。如下表所示:

过去分词	及物动词take		不及物动词go（主动语态）
	主动语态	被动语态	
	—	taken	gone

①The money was taken by his son.

钱被他儿子拿走了。(表被动)

②They have gone to Beijing.

他们已经去了北京。(表主动并完成)

过去分词短语通常可用作状语,修饰谓语,说明动作发生的背景或情况。比如:

①Seen by the hunter, the lion ran into the bushes immediately.

被猎人看见后,狮子立刻跑进了灌木丛。(作时间状语)

②Given more investment, our company will go public.

如有更多投资，我们公司就会上市。(作条件状语)

③Exhausted by working overtime, she decided to resign.

加班使她筋疲力尽，她决定辞职。(作原因状语)

④Repaired many times, the air conditioner still doesn't work.

修了好几次，空调还是不能用。(作让步状语)

⑤She entered the meeting room, followed by her partners.

她走进会议室，后面跟着合伙人。(表伴随，该用法无相对应的状语从句可替代)

（3）动词不定式（Infinitive）

动词不定式由 to 加动词原形构成，没有人称和数的变化，不受主语人称和谓语动词时态的影响，不能在句子中单独作谓语，不定式同它的宾语或状语构成不定式短语。如下表所示：

	主动形式	被动形式
一般式	to do	to be done
完成式	to have done	to have been done
进行式	to be doing	—
完成进行式	to have been doing	—

①Hope to see you again.

希望再次见到你。(表将来)

②I'm sorry to have kept you waiting so long.

很抱歉让你久等了。(表完成)

③He seems to be saying something.

他好像在说什么。(表进行)

不定式结构也可作状语，或作句子的独立成分，起到解释说明整个句子的作用。比如：

①In order to buy a house, he took a part-time job after work.

为了买房子，他下班后还去做兼职。(作目的状语)

②To lose weight, she eats very little these days.

为了减肥，她这些天吃得很少。(作目的状语)

③To my surprise, he learned the whole book by heart.

使我惊奇的是，他背熟了整本书。(独立成分，起解释说明作用)

④To my disappointment, he broke the contract.

令我失望的是，他违反了合同。(独立成分，起解释说明作用)

Section 8 独立主格结构（Absolute Construction）

在上一节中,非谓语动词作状语时,其逻辑主语与主句主语是一致的。若不一致时,非谓语动词则须另带主语,从而构成一个复合结构的形式作状语,这种结构被称为独立主格结构。该结构有自己的主语,与主句无结构上的关系,所以被称为独立主格结构。独立主格结构实质上是一个带有自己主语的非限定状语从句,在意义上为一个从属分句。

独立主格结构由两部分组成,前一部分为名词或代词,后一部分为非谓语动词(动名词、不定式、现在分词、过去分词)或者形容词、副词、名词或介词短语,前后两部分通常具有逻辑上的主谓关系。独立主格结构可表示时间、方式、原因、条件、目的或伴随等,用来修饰整个句子,主要用于书面语。独立主格结构表示时间、条件或原因时,相当于一个状语从句;表伴随状况或补充说明时,相当于一个并列句。

（1）名词/代词+现在分词
现在分词表示前面的名词/代词主动进行的动作或所处的状态。比如:

①Time permitting, we'll stay here one more day.
如果时间允许,我们将在这里多住一天。(作条件状语)

②There being no tickets, we can only come tomorrow.
没有票了,我们只能明天来。(作原因状语)

③It being Sunday, the restaurant is particularly crowded.
由于是星期日,饭店里人特别多。(作原因状语)

④The problem having been solved, we ended the conference call.
问题解决后,我们结束了电话会议。(作时间状语)

⑤She saw him come back from the army, tears running down her face.
看见他从军队回来,她的眼泪流了下来。(表伴随状况)

（2）名词/代词+过去分词
过去分词表示前面的名词/代词被动完成的动作或所处的状态。比如:

①His work done, he read the newspaper for a while.
工作做完后,他看了一会儿报纸。(作时间状语)

②The machine broken, we are not able to work today.
机器坏了,我们今天不能工作了。(作原因状语)

③People began to have spiritual pursuits, their per capita income risen greatly.
由于人均收入大大提高,人们开始有了精神追求。(作原因状语)

④He is deeply attracted to her, eyes fixed on her face.
他被她吸引住了,他的眼睛盯着她的脸。(表伴随状况)

（3）名词/代词+不定式

名词/代词与不定式之间如果是逻辑主谓关系，动词不定式用主动形式；如果是动宾关系，则用被动形式。动词不定式通常表示将要发生的动作。比如：

①So many people to help me, I'm sure to succeed.

　　有这么多人帮助我，我一定会成功的。（作原因状语）

②Two contracts to be revised, he is not able to sleep early tonight.

　　有两份合同要修改，他今晚没法早睡了。（作原因状语）

③Six guests have arrived, the rest to come later.

　　六位客人已经到了，其余的人稍后到。（作补充说明）

（4）名词/代词+形容词

形容词通常用来说明名词、代词的性质、特征或所处的状态。比如：

①His head dizzy, he decided not to drive.

　　由于头晕，他决定不开车了。（作原因状语）

②He gazed at the pretty girl, his mouth half open.

　　他半张着嘴，盯着那个漂亮的姑娘看。（作方式状语）

③The floor very clean, she still mopped it every day.

　　地板虽然很干净，她仍然每天拖地。（作让步状语）

（5）名词/代词+副词

副词通常用来说明名词、代词的性质、特征或所处的状态。比如：

①The meeting over, the shareholders still wouldn't leave.

　　会议虽然结束了，股东们仍然不愿离开。（作让步状语）

②Her family abroad, she had to take care of herself.

　　由于家人都在国外，她不得不自己照顾自己。（作原因状语）

③Lights out, we can't read any more.

　　熄灯了，我们不能再看书了。（作原因状语）

（6）名词/代词+名词

①The performance triumph, the Queen rewarded them.

　　演出大获成功，女王奖赏了他们。（作原因状语）

②Countless people died in the war, many of them civilians.

　　无数人在战争中丧生，其中许多是平民。（作补充说明）

③He struggled to the shore, the hands his only oars.

　　他挣扎着向岸边游去，双手是他唯一的船桨。（作补充说明）

（7）名词/代词+介词短语

介词短语通常用来说明伴随前面名词/代词的方式或状态。比如：

①His back against the wall, he began to cry.

他背靠着墙,开始哭泣。(作方式状语)

②Book in hand, she went into the library.

她手里拿着书,走进了图书馆。(表伴随状况)

③His hand on my shoulder, he excitedly told me the good news.

他的手搭在我肩膀上,激动地告诉我这个好消息。(表伴随状况)

（8）with/without+宾语（名词/代词）+宾语补足语

①With so much time to go on vacation, she was overjoyed.

有这么多时间去度假,她欣喜若狂。(作原因状语)

②He slept soundly with the door unlocked.

他没锁门,睡得很香。(表伴随状况)

③Without anyone knowing his identity, he boarded a private plane.

没有人知道他是谁,他登上了一架私人飞机。(作补充说明)

（with通常可以省略,without则不能）

④With his parents away, he watched TV all day.

由于父母不在,他整天看电视。(作原因状语)

⑤The boy with a letter in his hand is my brother.

手里拿着信的那个男孩是我弟弟。(独立主格结构作定语)

⑥I have all the symptoms of someone giving up drinking.

我有戒酒者所具备的所有症状。(独立主格结构作宾语)

（须结合句型分析来判断独立主格结构在句中的具体应用）

（9）each引导的强调型独立主格

①We all worked hard to get our company to go public, each one working late everyday.

为了公司上市,我们每天都很努力,每个人都工作到很晚。(作方式状语)

②The three of us agreed to split the profits equally, each to contribute greatly.

我们三人同意平分利润,每个人都有巨大的贡献。(作补充说明)

③The company has recruited many excellent employees, each with a master's degree.

公司招聘了许多优秀的员工,每个人都有硕士学位。(作补充说明)

Section 9 强调句型(Emphatic Sentence)

强调句型是一种采用修辞的特殊句式,用来表达说话者意愿或情感的一种形式。通过特定的方式对句中的某个部分进行强调,从而使该部分所含信息比其他部分显得更为重要。常用的强调结构为"It is/was+被强调部分+that/who+其他部分"。比如:

①It is the good news that makes him overjoyed.

　　正是这个好消息使他欣喜若狂。

②It was his son who gave him a hard time.

　　正是他的儿子让他如此头疼。

③It was last night that he experienced all this.

　　就在昨晚他经历了这一切。

④It is because the pandemic shows no sign of ending that he doesn't want to study abroad.

　　正是因为疫情没有结束的迹象,他才不想出国留学。

注:被强调的部分是人时,that 或 who 均可引导分句,其他情况只能用 that 引导;当强调原因状语从句时,从句只能用 because 引导,不能用 since 或 as 等。

（1）陈述句的强调句型

强调句通常可强调句中的主语、宾语或状语等成分。比如:

原始句型:Jane attended an important meeting with her supervisor yesterday.

　　　　简昨天和她的主管参加了一个重要会议。

强调主语:It was Jane who attended an important meeting with her supervisor yesterday.

　　　　昨天和主管参加重要会议的是简。

强调宾语:It was an important meeting that Jane attended with her supervisor yesterday.

　　　　昨天简和她的主管参加的是一个重要会议。

强调状语:It was with her supervisor that Jane attended an important meeting yesterday.

　　　　简昨天是和她的上司一起参加了一个重要会议。

强调状语:It was yesterday that Jane attended an important meeting with her supervisor.

　　　　简和她的主管是在昨天参加了一个重要的会议。

注:该句型结构不能强调句中的谓语部分,如需强调谓语时,则通常用助动词 do/does/did 来表示强调,后面的谓语动词须用原形。比如:

①I do know him well.

　　我确实很了解他。

②I'm sure she does understand everything.

　　我敢肯定她什么都懂。

③He did like to make friends with people in those days.

在那些日子里,他确实喜欢和人们交朋友。

④Do be careful when you drive at night.

晚上开车一定要小心。

（2）一般疑问句的强调句型

强调句的一般疑问句只需将be动词提前。比如：

原始句型：Jane attended an important meeting with her supervisor yesterday.

简昨天和她的主管参加了一个重要会议。

询问主语：Was it Jane who attended an important meeting with her supervisor yesterday?

昨天是简和她的主管参加了一个重要会议吗？

询问宾语：Was it an important meeting that Jane attended with her supervisor yesterday?

昨天简和她的主管参加的是一个重要会议吗？

询问状语：Was it with her supervisor that Jane attended an important meeting yesterday?

简昨天是和她的上司一起参加了一个重要会议吗？

询问状语：Was it yesterday that Jane attended an important meeting with her supervisor?

简和她的主管是在昨天参加了一个重要的会议吗？

（3）特殊疑问句的强调句型

强调句的特殊疑问句结构为"疑问代词/疑问副词（被强调部分）+is/was+it+that/who+其他部分"。比如：

原始句型：Jane attended an important meeting with her supervisor yesterday.

简昨天和她的主管参加了一个重要会议。

询问主语：Who was it that attended an important meeting with her supervisor yesterday?

昨天是谁和她的主管参加了一个重要会议？

询问宾语：What was it that Jane attended with her supervisor yesterday?

简昨天和她的上司一起参加了什么？

询问状语：Who was it that Jane attended an important meeting with yesterday?

昨天简和谁一起参加了一个重要会议？

询问状语：When was it that Jane attended an important meeting with her supervisor?

简是在什么时候和她的主管参加了一个重要会议？

（4）not ... until句型的强调句

该句型的强调句结构为"It is/was not until+被强调部分+that+其他部分"。比如：

原始句型：He didn't stop crying until his mother came back.

直到他妈妈回来,他才停止哭泣。

强调句型：It was not until his mother came back that he stopped crying.

直到他妈妈回来,他才停止哭泣。

原始句型:He didn't admit stealing until there was hard evidence against him.

直到有了确凿的证据,他才承认偷了东西。

强调句型:It was not until there was hard evidence against him that he admitted stealing.

直到有了对他不利的确凿证据,他才承认了偷窃行为。

(5)强调句型中的主谓一致

当强调句中的被强调部分为主语时,须注意主谓一致。比如:

①It is who I am disappointed by their decision deeply.

对他们的决定深感失望的人正是我。

②It was not you but she that was to blame for all this.

这一切的过错不在于你,而是她。

(6)强调句型的判断方式

判断句子是否为强调句,可将句中的It is/was和that/who去掉,同时将被强调部分还原至原来的位置,此时如果仍是一个完整的句子,则为强调句,反之则不是。比如:

①It is the good news that makes him overjoyed.

→The good news makes him overjoyed.

这个好消息使他欣喜若狂。

②It was last night that he experienced all this.

→He experienced all this last night.

他昨晚经历了这一切。

③It was with her best friend that she went shopping yesterday.

→She went shopping with her best friend yesterday.

她昨天和她最好的朋友去购物了。

④It is confusing that she said she didn't know me.

她说不认识我,这令人很困惑。(该句为主语从句)

⑤It is the best film that I have ever seen.

这是我看过的最好的电影。(该句为定语从句,it指代film,that可省略)

⑥It was midnight when I went to bed yesterday.

昨天我睡觉时已经是午夜了。(该句为状语从句,it指代时间)

注:构成强调句的it无词义,连接词只用that/who,在句子中不可省略,即使强调的部分是时间状语或地点状语,亦不能用when或where引导,须用that引导。在时态方面,现在时be动词用is,过去时用was。

（7）其他常用强调句型

强调句也可用"what ... be"句型来表达,该句型通常由 what 引导的主语从句作主语,be动词构成的系表结构作谓语。比如:

强调主语:What annoys me most is her deceit.

最让我恼火的是她的欺骗。

强调宾语:What we need most now is time.

我们现在最需要的是时间。

强调表语:What I feel is thoroughly disappointed.

我感到非常失望。

强调谓语:What we should do is (to) inform him at once.

我们应该做的是马上通知他。

Section 10 倒装(Inversion)

英语句子的基本语序为"主语+谓语",但有时根据语法所需,会将谓语的一部分或全部置于主语之前,这种语序被称为"倒装"。句子采用倒装的原因通常是由于语法结构所需或是采用修辞手法用来强调句中的某一部分,倒装的形式分为完全倒装和部分倒装。

完全倒装(Full Inversion)

完全倒装是指谓语的所有组成部分放在主语之前的倒装结构。句子采用完全倒装结构通常出现在以下几种情况当中:

（1）以 here、there、now、then、away、off、out、in、up、down 等表示方向、地点或时间的副词位于句首时,句子通常用完全倒装语序表示强调或提升句子的生动性。比如:

①Here comes the train.

火车来了。

②There is a hill.

有一座小山。

③There flows a stream in front of my house.

我家前面有一条小溪。

④Then occurred a new problem.

然后出现了一个新问题。

⑤Away went the teacher.

老师走了。

⑥Out rushed the crowd.

人群冲了出来。

⑦In came the students.

学生们进来了。

> 注：当主语为代词时，则不用该倒装结构。比如：
> ①Here it comes.
>   它来了。
> ②Away she went.
>   她离开了。

（2）主语前面有直接引语时，句子采用全部倒装。比如：

①"What did he say to you?" asked my friend.

  "他对你说了什么?"我的朋友问。

②"Let's eat out tonight." said my wife.

  "我们今晚出去吃饭吧。"我妻子说。

> 注：当主语为代词时，则不用该倒装结构。比如：
> ①"Can you dive?" he asked.
>   "你能潜水吗?"他问道。
> ②"I want to eat hot pot." she said.
>   "我想吃火锅。"她说。

（3）将表示地点、方向的状语（通常为介词短语）置于句首加以强调时，须采用倒装。比如：

①On the ground lay a beggar.

  地上躺着一个乞丐。

②Around the playground was running a soldier.

  一个士兵正在绕着操场跑。

③Under the bed was hidden a suitcase.

  床底下藏着一只手提箱。

④In the crowd stood his mother.

  人群中站着他的母亲。

（4）将表语（通常为介词短语）置于句首加以强调时，通常采用倒装语序。比如：

①Among them was his mother.

  他的母亲也在其中。

②On the table are the presents she's been waiting for.

桌上放着她期待已久的礼物。

③At the foot of the mountain is a temple with a long history.

山脚下有一座历史悠久的寺庙。

(5)当谓语部分的分词短语、动词不定式等置于句首加以强调时,通常采用完全倒装。比如:

①Forgotten in the forest is a magnificent castle.

被遗忘在森林里的是一座宏伟的城堡。

②Standing in the middle is our drillmaster.

站在中间的是我们的教官。

③To be solved firstly is this crucial problem.

首先要解决的是这个关键问题。

(6)在so(肯定句)和neither/nor(否定句)引导的句子中,采用完全倒装语序,表示前面的情况也适用于后者。比如:

①He is confident and so am I.

他很自信,我也很自信。

②If he can do it well, so can I.

如果他能把这件事做好,我也能。

③He has never been absent from school, neither have I.

他从来没有缺过课,我也没有。

④She doesn't wear makeup, nor do I.

她不化妆,我也不。

注:若so在句子后面表示强调、同意或重复前者的意思时,则不用倒装,此时so的含义相当于yes。比如:

①"He's quite smart." —"So he is."

"他很聪明。"——"是的,的确如此。"

②"He made a mistake." —"So he did."

"他犯了个错误。"——"是的,他做错了。"

部分倒装(Partial Inversion)

部分倒装是指只把谓语中的一部分(如助动词、系动词或情态动词等)放在主语之前,而谓语的其他部分仍保留在主语后面的倒装结构。如果句中的谓语没有助动词或情态动词,则需添加助动词do、does或did等,并将其置于主语之前。部分倒装通常有以下几种情况:

(1)具有否定意义的副词、连词及词组位于句首时,通常采用部分倒装。这类词如

not、not only、not until、few、little、seldom、rarely、hardly、scarcely、barely、never、no sooner、no longer等。比如：

①Not even once did he help me.

他一次也没帮过我。

②Not only did I invite him to dinner, but also invited him to the bar.

我不仅请他吃饭,还请他去酒吧。

③Not until today did he admit his mistake.

直到今天他才承认错误。

④Seldom does he get up late.

他很少晚起床。

⑤Never has he paid me back.

他从未还过我钱。

⑥No sooner had he said it than we burst into laughter.

他一说完,我们就哄堂大笑起来。

⑦At no time did I give any orders or permission.

我从来没有下过任何命令或给予任何允许。

⑧Under no circumstances should you lend money to him.

你无论如何都不应该借钱给他。

（2）"only+状语"位于句首时,通常采用部分倒装,该结构中only作副词。比如：

①Only in this way can you improve your logical thinking.

只有这样你才能提高自己的逻辑思维能力。

②Only in Japan can you find such a restaurant.

只有在日本你才能找到这样的餐馆。

③Only then did he realize how ridiculous he was.

直到那时他才意识到自己有多可笑。

④Only when he got off the plane did he learn what had happened in the company.

他下了飞机才知道公司里发生了什么事。

⑤Only because her best friend lied to her did she feel so upset.

只是因为她最好的朋友欺骗了她,她才感到如此沮丧。

注意:只有当only修饰状语时,句子才使用倒装,修饰其他成分时则不用。比如：

①Only he can answer your question.

只有他能回答你的问题。(only修饰主语,only作形容词)

②Only one or two student have finished their homework.

只有一两个学生完成了作业。(only修饰主语,only作形容词)

（3）"so+形容词/副词"位于句首时，通常采用倒装语序。比如：

①So hot was the weather that we had to keep the air conditioner on all day.

天气太热了，我们不得不整天开着空调。

②So angry was he that everyone in the office could feel his rage.

他太生气了，办公室里的每个人都能感觉到他的愤怒。

③So efficiently did the team finish the project that they got an extra reward.

这个团队如此高效地完成了这个项目，从而得到了额外的奖励。

④So loudly was the machine running that no one could hear what the boss said.

机器运转的声音太大了，没有人能听清老板说了什么。

> 注：在该倒装结构中，"so+形容词"为表语的前置，"so+副词"是状语的前置。若句中有such，并且置于句首时，通常也采用倒装语序。比如：
>
> ①Such is human nature that man always desires to own more money.
>
> 人总是渴望拥有更多的钱，这是人的本性。
>
> ②Such a harsh reality was there that I almost lost faith.
>
> 现实是如此残酷，我几乎失去了信心。
>
> ③Such was what he told me.
>
> 这就是他告诉我的。

（4）省略if的虚拟条件句中，须将had、were、should等词置于主语前，构成部分倒装句。比如：

①Had you gone yesterday, you would have had a good time.

如果你昨天去了，你会玩得很开心。

②Were I you, I wouldn't do that.

如果我是你，我就不会那样做。

③Should you need anything, please feel free to contact me.

如果您需要什么，请随时与我联系。

（5）由as引导的状语可采用部分倒装语序。比如：

①Fast as an arrow, he ran at full speed towards us.

他像箭一样快，全速向我们跑来。（省略其中一个as，引导比较状语）

②Child as he is, he is very mature.

他虽然还是个孩子，但很成熟。（引导让步状语）

③A green hand as she is in our company, we should help her.

她在我们公司是个新手，我们应该帮助她。（引导原因状语）

（6）频率副词如 often、always、many a time、now and then、once、twice、every other day 等位于句首时,通常采用部分倒装语序。比如:

①Often did he encourage me to be brave.

　　他经常鼓励我要勇敢。

②Always did she warn her children to keep away from the river.

　　她总是警告孩子们不要靠近那条河。

③Many a time have I been moved by this book.

　　我多次被这本书感动。

④Now and then does he lie to me.

　　他不时地对我撒谎。

（7）由 what/how 引导的感叹句中,以及表示祝愿的句子中,通常采用倒装语序。比如:

①How beautiful your dress is!

　　你的裙子真漂亮啊!

②What bright eyes you have!

　　你的眼睛真亮!

③Long live our friendship!

　　我们的友谊万岁!

④May you be tranquil and graceful.

　　愿你恬静优雅。

⑤May you succeed!

　　祝你成功!

Section 11　省略(Abbreviation)

　　在英语中,为了使语言简练或避免重复,通常会省略句中的某些成分,这种语法现象被称为"省略"。采用省略之后,句子结构往往更加清晰紧凑,上下文的连接更加紧密。同时,句中的重要信息更为突出,句意也更为明确。

　　省略的用法在英语中极其广泛,有些已形成习惯,被大家所认同和使用;有些则按修辞或语法所需已形成一定的规律。但采用省略、追求简练的同时,不可使句意产生歧义。以下,我们将对英语句法中的重点省略用法做归纳。

　　（1）简单句中,通常会省略某些句子成分。比如:

①(I) Thank you very much.

　　非常感谢!

②(You) Come this way, please.

请走这边。

③(I'm) Sorry to bother you.

很抱歉打扰你。

④(Is there) Any problem?

有什么问题吗？

⑤Would you like to go with us?—I'd like to (go with you).

你想一起去吗？——我很乐意。

⑥Are you a teacher?—Yes, I am (a teacher).

你是老师吗？——是的。

⑦How interesting (it is)!

多有趣呀！

⑧What a big house (it is)!

多么大的房子啊！

（2）并列句中，句中相同的成分通常采取省略。比如：

①I like hiking, but he doesn't (like hiking).

我喜欢徒步旅行，但他不喜欢。

②Some people in the company are hard working and some (are) lazy.

公司里有些人很努力，有些人很懒。

③It's easy to say, but (it is) hard to do.

说起来容易，做起来难。

④He told me to go inside and (to) sit down.

他叫我进来坐下。

⑤He wanted to argue with the manager, but his friend told him not to (do this).

他想和经理争论，但是他的朋友告诉他别这样做。

⑥My father must have been off work and my mother (must have been) cooking.

爸爸肯定已经下班了，妈妈肯定在做饭了。

（3）主语从句中，有 it 作形式主语时，从句中的 that 可省略。比如：

①It appears (that) I am not welcome here.

看来我在这里不受欢迎。

②It is reported (that) China will make great efforts to develop high-end manufacturing.

据报道，中国将大力发展高端制造业。

③It has been proved (that) he is the murderer.

已证实他就是凶手。

(4)宾语从句中,可适当省略重复部分或从属连词that。比如:

①He didn't inform me of the time of the meeting. I don't know why (he didn't).

　　他没有通知我开会的时间。我不知道为什么。

②I don't know when the thief got in, or how (the thief got in).

　　我不知道小偷是什么时候进去的,或者他是怎么进去的。

③I feel (that) the company's performance this year is better than last year.

　　我觉得公司今年的业绩比去年好。

(5)限制性定语从句中,可省略作宾语的关系代词that、which、who、whom。比如:

①All (that) she needs is impractical.

　　她所需要的这一切是不切实际的。

②The mobile phone (which) he bought yesterday was used.

　　他昨天买的手机是使用过的。

③I saw the man (who) you were looking for.

　　我看到了你要找的人。

④She is the film star (whom) we are talking about now.

　　她就是我们现在正在谈论的那个电影明星。

(6)状语从句中,可省略跟主句相同的主语及其后面的 be 动词;从句中若有 it be 或 there be 结构,通常也可省略。比如:

①When (you are) lonely, you can come and chat with me.

　　当你觉得孤独时,可以来找我聊天。

②He is very dedicated while (he is) working.

　　他工作时非常敬业。

③He looked very anxious, as if (he were) in trouble.

　　他看上去很焦虑,好像遇到了麻烦。

④Though (he was) tired, he still visited his clients.

　　尽管很累,他还是去拜访了客户。

⑤Whether (it is) right or not, we should agree with each other first.

　　不管对不对,我们都应该先达成一致。

⑥Do not disturb the senior officer unless (it is) necessary.

　　除非有必要,否则不要打扰高级军官。

⑦Problems, if (there are) any, should be solved without delay.

　　如果有问题,就应该立即解决。

⑧Could you lend me some money if (it is) possible?

　　如果可能的话,你能借我一些钱吗?

⑨The show is more interesting than (it is) expected.

这个表演比我们预期的要更有趣。

（7）虚拟条件句中，如有 had、were、should 等词，可将其置于主语前，同时省略 if。
比如：

①Had you gone yesterday, you would have had a good time.

如果你昨天去了，你会玩得很开心。

②Were I you, I wouldn't do that.

如果我是你，我就不会那样做。

③Should you need anything, please feel free to contact me.

如果您需要什么，请随时与我联系。

第四章 语篇解构

语篇学习 1

（参考第二章一般现在时）

（参考第二章现在进行时）

The best art critics
最佳艺术评论家

I am an art student and I paint a lot of pictures. Many people pretend that they understand modern art. They always tell you what a picture is "about". Of course, many pictures are not "about" anything. They are just pretty patterns. We like them in the same way that we like pretty curtain material. I think that young children often appreciate modern pictures better than anyone else. They notice more. My sister is only seven, but she always tells me whether my pictures are good or not. She came into my room yesterday.

"What are you doing?" she asked.

"I'm hanging this picture on the wall," I answered. "It's a new one. Do you like it?"

She looked at it critically for a moment. "It's all right," she said, "but isn't it upside down?"

I looked at it again. She was right! It was!

句型解构

句1 I am an art student and I paint a lot of pictures.

解构：一般现在时，表述现在的特征或状态。

句2 Many people pretend that they understand modern art.

解构：一般现在时，表述一种普遍的情况；pretend，动词，意为"假装"；modern art 意为"现代艺术，当代艺术"；that 引导的宾语从句，作 pretend 的宾语。

句3 They always tell you what a picture is "about".

解构：一般现在时，表述一个经常性的动作；always，频度副词；tell 作双宾语动词，you 为间接宾语，what 引导的宾语从句，作直接宾语；about 加引号，一是指此类人谈论画作时常用到该词,二是表示讽刺。

句4 They are just pretty patterns.

解构:just,副词,意为"仅仅,只是";pattern,名词,意为"图案"。

句5 We like them in the same way that we like pretty curtain material.

解构:in the same way that/as为连接短语,用于表示比较,意为"和……一样,正如";curtain material意为"窗帘材料,窗帘布"。

句6 I think that young children often appreciate modern pictures better than anyone else.

解构:that引导的宾语从句,作think的宾语;appreciate,动词,意为"欣赏,鉴别";else,形容词,意为"其他的,另外的",作不定代词anyone的后置定语。

句7 My sister is only seven, but she always tells me whether my pictures are good or not.

解构:whether引导的宾语从句,作tell的直接宾语;whether,连词,表选择,意为"是否",当or not与whether连用时,通常不用if。

句8 "What are you doing?" she asked.

解构:现在进行时,询问正在发生的动作。

句9 "I'm hanging this picture on the wall," I answered.

解构:现在进行时,表示正在进行的动作;hang,动词,意为"悬挂",区分hang/hung/hung(意为"悬挂")与hang/hanged/hanged(意为"绞死,上吊")的词义差异。

句10 She looked at it critically for a moment. "It's all right," she said, "but isn't it upside down?"

解构:critically,副词,意为"挑剔地,批判地";upside down意为"颠倒的,倒置的"。

参考译文

　　我是个学艺术的学生,画了很多画。有很多人装成很懂现代艺术的样子,总是告诉你一幅画的"意思"是什么。当然,有很多画是什么"意思"也没有的。它们就是些好看的图案,我们喜爱它们就像我们喜欢漂亮的窗帘布一样。我觉得小孩子们往往比其他任何人都更能欣赏现代绘画,他们观察到的东西更多。我的妹妹只有7岁,但她总能说出我的画是好还是坏。昨天她到我房里来了。

　　"你在干什么呢?"她问。

　　"我正把这幅画挂到墙上去。"我回答说,"这是幅新画,你喜欢吗?"

　　她用挑剔的目光看了一会儿。"还可以吧。"她说,"不过,是不是挂倒了?"

　　我再次看了看画。她说对了! 是挂倒了!

语篇学习 2

（参考第二章一般过去时）

Reward for virtue
对美德的奖赏

My friend, Hugh, has always been fat, but things got so bad recently that he decided to go on a diet. He began his diet a week ago. First of all, he wrote out a long list of all the foods which were forbidden. The list included most of the things Hugh loves: butter, potatoes, rice, beer, milk, chocolate, and sweets. Yesterday I paid him a visit. I rang the bell and was not surprised to see that Hugh was still as fat as ever. He led me into his room and hurriedly hid a large parcel under his desk. It was obvious that he was very embarrassed. When I asked him what he was doing, he smiled guiltily and then put the parcel on the desk. He explained that his diet was so strict that he had to reward himself occasionally. Then he showed me the contents of the parcel. It contained five large bars of chocolate and three bags of sweets!

句型解构

句1 My friend, Hugh, has always been fat, but things got so bad recently that he decided to go on a diet.

解构：Hugh 作 my friend 的同位语，表补充说明；has always been fat 现在完成时，表持续；so ... that... 意为"如此……以至于……"，that 引导的从句为结果状语从句；things，名词，意为"情况，形势"；get，动词，意为"变得"；decide to 意为"决定"；go on a diet 意为"节食，减肥"。

句2 He began his diet a week ago.

解构：时间状语 a week ago 暗示时态为一般过去时，开始讲述过去的事情，全文的时态在此转换为一般过去时。

句3 First of all, he wrote out a long list of all the foods which were forbidden.

解构：first of all 意为"首先"；write out 意为"详细写出，全部写出"；of all the foods 为介词短语，作 list 的定语；which 引导定语从句，限定修饰 foods；were forbidden 为被动语态，也可理解为系表结构；foods，名词，意为"不同种类的食物"。

句4 The list included most of the things Hugh loves.

解构:include,动词,意为"包含",宾语中的内容是所包含的其中一部分;most,代词,意为"大多数";Hugh loves 是定语从句,限定修饰 the things;此句中,主句的谓语动词 included 为一般过去时,讲述过去发生的事件,从句的谓语动词 love 用一般现在时,说明喜爱这些食物是一种习惯。

句5 Yesterday I paid him a visit.

解构:pay sb. a visit 意为"拜访某人",其中 pay 为动词,有"给予"的含义。

句6 I rang the bell and was not surprised to see that Hugh was still as fat as ever.

解构:ring the bell 意为"按门铃";was not surprised 两个并列句的主语一致,因而此处省略主语 I;that 引导的宾语从句,作 see 的宾语;as fat as ever 理解为 as fat as he ever was,as ... as ever 可译为"依旧,一直"。

句7 He led me into his room and hurriedly hid a large parcel under his desk.

解构:lead/led/led,动词,意为"指引,引领";hurriedly,副词,意为"匆忙地,仓促地";hide/hid/hidden,动词,意为"隐藏"。

句8 It was obvious that he was very embarrassed.

解构:it 为先行主语/形式主语,that 引导的从句作逻辑主语,此句为主语从句;embarrassed,形容词,意为"尴尬的"。

句9 When I asked him what he was doing, he smiled guiltily and then put the parcel on the desk.

解构:本句为 when 引导时间状语从句;ask 为双宾语动词,him 作间接宾语,what he was doing 从句作直接宾语;guiltily,副词,意为"惭愧地,内疚地"。

句10 He explained that his diet was so strict that he had to reward himself occasionally.

解构:explain,动词,意为"解释,说明";that 引导的宾语从句,作 explain 的宾语;strict,形容词,意为"严格的";had to 体现时态,不用 must;reward,动词,意为"奖励,奖赏",标题中的 reward 作名词;occasionally,副词,意为"偶尔"。

句11 Then he showed me the contents of the parcel.

解构:show,双宾语动词,me 作间接宾语,the contents 为直接宾语;contents,名词,意为"内容,物品"。

句12 It contained five large bars of chocolate and three bags of sweets!

解构:contain,动词,意为"包含",宾语中的内容是其所包含的全部。

　　我的朋友休一直很胖,但是近来情况变得愈加糟糕,以至他决定节食。他是一星期前开始节食的。首先,他开列了一张长长的单子,上面列了所有禁吃的食物。这张单子上的大多数食物都是休喜欢吃的:黄油、土豆、米饭、啤酒、牛奶、巧克力和糖果。昨天我去看望了他。我按响了门铃,当看到休仍和往常一样胖时,我并不感到惊奇。他把我领进屋,慌忙把一个大包藏到了桌子下面。显然他感到很尴尬。当我问他正干什么时,他内疚地笑了,然后把那个大包拿到了桌上。他解释说,他的饮食控制得太严格了,以至不得不偶尔奖赏自己一下。接着他给我看了包里的东西,里面装了五大块巧克力和三袋糖果!

语篇学习 3

（参考第二章一般将来时）

On strike
罢工

Busmen have decided to go on strike next week. The strike is due to begin on Tuesday. No one knows how long it will last. The busmen have stated that the strike will continue until general agreement is reached about pay and working conditions. Most people believe that the strike will last for at least a week. Many owners of private cars are going to offer "free rides" to people on their way to work. This will relieve pressure on the trains to some extent. Meanwhile, a number of university students have volunteered to drive buses while the strike lasts. All the students are expert drivers, but before they drive any of the buses, they will have to pass a special test. The students are going to take the test in two days' time. Even so, people are going to find it difficult to get to work. But so far, the public has expressed its gratitude to the students in letters to the Press. Only one or two people have objected that the students will drive too fast!

句型解构

句1 Busmen have decided to go on strike next week.
解构：have decided为现在完成时，表结果；go on strike意为"举行罢工"。

句2 The strike is due to begin on Tuesday.
解构：due，形容词，意为"预期的，约定的，定于……"，用一般现在时，表示预计会发生的事。

句3 No one knows how long it will last.
解构：how long it will last为宾语从句，作know的宾语；last，动词，意为"持续"。

句4 The busmen have stated that the strike will continue until general agreement is reached about pay and working conditions.
解构：have stated为现在完成时，表结果；state，动词，意为"声明，宣布"；that引导的宾语从句，作state的宾语；until引导时间状语从句，此句中用一般现在时表将来时；general agreement意为"总协定，全面协议"；is reached为被动语态，意为"被达到，被达成"；about pay and working conditions，介词短语，作general agreement的定语；pay，名词，意为"工资，薪水";working conditions意为"工作环境,工作条件"。

句5 Most people believe that the strike will last for at least a week.

解构:most,形容词,意为"大部分的,多数的";that引导的宾语从句,作believe的宾语;at least 意为"至少,起码"。

句6 Many owners of private cars are going to offer "free rides" to people on their way to work.

解构:owner,名词,意为"物主,主人";private cars意为"私家车";are going to意为"打算,将要";be going to表示事先经过考虑,打算或决定做某事;offer,动词,意为"提供";free rides意为"搭便车"。

句7 This will relieve pressure on the trains to some extent.

解构:will的将来时在句中表示对将来的预测,陈述将来事实;relieve,动词,意为"减轻,减除";pressure,名词,意为"压力";to some extent意为"在一定程度上,在某种程度上"。

句8 Meanwhile, a number of university students have volunteered to drive buses while the strike lasts.

解构:meanwhile,副词,意为"同时,期间";a number of意为"许多,一些";have volunteered为现在完成时,表结果,其中volunteer是动词,意为"自愿,主动";while引导的时间状语从句中,其通常引导一个时间段。

句9 All the students are expert drivers, but before they drive any of the buses, they will have to pass a special test.

解构:expert drivers意为"专业司机,开车能手";before引导时间状语从句;any,代词,意为"任一,任何";special,形容词,意为"专门的,特殊的";在一般将来时和一般过去时中,通常用will have to和had to来体现时态,而不用must。

句10 The students are going to take the test in two days' time.

解构:are going to意为"准备,打算";take the test意为"参加考试";in two days' time意为"两天后"。

句11 Even so, people are going to find it difficult to get to work.

解构:even so意为"即使如此";are going to do sth.,含有作者主观的判断、推测;it作形式宾语,to get to work为动词不定式短语,作逻辑宾语。

句12 But so far, the public has expressed its gratitude to the students in letters to the Press.

解构:so far意为"迄今为止";has expressed为现在完成时,表结果;express,动词,意为"表达";gratitude,名词,意为"感激,感谢";in letters为介词短语,作方式状语,意为"以书信的方式"；to the Press意为"向报社"。

句13 Only one or two people have objected that the students will drive too fast!

解构：have objected为现在完成时，表结果，object，动词，意为"反对，拒绝"，object to后面跟名词/动名词；that引导的宾语从句，作object的宾语；fast，副词，意为"快地"。

参考译文

公共汽车司机决定下星期罢工。罢工定于星期二开始，谁也不知道会持续多久。司机们声称此次罢工将一直持续到就工资和工作条件问题达成全面协议的时候为止。多数人认为此次罢工至少会持续一个星期。很多私人汽车的车主正准备为乘车上班的人们提供"免费乘车"服务，这将在某种程度上减轻对火车的压力。与此同时，有一部分大学生自愿在罢工期间驾驶公共汽车。所有的学生都是开车的能手，但在驾驶公共汽车之前，他们必须通过一项专门测验。学生们准备在两天后就接受测验。即使这样，人们仍会感到上班有困难。但到目前为止，公众已经向新闻界写信表达他们对学生们的感激之情了。只有一两个人提出反对意见，说学生们会把车开得太快！

语篇学习 4

(参考第二章过去将来时)
(参考第二章过去进行时)

By air
乘飞机

I used to travel by air a great deal when I was a boy. My parents used to live in South America and I used to fly there from Europe in the holidays. A flight attendant would take charge of me and I never had an unpleasant experience. I am used to traveling by air and only on one occasion have I ever felt frightened. After taking off, we were flying low over the city and slowly gaining height, when the plane suddenly turned round and flew back to the airport. While we were waiting to land, a flight attendant told us to keep calm and to get off the plane quietly as soon as it had touched down. Everybody on board was worried and we were curious to find out what had happened. Later we learnt that there was a very important person on board. The police had been told that a bomb had been planted on the plane. After we had landed, the plane was searched thoroughly. Fortunately, nothing was found and five hours later we were able to take off again.

句型解构

句1 I used to travel by air a great deal when I was a boy.

解构：used to意为"过去经常"，表示该状态或动作现已终止；a great deal意为"许多，大量"；when引导的时间状语从句，作全句的时间背景。

句2 My parents used to live in South America and I used to fly there from Europe in the holidays.

解构：句中两处运用used to，强调过去的习惯与现在的对比，该习惯现已终止。

句3 A flight attendant would take charge of me and I never had an unpleasant experience.

解构：would在此句中表示过去经常发生的事，但不强调该习惯的终止；flight attendant意为"客机乘务员，空乘"；take charge of意为"负责，照看"；experience，名词，此处意为"经历，体验"，为可数名词，但当意为"经验"时为不可数名词。

句 4 I am used to traveling by air and only on one occasion have I ever felt frightened.

解构:be used to 意为"习惯于",后接名词或动名词;only 副词构成的状语置于句首时,采用倒装语序,即助词 have 提前,用于加强语气;on one occasion 意为"有一次";have I ever felt frightened 为现在完成时,表影响、结果。

句 5 After taking off, we were flying low over the city and slowly gaining height, when the plane suddenly turned round and flew back to the airport.

解构:after taking off 为现在分词短语,作时间状语,其中 take off 意为"起飞";were flying/gaining height 为过去进行时,作时间背景;low,副词,意为"低地";gain height 意为"增加高度,爬升";when 引导瞬间动作,动作在后,此处有"突然"之意;turn round 意为"转身,掉头";fly back 意为"飞回"。

句 6 While we were waiting to land, a flight attendant told us to keep calm and to get off the plane quietly as soon as it had touched down.

解构:while 引导时间段,描述时间背景,主句的动作在此过程中发生;keep calm 意为"保持冷静";get off 意为"从……下来,离开";as soon as 意为"一……就……",引导时间状语从句;had touched down 为过去完成时,表示动作在先;touch down 意为"降落,着陆"。

句 7 Everybody on board was worried and we were curious to find out what had happened.

解构:on board 为介词短语,作定语,意为"在(飞机、火车、船)上";curious,形容词,意为"好奇的";find out 意为"找出,查明";what 引导的宾语从句,作 find out 的宾语;had happened 为过去完成时,表示动作在先。

句 8 Later we learnt that there was a very important person on board.

解构:learn,动词,意为"得知,获悉";that 引导的宾语从句,作 learn 的宾语。

句 9 The police had been told that a bomb had been planted on the plane.

解构:had been told/had been planted 为被动语态用于过去完成时;bomb,名词,意为"炸弹";plant,动词,意为"安置"。

句 10 After we had landed, the plane was searched thoroughly.

解构:had landed 为过去完成时,表示动作在先;was searched 为被动语态,意为"被搜查";thoroughly,副词,意为"彻底地,完全地"。

句 11 Fortunately, nothing was found and five hours later we were able to take off again.

解构:fortunately,副词,意为"幸运地";was found 为被动语态,意为"被找到";be able to 用于一般过去时,取代 could,意为"成功做某事"。

参考译文

　　我在幼年的时候,曾多次乘飞机旅行。我的父母曾经住在南美洲,所以假期里我常从欧洲乘飞机到他们那里。我总是由一位空中乘务员照管,从未遇到过不愉快的经历。我习惯了乘飞机旅行,只是有一次把我吓坏了。起飞之后,我们在城市上空低低地飞行,然后慢慢爬高。这时飞机突然调转头来,飞回了机场。在我们等待降落时,一位空中乘务员告诉我们要保持镇静,待飞机一着陆,就安静地离开飞机。飞机上的人都很着急,大家都急于想知道究竟出了什么事。后来我们才得知,飞机上坐了一位非常重要的人物。有人报告警察,说飞机上安放了一枚炸弹。我们降落之后,飞机被彻底搜查了一遍。幸运的是,什么也没有找到。5个小时后,我们又起飞了。

语篇学习 5

（参考第二章过去进行时）

Too late
为时太晚

The plane was late and detectives were waiting at the airport all morning. They were expecting a valuable parcel of diamonds from South Africa. A few hours earlier, someone had told the police that thieves would try to steal the diamonds. When the plane arrived, some of the detectives were waiting inside the main building while others were waiting on the airfield. Two men took the parcel off the plane and carried it into the Customs House. While two detectives were keeping guard at the door, two others opened the parcel. To their surprise, the precious parcel was full of stones and sand!

句型解构

句1 The plane was late and detectives were waiting at the airport all morning.

解构：all morning 为时间状语，表示时间段；were waiting 为过去进行时，表示过去某段时间内正在进行的动作；detective，名词，意为"侦探"。

句2 They were expecting a valuable parcel of diamonds from South Africa.

解构：expect，动词，意为"期待"；valuable，形容词，意为"贵重的"；parcel，名词，意为"包裹"；diamond，名词，意为"钻石"；were expecting 为过去进行时，表示过去某时正在进行的动作。

句3 A few hours earlier, someone had told the police that thieves would try to steal the diamonds.

解构：earlier，副词 early 的比较级；that 引导的宾语从句，作 told 的宾语，从句中的 would 为过去将来时，与主句谓语时态相一致；had told 为过去完成时，强调影响和结果，与从句的动作相比，该动作在先。

句4 When the plane arrived, some of the detectives were waiting inside the main building while others were waiting on the airfield.

解构：此句由3部分组成，when 引导整个句子的时间状语从句，some of ... building 为主句，while 引导的时间状语从句，表示与主句的动作同时进行；when 既可以引导时间点，也可以引导时间段，while 只能引导时间段，当从句和主句的动作同时发生且都用过去进行时，多用 while 引导；inside the main building 是地点状语，意为"在主楼内"；on the airfield 是地点状语，意为"在停机坪上"。

句 5 Two men took the parcel off the plane and carried it into the Customs House.

解构：take ... off... 意为"从……拿下"；Customs House 意为"海关"。

句 6 While two detectives were keeping guard at the door, two others opened the parcel.

解构：while 引导时间段，从句描述时间背景，主句的动作在此过程中发生。

句 7 To their surprise, the precious parcel was full of stones and sand!

解构：to their surprise 插入语在句中作独立成分，表补充说明；be full of/be filled with 意为"充满，装满"；sand，名词，意为"沙子"时不可数，sands 意为"沙滩，沙漠"。

参考译文

飞机误点了，侦探们在机场等了整整一上午。他们正期待从南非来的一个装着钻石的贵重包裹。数小时以前，有人向警方报告，说有人企图偷走这些钻石。当飞机到达时，一些侦探等候在主楼内，另一些侦探则守候在停机坪上。有两个人把包裹拿下飞机，进了海关。这时两个侦探把住门口，另外两个侦探打开了包裹。令他们吃惊的是，那珍贵的包裹里面装的全是石头和沙子！

语篇学习 *6*

（参考第二章将来进行时）

The Greenwood Boys
绿林少年

The Greenwood Boys are a group of pop singers. At present, they are visiting all parts of the country. They will be arriving here tomorrow. They will be coming by train and most of the young people in the town will be meeting them at the station. Tomorrow evening they will be singing at the Workers' Club. The Greenwood Boys will be staying for five days. During this time, they will give five performances. As usual, the police will have a difficult time. They will be trying to keep order. It is always the same on these occasions.

句型解构

句1 The Greenwood Boys are a group of pop singers.

解构：group，名词，意为"群体，团体"；pop是popular的缩写，意为"流行的，受欢迎的"。

句2 At present, they are visiting all parts of the country.

解构：at present是时间状语，等同于now；根据语义，visit在文中指"巡回演出"；all parts of the country意为"全国各地"。

句3 They will be arriving here tomorrow.

解构：will be arriving为将来进行时，表示计划好的事情或预计要发生的事情，陈述将来事实；一般将来时的be going to/will常带有意愿、意图等情态意义，而将来进行时只是单纯陈述即将发生的动作，不带有情态意义。

句4 They will be coming by train and most of the young people in the town will be meeting them at the station.

解构：will be coming为将来进行时，陈述将来事实；most，代词，意为"大多数，大部分"；in the town为介词短语，作定语；will be meeting为将来进行时，陈述将来事实。

句5 Tomorrow evening they will be singing at the Workers' Club.

解构：tomorrow evening表示时间段；will be singing为将来进行时，表示将来某段时间内正在进行的动作或状态。

句6 The Greenwood Boys will be staying for five days.

解构：for five days表示时间段；will be staying将来进行时，表示将来某段时间内正在进行的动作或状态。

句7 During this time, they will give five performances.

解构：performance，名词，意为"表演，演出"；will give是一般将来时，相比将来进行时，一般将来时表示主语的意愿，具有"蓄意为之"的情态含义。

句8 As usual, the police will have a difficult time.

解构：as usual/as always意为"如同往常，照例"；have a difficult time意为"有困难，过得很艰难"。

句9 They will be trying to keep order.

解构：will be trying为将来进行时，陈述将来事实；keep order意为"维持秩序"。

句10 It is always the same on these occasions.

解构：same，代词，"同样的事物"，通常与the连用，the same在句中作表语；occasion，名词，意为"场合，时机"，常与介词on连用。

参考译文

"绿林少年"是一个流行歌曲演唱团。目前他们正在全国各地巡回演出，明天就要到达此地。他们将乘火车来，镇上的大部分青年人将到车站迎接他们。明晚他们将在工人俱乐部演出。"绿林少年"准备在此逗留5天。在此期间，他们将演出5场。同往常一样，警察的日子不好过，他们将设法维持秩序。每逢这种场合，情况都这样。

语篇学习 7

（参考第二章现在完成时）

No parking
禁止停车

Jasper White is one of those rare people who believes in ancient myths. He has just bought a new house in the city, but ever since he moved in, he has had trouble with cars and their owners. When he returns home at night, he always finds that someone has parked a car outside his gate. Because of this, he has not been able to get his own car into his garage even once. Jasper has put up "No Parking" signs outside his gate, but these have not had any effect. Now he has put an ugly stone head over the gate. It is one of the ugliest faces I have ever seen. I asked him what it was and he told me that it was Medusa, the Gorgon. Jasper hopes that she will turn cars and their owners to stone. But none of them has been turned to stone yet!

句型解构

句 1 Jasper White is one of those rare people who believes in ancient myths.

解构：关系代词who引导定语从句，修饰限制one，因此谓语动词believe用第三人称单数形式；one of后面的名词须用复数。

句 2 He has just bought a new house in the city, but ever since he moved in, he has had trouble with cars and their owners.

解构：just，副词，意为"刚刚"；has bought是现在完成时的已完成用法，表结果；ever加强语气，since+时间点，表时间段；has为助动词，had为过去分词，构成现在完成时，表动作的持续；have trouble with意为"与……有纠纷，因……而苦恼"。

句 3 When he returns home at night, he always finds that someone has parked a car outside his gate.

解构：when引导时间状语从句，that引导宾语从句；has parked构成现在完成时，表结果，强调对现在的影响。

句 4 Because of this, he has not been able to get his own car into his garage even once.

解构：because of后面跟名词或代词等；be able to与can均可表示"能够"，但be able to可用于各种时态，该句中用于现在完成时，表结果；get意为"使得"，为使役动词用法；even加强语气。

句5 Jasper has put up "No Parking" signs outside his gate, but these have not had any effect.

解构：put up意为"挂起"；have effect意为"有效果，有作用"；has put up与have not had any effect构成现在完成时，表影响和结果。

句6 Now he has put an ugly stone head over the gate.

解构：has put为现在完成时，表结果；now也可作为现在完成时的时间标志。

句7 It is one of the ugliest faces I have ever seen.

解构：I have ever seen作定语从句，意为"我曾见过的"，在过往的经历中做比较，用最高级。

句8 I asked him what it was and he told me that it was Medusa, the Gorgon.

解构：ask为双宾语动词，him作间接宾语，what it was宾语从句作直接宾语；told为双宾语动词，me作间接宾语，that引导的宾语从句作直接宾语；the Gorgon为蛇发三姐妹，Medusa是其中之一，the Gorgon作同位语。

句9 Jasper hopes that she will turn cars and their owners to stone.

解构：that引导的宾语从句作hope的宾语，turn ... to意为"把……变成"。

句10 But none of them has been turned to stone yet!

解构：none，代词，意为"没有人，全无"；yet，副词，意为"还"，常用于表疑问或否定的完成时中。

参考译文

贾斯珀·怀特是少有的相信古代神话的人之一。他刚在城里买下一所新房子，但自从搬进去后，他就和车主们发生了摩擦。当他夜里回到家时，总是发现有人把车停在他家大门外。为此，他甚至一次也没能把自己的车开进车库。贾斯珀曾把几块"禁止停车"的牌子挂在大门外边，但没有任何效果。现在他把一个丑陋的石雕头像放在了大门上边，这是我见过的最丑陋的头像之一。我问他那是什么，他告诉我那是蛇发女怪美杜莎。贾斯珀希望她把汽车和车主们都变成石头。但到目前为止还没有一个变成石头呢！

语篇学习 *8*

（参考第二章过去完成时）

Everything except the weather
唯独没有考虑到天气

My old friend, Harrison, had lived in the Mediterranean for many years before he returned to England. He had often dreamed of retiring in England and had planned to settle down in the country. He had no sooner returned than he bought a house and went to live there. Almost immediately he began to complain about the weather, for even though it was still summer, it rained continually and it was often bitterly cold. After so many years of sunshine, Harrison got a shock. He acted as if he had never lived in England before. In the end, it was more than he could bear. He had hardly had time to settle down when he sold the house and left the country. The dream he had had for so many years ended there. Harrison had thought of everything except the weather.

句型解构

句 1 My old friend, Harrison, had lived in the Mediterranean for many years before he returned to England.

解构：Harrison 为 my old friend 的同位语，表补充说明，指同一人；had lived 为过去完成时表持续，for+一段时间，也说明该完成时表动作的持续；the Mediterranean 意为"地中海"，江河、海洋等名称前须用定冠词 the；before 引导时间状语从句，该从句的动作在前。

句 2 He had often dreamed of retiring in England and had planned to settle down in the country.

解构：dream of 意为"幻想"；plan to 意为"计划"；settle down 意为"定居，安顿"；country 指"乡村"；had dreamed 与 had planned 构成过去完成时，是完成时的已完成用法，强调结果，表示对 Harrison 之后的选择和生活产生影响。

句 3 He had no sooner returned than he bought a house and went to live there.

解构：no sooner ... than... 意为"刚……就……"，常与过去完成时连用，no sooner 引导的动词表示的动作在先，因此用过去完成时，than 引导的动词表示的动作在后，用一般过去时。

句 4 Almost immediately he began to complain about the weather, for even though it was still summer, it rained continually and it was often bitterly cold.

解构：almost，程度副词，意为"几乎"；immediately，时间副词，意为"立刻"；begin to/begin doing 意为"开始"；complain about/of 意为"抱怨"；for，连词，意为"由于"，引导原因状语从句，for 与 because 不同，通常不用于句首；even though 表示"尽管"，引导让步状语从句，此处为让步状语从句用于原因状语从句之中；continually，频度副词，意为"不断地，频繁地"；bitterly，程度副词，意为"痛苦地，激烈地，严寒地"。

句5 After so many years of sunshine, Harrison got a shock.

解构：after 引导时间状语从句；so many 后跟可数名词；get a shock/get shocked 意为"大吃一惊"。

句6 He acted as if he had never lived in England before.

解构：as if/though 意为"似乎，好像"，引导方式状语从句，常用于虚拟语气，从句表示与过去的事实相反，谓语动词用过去完成时。

句7 In the end, it was more than he could bear.

解构：区分 in the end 与 at the end of 的用法；more than 意为"超出……的范围"；bear，动词，意为"忍受"。

句8 He had hardly had time to settle down when he sold the house and left the country.

解构：hardly ... when... 意为"几乎未来得及……就……"，常用过去完成时，hardly 引导的动词表示的动作在先，用过去完成时，when 引导的动词表示的动作在后，用一般过去时。

句9 The dream he had had for so many years ended there.

解构：he had had for so many years 为定语从句，修饰限定先行词 dream，从句中第一个 had 作过去完成时的助词，后一个 had 作实义动词，表示"拥有"，为过去分词，此处用过去完成时表持续。

句10 Harrison had thought of everything except the weather.

解构：had thought of 为过去完成时，表结果；think of 意为"考虑，想到"；except，介词，意为"除了"。

参考译文

　　我的老朋友哈里森在回到英国以前曾多年居住在地中海地区。过去他常幻想退休后到英国，并计划在乡间安顿下来。他一回到英国便买下了一幢房子住了进去。但紧接着他就开始抱怨那里的天气了。因为即使那时仍为夏季，但雨总是下个不停，而且常常冷得厉害。在阳光下生活了那么多年的哈里森对此感到惊奇。他的举动就好像他从未在英国生活过一样。最后，他再也忍受不住，还没等安顿下来就卖掉了房子，离开了这个国家。他多年来的幻想从此破灭。哈里森把每件事情都考虑到了，唯独没想到天气。

语篇学习 9

（参考第二章将来完成时）

The Olympic Games
奥林匹克运动会

The Olympic Games will be held in our country in four years' time. As a great many people will be visiting the country, the government will be building new hotels, an immense stadium, and a new Olympic-standard swimming pool. They will also be building new roads and a special railway line. The Games will be held just outside the capital and the whole area will be called "Olympic City". Workers will have completed the new roads by the end of this year. By the end of next year, they will have finished work on the new stadium. The fantastic modern buildings have been designed by Kurt Gunter. Everybody will be watching anxiously as the new buildings go up. We are all very excited and are looking forward to the Olympic Games because they have never been held before in this country.

句型解构

句1 The Olympic Games will be held in our country in four years' time.

解构：Games作专有名词的一部分，首字母需大写；will be held为被动语态用于一般将来时；in four years' time等同于in four years，其中in是介词，意为"在……之后"。

句2 As a great many people will be visiting the country, the government will be building new hotels, an immense stadium, and a new Olympic-standard swimming pool.

解构：as表示"由于"，引导原因状语从句，通常位于句首，as引导的状语从句往往是人们已知的原因，而because引导的原因往往是大家未知的；a great many/a great number of后跟可数名词；will be visiting/will be building将来进行时，表示计划或安排好的事，单纯陈述将来事实；new hotels、an immense stadium和and a new Olympic-standard swimming pool为三个并列宾语；Olympic-standard为复合形容词，作定语。

句3 They will also be building new roads and a special railway line.

解构：will also be building为将来进行时，表示预计将要发生的事情；special意为"专门的，特设的"，a special railway line意为"一条铁路专线"。

句4 Workers will have completed the new roads by the end of this year.

解构：by+时间点，表示"在……之前"，by the end of this year表示"在今年年底前"，为将来完成时时间标志；will have completed为将来完成时，表示今年年底前将会完成的动作。

句5 By the end of next year, they will have finished work on the new stadium.

解构：by the end of next year意为"到明年年底"；will have finished表示明年年底前将会完成的动作；work，名词，表示"工作"。

句6 The fantastic modern buildings have been designed by Kurt Gunter.

解构：have been designed为被动语态用于现在完成时，表示动作已完成，强调结果。

句7 Everybody will be watching anxiously as the new buildings go up.

解构：watch意为"关注"，will be watching anxiously为将来进行时，陈述将来事实，意为"将会急切地关注"；as意为"当"，也可用when/while，引导时间状语从句；go up意为"兴建"。

句8 We are all very excited and are looking forward to the Olympic Games because they have never been held before in this country.

解构：excited，过去分词作形容词，常与人称主语连用，表示人的自我感受和对事物的感觉；look forward to+名词/代词/动名词，意为"期待……"，其中to是介词。

参考译文

4年以后，奥林匹克运动会将在我们国家举行。由于届时将有大批的人到我们国家来，所以政府准备建造一些新的饭店、一个大型体育场和一个新的奥运会标准的游泳池。他们还将修筑一些新的道路和一条铁路专线。奥运会就在首都市郊举办，整个地区将被称作"奥林匹克城"。工人们将在今年年底前把新路铺好；到明年年底，他们将把新体育场建成。这些巨大的现代化建筑是由库尔特·冈特设计的。大家都将急切地关注新建筑的建成。我们都非常激动，盼望着奥运会的到来，因为这个国家还从未举办过奥运会。

语篇学习 *10*

（参考第二章过去将来时）

（参考第二章过去将来完成时）

（参考第二章常用 if 条件句归纳）

The Channel Tunnel
英吉利海峡隧道

In 1858, a French engineer, Aime Thome de Gamond, arrived in England with a plan for a twenty-one-mile tunnel under the English Channel. He said that it would be possible to build a platform in the centre of the Channel. This platform would serve as a port and a railway station. The tunnel would be well-ventilated if tall chimneys were built above sea level. In 1860, a better plan was put forward by an Englishman, William Low. He suggested that a double railway-tunnel should be built. This would solve the problem of ventilation, for if a train entered this tunnel, it would draw in fresh air behind it. Forty-two years later a tunnel was actually begun. If, at the time, the British had not feared invasion, it would have been completed. The world had to wait almost another 100 years for the Channel Tunnel. It was officially opened on March 7th, 1994, finally connecting Britain to the European continent.

句型解构

句1 In 1858, a French engineer, Aime Thome de Gamond, arrived in England with a plan for a twenty-one-mile tunnel under the English Channel.

解构：Aime Thome de Gamond 作 a French engineer 的同位语，补充说明具体名字；for a twenty-one-mile tunnel under the English Channel 为介词短语，作 plan 的定语；twenty-one-mile 是复合形容词，其中 mile 需用单数。

句2 He said that it would be possible to build a platform in the centre of the Channel.

解构：that 引导的宾语从句，作 said 的宾语；would 为过去将来时；be possible to 表示"有可能……"；从句中的 it 为形式主语，to 的动词不定式作从句的逻辑主语。

句3 This platform would serve as a port and a railway station.

解构：serve as/for 表示"用作……充当……"，与 be used for/act as 同义。

句 4 The tunnel would be well-ventilated if tall chimneys were built above sea level.

解构：理解为第二类非真实条件句，虚拟语气，与现实情况相反，if从句用一般过去时，主句用过去将来时，也可以理解为第一类真实条件句用于过去时；well-ventilated 为副词＋过去分词，构成复合形容词。

句 5 In 1860, a better plan was put forward by an Englishman, William Low.

解构：put forward意为"提出（观点、建议、方案、计划等）"，was put forward是被动语态，其中 put 为过去分词，by后跟动作执行者。

句 6 He suggested that a double railway-tunnel should be built.

解构：suggest/insist/command/recommend 等词后面常用虚拟语气，should 可省略，that 引导的宾语从句，作 suggested 的宾语；"建议某事/做某事"也常用 suggest＋名词/动名词结构。

句 7 This would solve the problem of ventilation, for if a train entered this tunnel, it would draw in fresh air behind it.

解构：for表示"因为"，引导原因状语从句；if从句为第一类条件句，文中用于过去的语境中，故时态做相应变化，描述在满足此条件下较容易实现的情况；enter表示"进入"，及物动词，不加介词；draw意为"拖，拉"，draw in意为"使……进入"。

句 8 Forty-two years later a tunnel was actually begun.

解构：was begun 为被动语态。

句 9 If, at the time, the British had not feared invasion, it would have been completed.

解构：at the time意为"在当时，在那时"，插入语；第三类if条件句是对过去事物的一种假设，其中if条件句谈论想象中的事情，主句讲述想象的结果，实际上这种情况在过去并没有发生，因此与过去的事实相反。

句 10 The world had to wait almost another 100 years for the Channel Tunnel.

解构：had to体现时态，不能用must；almost为程度副词。

句 11 It was officially opened on March 7th, 1994, finally connecting Britain to the European continent.

解构：officially，副词，表示"正式地，官方地"；was opened 为被动语态；on March 7th, 1994，具体的某一日期前须用介词on；connecting是现在分词短语，作状语，相当于并列句 and finally connects Britain to the European continent; connect to/with表示"连接，链接"。

参考译文

　　1858年,一位名叫埃梅·托梅·德·干蒙的法国工程师带着建造一条长21英里、穿越英吉利海峡的隧道计划到了英国。他说,可以在隧道中央建造一座平台,这座平台将被用作港口和火车站。如果再建些伸出海面的高大的烟囱状通风管,隧道就具备了良好的通风条件。1860年,一位名叫威廉·洛的英国人提出了一项更好的计划。他提议建一条双轨隧道,这样就解决了通风问题。因为如果有一列火车开进隧道,它就把新鲜空气随之抽进了隧道。42年以后,隧道实际已经开始建了。如果不是因为那时英国人害怕德国入侵,隧道早已建成了。世界不得不再等将近100年才看到海峡隧道竣工。这条隧道于1994年3月7日正式开通,将英国与欧洲大陆连到了一起。

语篇学习 *11*

（参考第二章现在完成进行时）

April Fools' Day
愚人节

"To end our special news bulletin," said the voice of the television announcer, "we're going over to the macaroni fields of Calabria. Macaroni has been grown in this area for over six hundred years. Two of the leading growers, Giuseppe Moldova and Riccardo Brabante, tell me that they have been expecting a splendid crop this year and harvesting has begun earlier than usual. Here you can see two workers who, between them, have just finished cutting three cartloads of golden brown macaroni stalks. The whole village has been working day and night gathering and threshing this year's crop before the September rains. On the right, you can see Mrs. Brabante herself. She has been helping her husband for thirty years now. Mrs. Brabante is talking to the manager of the local factory where the crop is processed. This last scene shows you what will happen at the end of the harvest: the famous Calabrian macaroni-eating competition! Signor Fratelli, the present champion, has won it every year since 1991. And that ends our special bulletin for today, Thursday, April 1st. We're now going back to the studio."

句型解构

句1 To end our special news bulletin,

解构：其为动词不定式短语,作目的状语;special news bulletin表示"特别新闻节目,专题新闻报道"。

句2 we're going over to the macaroni fields of Calabria.

解构：go over意为"朝……走过去";macaroni是意大利语,意为"通心粉",是指经过加工的面粉,并非长在田里,但由于有人可能没听说过,文章便以通心粉长在田里为前提进行描述,从而作为愚人节的新闻专题。

句3 Macaroni has been grown in this area for over six hundred years.

解构：has been grown为被动语态用于现在完成时,表示动作的持续。

句 4 Two of the leading growers, Giuseppe Moldova and Riccardo Brabante, tell me that they have been expecting a splendid crop this year and harvesting has begun earlier than usual.

解构:leading 为现在分词作定语,意为"主要的";Giuseppe Moldova 和 Riccardo Brabante 是两个意大利人名,作同位语,补充说明具体姓名;tell 双宾语动词,作谓语动词,me 为间接宾语,that 引导的宾语从句,作直接宾语;have been expecting 是现在完成进行时,表动作持续进行;crop,名词,意为"产量,收成";harvesting,动名词,意为"收割工作",作主语;has begun 为现在完成时,表结果;earlier,副词,early 的比较级。

句 5 Here you can see two workers who, between them, have just finished cutting three cartloads of golden brown macaroni stalks.

解构:关系代词 who 引导定语从句,修饰限定 two workers;have just finished 为现在完成时,表结果;finish+名词/动名词,表示"完成某事/做某事";between them 作定语从句中的插入语,between 在此处作介词,意为"作为……的共同努力的结果,协力"。

句 6 The whole village has been working day and night gathering and threshing this year's crop before the September rains.

解构:has been working 为现在完成进行时,表动作持续进行;gathering and threshing 为现在分词短语,作状语;the September rains 意为"9月雨季",表达雨季通常用 rain 的复数。

句 7 On the right, you can see Mrs. Brabante herself.

解构:herself,反身代词,意为"本人,自己"。

句 8 She has been helping her husband for thirty years now.

解构:has been helping 为现在完成进行时,表持续进行;for+时间段,表该状态的时间长度。

句 9 Mrs. Brabante is talking to the manager of the local factory where the crop is processed.

解构:关系副词 where 引导定语从句,修饰限定 the local factory;is processed 构成被动语态。

句 10 This last scene shows you what will happen at the end of the harvest: the famous Calabrian macaroni-eating competition!

解构:show,双宾语动词,you 为间接宾语,what will happen 宾语从句作直接宾语;macaroni-eating 名词+现在分词,构成复合形容词。

句 11 Signor Fratelli, the present champion, has won it every year since 1991.

解构:the present champion 为同位语,表补充说明;has won it every year 为现在完成时,在此表示经常性、重复性完成的动作。

参考译文

　　"作为我们专题新闻节目的结尾,"电视播音员说,"我们现在到卡拉布利亚的通心粉田里。通心粉在这个地区已经种植了600多年了。两个主要种植者,朱塞皮·莫尔道瓦和里卡多·布拉班特告诉我,他们一直期待着今年获得一个大丰收,收割工作比往年开始得要早些。这里您可以看到两个工人,他们协力割下了3车金黄色的通心粉梗。全村的人都日夜奋战,要赶在9月的雨季之前把今年的庄稼收割上来,打完场。在屏幕的右侧,您可以看到布拉班特太太本人,她已经帮助她的丈夫30年了。布拉班特太太现在正和负责通心粉加工的当地加工厂的经理交谈。这最后一个镜头向您展示了收获之后将发生的事情:著名的卡拉布利亚人吃通心粉大赛!目前的冠军弗拉特里先生,自1991年以来,年年获胜。今天——4月1日,星期四——的专题新闻节目到此结束。现在我们回到电视演播室。"

语篇学习 *12*

（参考第二章过去完成进行时）

Out of control
失控

As the man tried to swing the speedboat round, the steering wheel came away in his hands. He waved desperately to his companion, who had been water skiing for the last fifteen minutes. Both men had hardly had time to realize what was happening when they were thrown violently into the sea. The speedboat had struck a buoy, but it continued to move very quickly across the water. Both men had just begun to swim towards the shore, when they noticed with dismay that the speedboat was moving in a circle. It now came straight towards them at tremendous speed. In less than a minute, it roared past them only a few feet away. After it had passed, they swam on as quickly as they could because they knew that the boat would soon return. They had just had enough time to swim out of danger when the boat again completed a circle. On this occasion, however, it had slowed down considerably. The petrol had nearly all been used up. Before long, the noise dropped completely and the boat began to drift gently across the water.

句型解构

句1 As the man tried to swing the speedboat round, the steering wheel came away in his hands.

解构：as，连词，表示"当……时"，引导时间状语从句；swing/turn round 意为"掉头，转身"；steering wheel 意为"方向盘，舵轮"；come away 意为"脱落，离开"。

句2 He waved desperately to his companion, who had been water skiing for the last fifteen minutes.

解构：wave to 意为"向……挥手"，companion，名词，意为"同伴，朋友"；关系代词 who 引导非限定性定语从句，作先行词 his companion 的附加说明，用逗号与主句隔开，去掉不影响主句意思；had been water skiing 为过去完成进行时，表动作在过去一段时间内持续进行；for+时间段，表示该动作的持续时长。

句 3 Both men had hardly had time to realize what was happening when they were thrown violently into the sea.

解构：hardly ... when... 意为"未来得及……就……，刚……就……"，通常用于过去完成时，hardly 引导的动词表示的动作在先，用过去完成时，when 引导的动词表示的动作在后，用一般过去时；what was happening 为宾语从句，作 realize 的宾语；were thrown 为被动语态。

句 4 The speedboat had struck a buoy, but it continued to move very quickly across the water.

解构：had struck 为过去完成时，表结果，struck 为过去分词，原形为 strike，意为"打击，撞击"；buoy，名词，意为"浮标"；across，介词，通常指在表面穿过。

句 5 Both men had just begun to swim towards the shore, when they noticed with dismay that the speedboat was moving in a circle.

解构：just ... when 意为"刚……就……"，时间背景为过去时的两个动作，动作在先可用过去完成时，动作在后用一般过去时表示，"had just begun"动作在先，"noticed"动作在后；with dismay 为介词短语，作状语，意为"带着惊慌，带着沮丧"；that 引导的宾语从句，作 notice 的宾语。

句 6 It now came straight towards them at tremendous speed.

解构：come straight towards 意为"直冲向"；tremendous，形容词，意为"巨大的"。

句 7 In less than a minute, it roared past them only a few feet away.

解构：less than 意为"不到，少于"；roar，动词，意为"咆哮，呼啸"。

句 8 After it had passed, they swam on as quickly as they could because they knew that the boat would soon return.

解构：had passed 为过去完成时，表示动作先完成；on，副词，意为"继续，向前"；because 引导原因状语从句；that 引导的宾语从句，作 knew 的宾语；would 为过去将来时。

句 9 They had just had enough time to swim out of danger when the boat again completed a circle.

解构：just ... when 表示"刚……就……"；had just had enough time to 前一个 had 作助动词，构成过去完成时，表示动作在先，后一个 had 为过去分词；completed 一般过去时表示动作在后；have enough time to 意为"有足够的时间做某事"；out of danger 意为"脱离危险"。

句 10 On this occasion, however, it had slowed down considerably.

解构：on this occasion 意为"这一次"；had slowed down 为过去完成时，表结果，slow down 意为"减速"；considerably，副词，意为"相当地，非常地"。

句 11 The petrol had nearly all been used up.

解构：had been used up 为被动语态用于过去完成时，表结果；use up 意为"用完，耗尽"。

句 12 Before long, the noise dropped completely and the boat began to drift gently across the water.

解构：before long 意为"不久之后"；drop，动词，意为"下降，骤减，终止"；drift，动词，意为"漂流"。

参考译文

当那人试图让快艇转弯时，方向盘脱手了。他绝望地向他的伙伴挥手，他的伙伴在过去的 15 分钟里一直在滑水。他们两个还没来得及意识到究竟发生了什么事情，就被猛地抛入了海里。快艇撞上了一个浮标，但它仍在水面上快速行驶着。两个人刚开始向岸边游去，就突然惊愕地发现快艇正在转着圈行驶，它现在正以惊人的速度直冲他们驶来。不到 1 分钟的工夫，它就从离他们只有几英尺远的地方呼啸着驶了过去。快艇过去之后，他们以最快的速度向前游去，因为他们知道快艇马上就要转回来。他们刚刚来得及游出危险区，快艇就又转完了一圈。然而这一次它的速度慢多了。汽油几乎已经用光。没过多久，噪音便彻底消失，快艇开始在水面上慢悠悠地漂流。

语篇学习 *13*

（参考第二章将来完成进行时）

Never too old to learn
活到老学到老

I have just received a letter from my old school, informing me that my former headmaster, Mr. Stuart Page, will be retiring next week. Pupils of the school, old and new, will be sending him a present to mark the occasion. All those who have contributed towards the gift will sign their names in a large album which will be sent to the headmaster's home. We shall all remember Mr. Page for his patience and understanding and for the kindly encouragement he gave us when we went so unwillingly to school. A great many former pupils will be attending a farewell dinner in his honour next Thursday. It is a curious coincidence that the day before his retirement, Mr. Page will have been teaching for a total of forty years. After he has retired, he will devote himself to gardening. For him, this will be an entirely new hobby. But this does not matter, for, as he has often remarked, one is never too old to learn.

句型解构

句 1 I have just received a letter from my old school, informing me that my former headmaster, Mr. Stuart Page, will be retiring next week.

解构：just，副词，表示"刚刚"；have received 为现在完成时，表结果；old school/Alma Mater 意为"母校"；informing 为现在分词短语，作目的状语；Mr. Stuart Page 作 my former headmaster 的同位语；will be retiring 为将来进行时，表示预计会发生的事情，陈述将来事实。

句 2 Pupils of the school, old and new, will be sending him a present to mark the occasion.

解构：old and new 有两种理解，第一种理解为作 pupils of the school 的同位语，补充说明，第二种理解为非限定性定语从句，(which are)old and new，有逗号分隔，去掉该句不影响对整体内容的理解；will be sending 为将来进行时，陈述将来事实；to 引导的动词不定式短语作目的状语；mark，动词，意为"纪念"，occasion，名词，意为"时刻，日子"。

句3 All those who have contributed towards the gift will sign their names in a large album which will be sent to the headmaster's home.

解构：关系代词who引导定语从句，修饰限定主语all those；have contributed towards the gift是现在完成时，表结果，意为"凑钱买该礼物"；contribute towards意为"对……有贡献，为……捐款，捐给"；gift相比present更为正式；will sign作主句的谓语部分；关系代词which引导定语从句，修饰限定a large album；will be sent为被动语态用于一般将来时。

句4 We shall all remember Mr. Page for his patience and understanding and for the kindly encouragement he gave us when we went so unwillingly to school.

解构：remember ... for意为"因某事而记住某人"，介词for后面跟随3个并列宾语，即patience、understanding 和 encouragement；he gave us是定语从句，修饰限定宾语encouragement；when引导的时间状语从句，作定语从句的时间背景；kindly这里为形容词，意为"亲切的，和蔼的"；unwillingly，副词，意为"不情愿地，勉强地"。

句5 A great many former pupils will be attending a farewell dinner in his honour next Thursday.

解构：a great many/a great number of+可数名词，表示"大量的"；will be attending 为将来进行时，陈述将来事实；farewell dinner意为"告别宴会"；in one's honour/in honour of 为介词短语，作定语，表示"为向某人表示敬意，为纪念某人"。

句6 It is a curious coincidence that the day before his retirement, Mr. Page will have been teaching for a total of forty years.

解构：it作形式主语，that引导的主语从句，作句子的逻辑主语；will have been teaching 为将来完成进行时，强调动作持续进行到将来某一时间；for+一段时间，表示动作持续的长度。

句7 After he has retired, he will devote himself to gardening.

解构：状语从句中，需用现在完成时替代将来完成时，has retired在此句中表将来完成；devote ... to意为"致力于，专心于"，其中to为介词，后接名词或动名词。

句8 But this does not matter, for, as he has often remarked, one is never too old to learn.

解构：for，连词，引导原因状语从句；as he has often remarked为as引导的非限定性定语从句，as作remarked的宾语，代替主句内容，as意为"正如，像"。

参考译文

我刚刚收到母校的一封信，通知我说以前的校长斯图亚特·佩奇先生下星期就退休了。为了纪念这个日子，学校的学生——无论老同学还是新同学——将送他一件礼物。

所有凑钱买此礼品的人都将把自己的名字签在一本大签名簿上，签名簿将被送到校长的家里。我们不会忘记对我们既有耐心又充满理解的佩奇先生，也不会忘记在我们不愿去上学时他给予我们的亲切鼓励。很多老同学都准备参加下星期四为他举行的告别宴会。佩奇先生退休的前一天正好是他执教满40年的日子，这真是奇妙的巧合。他退休后，将致力于园艺。对于他来说，这将是一种全新的爱好。但这没有关系，因为正如他常说的那样，人要活到老学到老。

语篇学习 *14*

（参考第二章情态动词+have done结构）

Jumbo versus the police
小象对警察

Last Christmas, the circus owner, Jimmy Gates, decided to take some presents to a children's hospital. Dressed up as Father Christmas and accompanied by a "guard of honour" of six pretty girls, he set off down the main street of the city riding a baby elephant called Jumbo. He should have known that the police would never allow this sort of thing. A policeman approached Jimmy and told him he ought to have gone along a side street as Jumbo was holding up the traffic. Though Jimmy agreed to go at once, Jumbo refused to move. Fifteen policemen had to push very hard to get him off the main street. The police had a difficult time, but they were most amused. "Jumbo must weigh a few tons," said a policeman afterwards, "so it was fortunate that we didn't have to carry him. Of course, we should arrest him, but as he has a good record, we shall let him off this time."

句型解构

句1 标题 Jumbo versus the police

解构：versus来源于拉丁文，意为"对，对抗，与……相对"。

句2 Dressed up as Father Christmas and accompanied by a "guard of honour" of six pretty girls, he set off down the main street of the city riding a baby elephant called Jumbo.

解构：dressed up和accompanied by是非谓语动词在复合句中的重要用法，此处为过去分词短语，作状语，表伴随状况；as，介词，意为"像，如同"；Father Christmas/Santa Claus意为"圣诞老人"，Father大写表示尊称；guard of honour/honour guard意为"仪仗队"；of six pretty girls中的of表示"由……组成"；set off意为"出发，动身"；down，介词，意为"沿着，顺着"；riding a baby elephant为现在分词短语，作状语，表伴随状况；called Jumbo为过去分词短语，作后置定语。

句3 He should have known that the police would never allow this sort of thing.

解构：should have known表示本该知道（实际上不知道），虚拟语气；that引导的宾语从句，作known的宾语；police，集合名词，单复数同形。

句4 A policeman approached Jimmy and told him he ought to have gone along a side street as Jumbo was holding up the traffic.

解构：approach，动词，意为"走进，接近"；side street 意为"小路，边道"；hold up 意为"阻挡，阻碍"；tell 为双宾语动词，him 作间接宾语；he ought to 是宾语从句，作直接宾语；ought to have gone along 为虚拟语气，表示本该做而实际未做某事，ought to 比 should 语气更强，通常表示法律、法规所规定的责任和义务；as，连词，为"由于，因为"，引导原因状语从句。

句5 Though Jimmy agreed to go at once, Jumbo refused to move.

解构：though，连词，意为"虽然，尽管"，引导让步状语从句，though 不能与 but 连用；agree to 意为"同意……"；refuse to 意为"拒绝……"。

句6 Fifteen policemen had to push very hard to get him off the main street.

解构：had to 体现一般过去时，不能用 must；hard，副词，意为"辛苦地，用力地"；get off 意为"从……移除，使……离开"。

句7 The police had a difficult time, but they were most amused.

解构：have a difficult time 表示"……有困难"；most，副词，意为"非常"，相当于 very；amused 意为"被逗乐的"，是过去分词作表语，也可将 were amused 视为被动语态。

句8 "Jumbo must weigh a few tons,"

解构：must 意为"肯定"，表推测；weigh，动词，意为"重，有……重"；a few 意为"一些"，后接可数名词。

句9 "so it was fortunate that we didn't have to carry him. Of course, we should arrest him, but as he has a good record, we shall let him off this time."

解构：it 为形式主语，that 引导的主语从句作逻辑主语；as 引导原因状语从句；record，名词，意为"履历，历史，档案"；let off 意为"放过，绕过"。

参考译文

去年圣诞节，马戏团老板吉米·盖茨决定送些礼物给儿童医院。他打扮成圣诞老人，在由6个漂亮姑娘组成的"仪仗队"的陪同下，骑上一头名叫江伯的小象，沿着城里的主要街道出发了。他本该知道警察绝不会允许这类事情发生。一个警察走过来告诉吉米，他应该走一条小路，因为江伯阻碍了交通。虽然吉米同意马上就走，但江伯拒绝移动。15个警察不得不用很大的力气把他推离主要街道。警察虽然吃了苦头，但他们还是感到很有趣。"江伯一定有好几吨重，"一个警察事后这样说，"值得庆幸的是他没让我们抬他走。当然，我们应该逮捕他，但由于他一贯表现很好，这次我们饶了他。"

语篇学习 *15*

（参考第三章并列句）
（参考第三章复合句）
（参考第三章非谓语短语）

The end of a dream
美梦告终

Tired of sleeping on the floor, a young man in Teheran saved up for years to buy a real bed. For the first time in his life, he became the proud owner of a bed which had springs and a mattress. Because the weather was very hot, he carried the bed on to the roof of his house. He slept very well for the first two nights, but on the third night, a storm blew up. A gust of wind swept the bed off the roof and sent it crashing into the courtyard below. The young man did not wake up until the bed had struck the ground. Although the bed was smashed to pieces, the man was miraculously unhurt. When he woke up, he was still on the mattress. Glancing at the bits of wood and metal that lay around him, the man sadly picked up the mattress and carried it into his house. After he had put it on the floor, he promptly went to sleep again.

句型解构

句1 Tired of sleeping on the floor, a young man in Teheran saved up for years to buy a real bed.

解构：tired of sleeping on the floor是形容词短语，作原因状语，该短语本质上为省略了being的现在分词短语，代替原因状语从句；in Teheran为介词短语，作定语；save up意为"储蓄，攒钱"；to buy a real bed是动词不定式短语，作目的状语。

句2 For the first time in his life, he became the proud owner of a bed which had springs and a mattress.

解构：for the first time in his life是介词短语，作时间状语；关系代词which引导定语从句，修饰限定先行词a bed，which在定语从句中作主语，不能省略；spring，名词，意为"弹簧"；mattress，名词，意为"床垫"。

句3 Because the weather was very hot, he carried the bed on to the roof of his house.
解构：because引导原因状语从句；on to/onto表示动作的过程，描述一种动态。

句 4 He slept very well for the first two nights, but on the third night, a storm blew up.

解构：but连接前后两个简单句，构成并列句；blow up意为"吹风，刮起"。

句 5 A gust of wind swept the bed off the roof and sent it crashing into the courtyard below.

解构：gust，名词，意为"一阵狂风"；sweep，动词，意为"吹走，横扫，席卷"；and连接前后两个简单句，构成并列句，两个简单句的主语一致，因而sent前面省略了主语a gust of wind；crashing into the courtyard below为现在分词短语，作宾语补足语；crash，动词，意为"坠毁，摔碎"；courtyard，名词，意为"院子"；below，副词，作后置定语。

句 6 The young man did not wake up until the bed had struck the ground.

解构：not ... until意为"直到……才"，until引导时间状语从句；had struck为过去完成时，该动作在先；strike，动词，意为"撞击，打击"。

句 7 Although the bed was smashed to pieces, the man was miraculously unhurt.

解构：although引导让步状语从句；was smashed为被动语态，其中smash是动词，意为"摔碎，粉碎"；miraculously，副词，意为"奇迹般地，出乎意料地"；unhurt，形容词，意为"未受伤的"。

句 8 When he woke up, he was still on the mattress.

解构：when引导时间状语从句，wake的过去式是woke，过去分词形式是woken，意为"醒来"。

句 9 Glancing at the bits of wood and metal that lay around him, the man sadly picked up the mattress and carried it into his house.

解构：glancing at the bits of wood and metal是现在分词短语，作时间状语，其中glance at意为"扫视"；that lay around him是定语从句，修饰限定the bits，that在定语从句中作主语，不能省略；of构成同位语结构，wood and metal作the bits的同位语；lie的过去式是lay，过去分词形式是lain，意为"位于"。

句 10 After he had put it on the floor, he promptly went to sleep again.

解构：after引导的句子为时间状语从句，had put是过去完成时，表示该动作在先，通常before/after已表达了动作的先后关系，从句中用一般过去时即可；promptly，副词，意为"立即"。

参考译文

德黑兰的一个年轻人由于对睡地板感到厌倦，于是用多年积蓄买了一张真正的床。他平生第一次自豪地拥有了一张既有弹簧又带床垫的床。由于天气很热，他便把床搬到了他的屋顶上。头两天晚上,他睡得非常好。但第三天晚上起了风暴,一阵狂风把床从屋顶上刮了下来,把它摔碎在下面的院子里。那年轻人直到床撞到地上才醒了过来。尽管床摔成了碎片,但年轻人奇迹般地没有受伤。他醒来时,仍然躺在床垫上。年轻人看了一眼周围的碎木片和碎金属片,伤心地捡起了床垫,把它拿进了屋。他把床垫往地板上一放,很快又睡着了。

语篇学习 *16*

（参考第三章并列句）
（参考第三章复合句）
（参考第三章非谓语短语）

The record-holder
纪录保持者

Children who play truant from school are unimaginative. A quiet day's fishing, or eight hours in a cinema seeing the same film over and over again, is usually as far as they get. They have all been put to shame by a boy who, while playing truant, travelled 1,600 miles. He hitchhiked to Dover and, towards evening, went into a boat to find somewhere to sleep. When he woke up next morning, he discovered that the boat had, in the meantime, travelled to Calais. No one noticed the boy as he crept off. From there, he hitchhiked to Paris in a lorry. The driver gave him a few biscuits and a cup of coffee and left him just outside the city. The next car the boy stopped did not take him into the centre of Paris as he hoped it would, but to Perpignan on the French-Spanish border. There he was picked up by a policeman and sent back to England by the local authorities. He has surely set up a record for the thousands of children who dream of evading school.

句型解构

句1 Children who play truant from school are unimaginative.

解构：关系代词who引导定语从句，修饰限定先行词children；play truant意为"逃学"；unimaginative，形容词，意为"缺乏想象力的"。

句2 A quiet day's fishing, or eight hours in a cinema seeing the same film over and over again, is usually as far as they get.

解构：a quiet day's为所有格作动名词fishing的定语；eight hours in a cinema前面省略动名词sitting for；seeing the same film over and over again为现在分词短语，表伴随状态；or连接两个短语，表示选择；over and over again意为"反复多次地，一再地"；as far as "到……的程度/限度"。

句 3 They have all been put to shame by a boy who, while playing truant, travelled 1,600 miles.

解构：put to shame 意为"使蒙羞，使某人自愧不如"；have been put to shame 为被动语态用于现在完成时，表结果；who travelled 1,600 miles 是定语从句，修饰限定先行词 a boy；插入语 while playing truant 为现在分词短语，作状语，相当于状语从句 while he was playing truant。

句 4 He hitchhiked to Dover and, towards evening, went into a boat to find somewhere to sleep.

解构：hitchhiked，动词，意为"搭便车旅行，搭顺风车"；towards evening 意为"临近傍晚"；to find somewhere to sleep 为动词不定式，作目的状语。

句 5 When he woke up next morning, he discovered that the boat had, in the meantime, travelled to Calais.

解构：when 引导时间状语从句；that 引导的宾语从句，作 discovered 的宾语；had travelled 为过去完成时，表结果；in the meantime，插入语，意为"在此期间，与此同时"。

句 6 No one noticed the boy as he crept off.

解构：as he crept off 为时间状语从句，其中 creep off 意为"爬出"。

句 7 From there, he hitchhiked to Paris in a lorry.

解构：from there 作地点状语，in a lorry 作方式状语，其中 lorry 是名词，意为"卡车，货车"。

句 8 The driver gave him a few biscuits and a cup of coffee and left him just outside the city.

解构：give 双宾语动词，him 作间接宾语，a few biscuits and a cup of coffee 作直接宾语；后一个 and 连接前后两个简单句，构成并列句，left 前面省略相同主语 the drive；leave 的过去式和过去分词均是 left，意为"留，留下"。

句 9 The next car the boy stopped did not take him into the centre of Paris as he hoped it would, but to Perpignan on the French-Spanish border.

解构：the boy stopped 是定语从句，修饰限定 the next car；the centre of 意为"……的中心"；as 引导方式状语从句，意为"如同，像……一样"；would 后省略相同成分 take him into the centre of Paris；not ... but 意为"不是……而是"；border，名词，意为"边境，边界"。

句 10 There he was picked up by a policeman and sent back to England by the local authorities.

解构：there 作地点状语；pick up 意为"抓住"；send back 意为"送回"；local authorities 意为"当地政府"。

句 11 He has surely set up a record for the thousands of children who dream of evading school.

解构：has set up 为现在完成时，表结果；surely，副词，意为"无疑"；record，名词，意为"纪录"；who引导定语从句，修饰限定先行词children；dream of意为"梦想……"；evade，动词，意为"逃避，规避"。

参考译文

　　逃学的孩子们都缺乏想象力。他们通常能够做到的，至多也就是安静地钓上一天鱼，或在电影院里坐上8个小时，一遍遍地看同一部电影。而有那么一个小男孩，他在逃学期间旅行了1600英里，从而使上述所有逃学的孩子们都相形见绌了。他搭便车到了多佛，天快黑时钻进了一条船，想找个地方睡觉。第二天早上醒来时，他发现船在这段时间已经到了加来。当男孩从船里爬出来时，谁也没有发现他。从那里他又搭上卡车到了巴黎。司机给了他几块饼干和一杯咖啡，就把他丢在了城外。男孩截住的下一辆车，没有像他希望的那样把他带到巴黎市中心，而是把他带到了法国和西班牙边界上的佩皮尼昂。他在那儿被一个警察抓住了，之后被当局送回了英国。他无疑为成千上万梦想逃避上学的孩子们创造了一项纪录。

语篇进阶 **1**

The double life of Alfred Bloggs
艾尔弗雷德·布洛格斯的双重生活

These days, people who do manual work often receive far more money than people who work in offices. People who work in offices are frequently referred to as "white-collar workers" for the simple reason that they usually wear a collar and tie to go to work. Such is human nature, that a great many people are often willing to sacrifice higher pay for the privilege of becoming white-collar workers. This can give rise to curious situations, as it did in the case of Alfred Bloggs who worked as a dustman for the Ellesmere Corporation.

When he got married, Alf was too embarrassed to say anything to his wife about his job. He simply told her that he worked for the Corporation. Every morning, he left home dressed in a smart black suit. He then changed into overalls and spent the next eight hours as a dustman. Before returning home at night, he took a shower and changed back into his suit. Alf did this for over two years and his fellow dustmen kept his secret. Alf's wife has never discovered that she married a dustman and she never will, for Alf has just found another job. He will soon be working in an office. He will be earning only half as much as he used to, but he feels that his rise in status is well worth the loss of money. From now on, he will wear a suit all day and others will call him "Mr. Bloggs", not "Alf ".

句型解构

句1 These days, people who do manual work often receive far more money than people who work in offices.

解构：两个关系代词 who 引导的定语从句，均修饰限定先行词 people；manual work 意为"体力劳动"；far/much，程度副词，用于修饰和加强比较级的程度和语气，不能用 very 代替。

句2 People who work in offices are frequently referred to as "white-collar workers" for the simple reason that they usually wear a collar and tie to go to work.

解构：refer to ... as/regard ... as 意为"把……当作，把……称作"，as 后为宾语补足语；white-collar workers 意为"白领工人"，指脑力劳动者，对应 blue-collar workers（意为"蓝领

工人"），指体力劳动者，此处为隐喻手法；for引导原因状语，多用于书面语；that引导同位语从句，补充说明reason的具体含义。

句 3 Such is human nature, that a great many people are often willing to sacrifice higher pay for the privilege of becoming white-collar workers.

解构：代词such前置，起强调作用，后面采用倒装语序；that引导同位语从句，解释说明such；a great many意为"许多"，修饰可数名词；be willing to意为"乐意……，愿意……"；sacrifice ... for/to...意为"为……牺牲……"；pay，名词，意为"工资，薪水"；privilege，名词，意为"特权，优待"。

句 4 This can give rise to curious situations, as it did in the case of Alfred Bloggs who worked as a dustman for the Ellesmere Corporation.

解构：give rise to意为"引起，导致"；curious situations意为"奇怪的现象"；as引导方式状语从句；it指主句中this所代替的具体内容，即上一句中的that a great many people are often willing to...，did指give rise to curious situations；in the case of意为"在……情况中"；who引导定语从句；work as意为"担任"；dustman，名词，意为"清洁工"。

句 5 When he got married, Alf was too embarrassed to say anything to his wife about his job.

解构：too ... to...意为"太……以致不能……"，其中too为副词，to引导的动词不定式作结果状语；embarrassed，形容词，意为"尴尬的，窘迫的"。

句 6 He simply told her that he worked for the Corporation.

解构：that引导宾语从句；simply，副词，意为"仅仅"；corporation，名词，意为"公司"。

句 7 Every morning, he left home dressed in a smart black suit.

解构：dressed in a smart black suit为过去分词短语，作状语，表方式。

句 8 He then changed into overalls and spent the next eight hours as a dustman.

解构：change into意为"换上"；overalls，名词，意为"工作服"；as，介词，意为"作为"。

句 9 Before returning home at night, he took a shower and changed back into his suit.

解构：before returning是介词+动名词形式，构成介宾短语，作时间状语；take a shower意为"洗澡，淋浴"；change back into意为"换回"。

句 10 Alf did this for over two years and his fellow dustmen kept his secret.

解构：this，代词，指代前文内容。

句 11 Alf's wife has never discovered that she married a dustman and she never will, for Alf has just found another job.

解构：has never discovered为现在完成时，表结果；that引导的宾语从句，作discovered

的宾语;she never will后省略了与前一句相同的成分discover that she married a dustman;for引导原因状语从句。

句12 He will soon be working in an office.

解构:will be working为将来进行时,陈述将来事实,文中表示确定将发生的事件。

句13 He will be earning only half as much as he used to, but he feels that his rise in status is well worth the loss of money.

解构:half,副词,表示"一半地";only half作状语,修饰as much as he used to (earn),意为"只有他过去挣的一半",其中used to意为"过去常常";that引导宾语从句;rise,名词,意为"提升,晋升";status,名词,意为"地位,身份";well,副词,加强语气;be worth+名词/动名词,意为"值得……的,价值相当于……";loss,名词,意为"损失,减少"。

句14 From now on, he will wear a suit all day and others will call him "Mr. Bloggs", not "Alf".

解构:from now on是时间状语,意为"从现在起";"Mr. Bloggs" not "Alf"指身份和地位的提升。

参考译文

如今,从事体力劳动的人的收入一般要比坐办公室的人高出许多。坐办公室的人之所以常常被称作"白领工人",就是因为他们通常是穿着硬领白衬衫、系着领带去上班。许多人常常情愿放弃较高的薪水以换取做白领工人的殊荣,此乃人之常情。而这常常会引起种种奇怪的现象,在埃尔斯米尔公司当清洁工的艾尔弗雷德·布洛格斯就是一个例子。

艾尔弗结婚时,为自己的职业感到非常难为情,而没有将实情告诉妻子。他只说在埃尔斯米尔公司上班。每天早晨,他穿上一身漂亮的黑色西装离家上班,然后换上工作服,当8个小时清洁工。晚上回家前,他洗个淋浴,重新换上那身黑色西服。2年多以来,艾尔弗一直这样,他的同事也为他保守秘密。艾尔弗的妻子一直不知道她嫁给了一个清洁工,而且她也永远不会知道了,因为艾尔弗已找到新职,不久就要坐在办公室里工作了。他将来挣的钱只有他现在的一半。不过他觉得,地位升高了,损失点儿钱也值得。从此,艾尔弗可以一天到晚穿西服了。别人将称呼他为"布洛格斯先生",而不再叫他"艾尔弗"了。

语篇进阶 2

The loss of the *Titanic*
"泰坦尼克号"的沉没

The great ship, *Titanic*, sailed for New York from Southampton on April 10th, 1912. She was carrying 1,316 passengers and a crew of 891. Even by modern standards, the 46,000 ton *Titanic* was a colossal ship. At that time, however, she was not only the largest ship that had ever been built, but was regarded as unsinkable, for she had sixteen watertight compartments. Even if two of these were flooded, she would still be able to float. The tragic sinking of this great liner will always be remembered, for she went down on her first voyage with heavy loss of life.

Four days after setting out, while the *Titanic* was sailing across the icy waters of the North Atlantic, a huge iceberg was suddenly spotted by a lookout. After the alarm had been given, the great ship turned sharply to avoid a direct collision. The *Titanic* turned just in time, narrowly missing the immense wall of ice which rose over 100 feet out of the water beside her. Suddenly, there was a slight trembling sound from below, and the captain went down to see what had happened. The noise had been so faint that no one thought that the ship had been damaged. Below, the captain realized to his horror that the *Titanic* was sinking rapidly, for five of her sixteen watertight compartments had already been flooded! The order to abandon ship was given and hundreds of people plunged into the icy water. As there were not enough lifeboats for everybody, 1,500 lives were lost.

句型解构

句1 The great ship, *Titanic*, sailed for New York from Southampton on April 10th, 1912.

解构：Titanic作the great ship的同位语，补充说明船名；sail for意为"驶往，开往"。

句2 She was carrying 1,316 passengers and a crew of 891.

解构：she指the great ship，将其拟人化；crew，集合名词，意为"全体船员，全体人员"。

句3 Even by modern standards, the 46,000 ton *Titanic* was a colossal ship.

解构：by，介词，意为"按照，依照"；colossal，形容词，意为"巨大的"。

句4 At that time, however, she was not only the largest ship that had ever been built, but was regarded as unsinkable, for she had sixteen watertight compartments.

解构：at that time 为时间状语,意为"在那时,当时";that had ever been built 是定语从句,that 作从句主语;had ever been built 为被动语态用于过去完成时,意为"有史以来建造过的……,曾建造过的……";regarded ... as... 意为"把……当作……",as 后的 unsinkable 为补语;for 引导原因状语从句;watertight,形容词,意为"防水的",compartment,名词,意为"密封舱,隔间"。

句5 Even if two of these were flooded, she would still be able to float.

解构：even if/though 意为"即使,虽然",引导让步状语从句;were flooded 为被动语态,意为"被水淹,充满水";float,动词,意为"漂浮,漂流"。

句6 The tragic sinking of this great liner will always be remembered, for she went down on her first voyage with heavy loss of life.

解构：tragic,形容词,意为"悲惨的,不幸的";sinking,动名词,意为"沉没";liner,名词,意为"班轮,班机";be remembered 为被动语态,意为"被铭记";for 引导原因状语从句;go down 意为"下沉";on her first voyage 为时间状语,其中 voyage 为名词,意为"航行,航程";with 构成的介词短语,作结果状语,修饰 went down。

句7 Four days after setting out, while the *Titanic* was sailing across the icy waters of the North Atlantic, a huge iceberg was suddenly spotted by a lookout.

解构：set out 意为"出发";while 引导时间状语从句,表示时间背景;sail across 意为"横渡";the North Atlantic 意为"北大西洋";was spotted 为被动语态,意为"被发现";lookout,名词,意为"瞭望员,守望者"。

句8 After the alarm had been given, the great ship turned sharply to avoid a direct collision.

解构：被动语态用于过去完成时,表示动作在先;give an/the alarm 意为"发出警报";sharply,副词,意为"急剧地";to 引导的动词不定式,作目的状语,修饰 turned;collision,名词,意为"碰撞"。

句9 The *Titanic* turned just in time, narrowly missing the immense wall of ice which rose over 100 feet out of the water beside her.

解构：in time 意为"及时";narrowly missing 为现在分词短语,作结果状语,其中 narrowly 是副词,意为"勉强地";immense,形容词,意为"巨大的";which 引导定语从句,修饰限定先行词 the immense wall。

句10 Suddenly, there was a slight trembling sound from below, and the captain went down to see what had happened.

解构：slight，形容词，意为"轻微的"，trembling，现在分词，作形容词定语，意为"颤动的，震动的"；from below，介词短语，作地点状语；to引导的动词不定式，作目的状语；what引导的宾语从句，作see的宾语。

句11 The noise had been so faint that no one thought that the ship had been damaged.

解构：so ... that... 意为"如此……以至于……"，其中so为副词，修饰程度，that为连词，引导结果状语从句；faint，形容词，意为"微弱的，微小的"；后一个that引导宾语从句，作thought的宾语。

句12 Below, the captain realized to his horror that the *Titanic* was sinking rapidly, for five of her sixteen watertight compartments had already been flooded!

解构：below，副词，意为"在下面"，作地点状语；to his horror为介词短语，作状语，意为"惊恐地"，修饰realized；that引导的宾语从句，作realized的宾语；for引导原因状语从句。

句13 The order to abandon ship was given and hundreds of people plunged into the icy water.

解构：to abandon ship为动词不定式短语，作order的定语；abandon，动词，意为"放弃，离开"，plunge，动词，意为"跳进"。

句14 As there were not enough lifeboats for everybody, 1,500 lives were lost.

解构：as是从属连词，引导原因状语从句；lifeboat，名词，意为"救生艇"；lost，形容词，作表语，意为"丧生的，死亡的"。

参考译文

巨轮"泰坦尼克号"于1912年4月10日从南安普敦起锚驶向纽约。船上载有1316名乘客与891名船员。即便用现代标准来衡量，46000吨的"泰坦尼克号"也算得上一艘巨轮了。当时，这艘轮船不仅是造船史上建造的最大的一艘船，而且也被认为是不会沉没的。因为船由16个密封舱组成，即使有两个舱进水，仍可漂浮在水面上。然而，这艘巨轮首航就下沉，造成大批人员死亡。人们将永远记着这艘巨轮的沉没惨剧。

"泰坦尼克号"起航后的第4天，它正行驶在北大西洋冰冷的海面上。突然，瞭望员发现了一座冰山。警报响过不久，巨轮急转弯，以避免与冰山正面相撞。"泰坦尼克号"这个弯拐得及时，紧贴着高出海面100英尺的巨大的冰墙擦过去。突然，从船舱下部传来一声轻微的颤音，船长走下船舱去查看究竟。由于这个声音非常轻，没人想到船身已遭损坏。在下面，船长惊恐地发现"泰坦尼克号"正在急速下沉，16个密封舱已有5个进水。于是，他发出弃船的命令，几百人跳进了冰冷刺骨的海水里。由于没有足够的救生艇运载所有乘客，结果导致1500人丧生。

语篇进阶 3

Not guilty
无罪

Customs Officers are quite tolerant these days, but they can still stop you when you are going through the Green Channel and have nothing to declare. Even really honest people are often made to feel guilty. The hardened professional smuggler, on the other hand, is never troubled by such feelings, even if he has five hundred gold watches hidden in his suitcase. When I returned form abroad recently, a particularly officious young Customs Officer clearly regarded me as a smuggler.

"Have you anything to declare?" he asked, looking me in the eye.

"No," I answered confidently.

"Would you mind unlocking this suitcase please?"

"Not at all," I answered.

The Officer went through the case with great care. All the things I had packed so carefully were soon in a dreadful mess. I felt sure I would never be able to close the case again. Suddenly, I saw the Officer's face light up. He had spotted a tiny bottle at the bottom of my case and he pounced on it with delight.

"Perfume, eh?" he asked sarcastically. "You should have declared that. Perfume is not exempt from import duty."

"But it isn't perfume," I said. "It's hair gel." Then I added with a smile, "It's a strange mixture I make myself."

As I expected, he did not believe me.

"Try it!" I said encouragingly.

The officer unscrewed the cap and put the bottle to his nostrils. He was greeted by an unpleasant smell which convinced him that I was telling the truth. A few minutes later, I was able to hurry away with precious chalk marks on my baggage.

句型解构

句1 Customs Officers are quite tolerant these days, but they can still stop you when you are going through the Green Channel and have nothing to declare.

解构：Customs Officers意为"海关官员"；tolerant，形容词，意为"宽容的，容忍的"；go through意为"通过，经过"；the Green Channel意为"绿色通道"；declare，动词，意为"申报"，

to declare为动词不定式作定语,修饰nothing。

句2 Even really honest people are often made to feel guilty.

解构:to feel guilty为动词不定式作补语;主动语态中,make后面的复合宾语需使用不带to的动词不定式,被动语态中,宾语后的动词不定式需还原to。

句3 The hardened professional smuggler, on the other hand, is never troubled by such feelings, even if he has five hundred gold watches hidden in his suitcase.

解构:hardened,形容词,意为"老练的,坚定的";smuggler,名词,意为"走私者";on the other hand是插入语,意为"另一方面,但,而";even if意为"即使,虽然",引导让步状语从句;hidden in his suitcase为过去分词短语,作定语,修饰限定watches。

句4 When I returned form abroad recently, a particularly officious young Customs Officer clearly regarded me as a smuggler.

解构:particularly,副词,意为"尤其,特别";officious,形容词,意为"好管闲事的,摆官架子的"。

句5 "Have you anything to declare?" he asked, looking me in the eye.

解构:have提前构成一般疑问句为英式用法,相当于"Do you have anything to declare?";looking me in the eye为现在分词短语,作方式状语,修饰asked,意为"直视着我的眼睛"。

句6 "Would you mind unlocking this suitcase please?"

解构:mind+名词/动名词,意为"介意";unlock,动词,意为"打开,解锁"。

句7 The Officer went through the case with great care.

解构:go through意为"检查";with great care为介词短语,作方式状语,意为"相当仔细地"。

句8 All the things I had packed so carefully were soon in a dreadful mess.

解构:I had packed so carefully是定语从句,修饰things;in a dreadful mess为介词短语,作表语,意为"乱作一团"。

句9 I felt sure I would never be able to close the case again.

解构:I would never是宾语从句。

句10 Suddenly, I saw the Officer's face light up.

解构:light up本意为"照亮,点亮",此处意为"露出得意的神色"。

句11 He had spotted a tiny bottle at the bottom of my case and he pounced on it with delight.

解构:had spotted为过去完成时,表结果,其中spot为动词,意为"认出,发现";at the bottom of意为"在……的底部";pounce on/upon意为"猛扑,猛抓";with delight意为"高兴地”,作状语,表伴随。

句 12 "Perfume, eh?" he asked sarcastically. "You should have declared that. Perfume is not exempt from import duty."

解构:perfume,名词,意为"香水";sarcastically,副词,意为"讽刺地,挖苦地";should have+过去分词,表示本该做某事而实际未做;exempt,形容词,意为"被免除的";import duty意为"进口税"。

句 13 "But it isn't perfume," I said. "It's hair gel." Then I added with a smile, "It's a strange mixture I make myself."

解构:hair gel意为"发胶";mixture,名词,意为"混合物,混合剂"。

句 14 As I expected, he did not believe me.

解构:as为关系代词,引导非限制性定语从句,指代整个主句的内容。

句 15 "Try it!" I said encouragingly.

解构:encouragingly,副词,意为"鼓励地"。

句 16 The officer unscrewed the cap and put the bottle to his nostrils.

解构:unscrew,动词,意为"旋开,拧开";cap,名词,意为"盖子";nostril,名词,意为"鼻孔"。

句 17 He was greeted by an unpleasant smell which convinced him that I was telling the truth.

解构:greet,动词,意为"迎接";which引导定语从句,修饰smell;convince,动词,意为"使确信,说服"。

句 18 A few minutes later, I was able to hurry away with precious chalk marks on my baggage.

解构:be able to用于过去式,表示成功地做某事;hurry away/off意为"匆匆离去";with precious chalk marks on my baggage为独立主格结构,作状语,表伴随,修饰hurry away。

参考译文

　　现在的海关官员往往相当宽容。但是,当你通过绿色通道,没有任何东西需要申报时,他们仍可以拦住你。甚至是最诚实的人也常被弄得觉得有罪似的,而老练的职业走私犯即使在手提箱里藏着500只金表,却也"处之泰然"。最近一次,我出国归来,碰上一位特别好管闲事的年轻海关官员,他显然把我当成了走私犯。

　　"您有什么需要申报的吗?"他直盯着我的眼睛问。

"没有。"我自信地回答说。

"请打开这只手提箱好吗?"

"好的。"我回答说。

那位官员十分仔细地把箱子检查了一遍。所有细心包装好的东西一会儿工夫就乱成一团。我相信那箱子再也关不上了。突然,我看到官员脸上露出了得意的神色。他在我的箱底发现了一只小瓶,高兴地一把抓了起来。

"香水,嗯?"他讥讽地说道,"你刚才应该申报,香水要上进口税的。"

"不,这不是香水,"我说,"是发胶。"接着我脸带微笑补充说:"这是一种我自己配制的奇特的混合物。"

"你就闻一闻吧!"我催促说。

海关官员拧开瓶盖,把瓶子放到鼻子底下。一股怪味袭来,使他相信了我说的是真话。几分钟后,我终于被放行,手提画着宝贵的粉笔记号的行李,匆匆离去。

语篇进阶 *4*

A very dear cat
一只贵重的宝贝猫

Kidnappers are rarely interested in animals, but they recently took considerable interest in Mrs. Eleanor Ramsay's cat. Mrs. Eleanor Ramsay, a very wealthy old lady, has shared a flat with her cat, Rastus, for a great many years. Rastus leads an orderly life. He usually takes a short walk in the evenings and is always home by seven o'clock. One evening, however, he failed to arrive. Mrs. Ramsay got very worried. She looked everywhere for him but could not find him.

Three days after Rastus' disappearance, Mrs. Ramsay received an anonymous letter. The writer stated that Rastus was in safe hands and would be returned immediately if Mrs. Ramsay paid a ransom of £1,000. Mrs. Ramsay was instructed to place the money in a cardboard box and to leave it outside her door. At first, she decided to go to the police, but fearing that she would never see Rastus again—the letter had made that quite clear—she changed her mind. She withdrew £1,000 from her bank and followed the kidnapper's instructions. The next morning, the box had disappeared but Mrs. Ramsay was sure that the kidnapper would keep his word. Sure enough, Rastus arrived punctually at seven o'clock that evening. He looked very well, though he was rather thirsty, for he drank half a bottle of milk. The police were astounded when Mrs. Ramsay told them what she had done. She explained that Rastus was very dear to her. Considering the amount she paid, he was dear in more ways than one!

句型解构

句 1 Kidnappers are rarely interested in animals, but they recently took considerable interest in Mrs. Eleanor Ramsay's cat.

解构：kidnapper，名词，意为"绑匪"；be interested in 意为"对……感兴趣"；take interested in意为"对……发生兴趣"；considerable，形容词，意为"相当大的"。

句 2 Mrs. Eleanor Ramsay, a very wealthy old lady, has shared a flat with her cat, Rastus, for a great many years.

解构：a very wealthy old lady 是同位语，表示补充说明；has shared 为现在完成时，

share ... with... 意为"与……分享,与……合用,与……共有";Rastus作cat的同位语,表示补充说明;for+时间段,作时间状语;has shared表示动作的持续。

句3 Rastus leads an orderly life.
解构:lead a life意为"过着……的生活";orderly,形容词,意为"有规律的"。

句4 He usually takes a short walk in the evenings and is always home by seven o'clock.
解构:take a short walk意为"溜达,散步";in the evenings中的evening加s泛指每晚;频度副词usually/always体现经常性、习惯性的动作。

句5 One evening, however, he failed to arrive. Mrs. Ramsay got very worried.
解构:fail to意为"未能";get worried是系表结构,意为"感到担心"。

句6 She looked everywhere for him but could not find him.
解构:look for意为"寻找";everywhere,副词,作地点状语,修饰look;everywhere提至for him之前,起到强调作用。

句7 Three days after Rastus' disappearance, Mrs. Ramsay received an anonymous letter.
解构:disappearance,名词,意为"失踪,消失";anonymous,形容词,意为"匿名的"。

句8 The writer stated that Rastus was in safe hands and would be returned immediately if Mrs. Ramsay paid a ransom of £1,000.
解构:and连接两个宾语从句,均作stated的宾语,第一个宾语从句由that引导,第二个宾语从句为条件状语从句;in safe hands意为"安然无恙,妥善照管中";ransom,名词,意为"赎金";would前面省略Rastus。

句9 Mrs. Ramsay was instructed to place the money in a cardboard box and to leave it outside her door.
解构:be instructed to是被动语态,意为"被指示/命令做某事,奉命";place,动词,意为"放置";cardboard,名词,意为"硬纸板";句中两个动词不定式均作主语Mrs. Ramsay的补足语。

句10 At first, she decided to go to the police, but fearing that she would never see Rastus again—the letter had made that quite clear—she changed her mind.
解构:fearing that为现在分词短语,作原因状语,说明she changed her mind的原因;the letter had made that quite clear插入语,其中that为代词,指"如果报警,就再也见不到Rastus",quite clear作宾语补足语。

句11 She withdrew £1,000 from her bank and followed the kidnapper's instructions.
解构:withdrew,动词,意为"取钱";instruction,名词,意为"指令,指示"。

句12 The next morning, the box had disappeared but Mrs. Ramsay was sure that the kidnapper would keep his word.

解构：that引导宾语从句，作形容词的宾语；keep one's word意为"守信，遵守承诺"，word通常使用单数形式，指"诺言"。

句13 Sure enough, Rastus arrived punctually at seven o'clock that evening.

解构：sure enough意为"果然，无疑"；punctually，副词，意为"准时地，如期地"。

句14 He looked very well, though he was rather thirsty, for he drank half a bottle of milk.

解构：he looked very well为主句；though引导让步状语从句；for引导原因状语从句。

句15 The police were astounded when Mrs. Ramsay told them what she had done.

解构：astounded为过去分词，作形容词，意为"感到震惊的"；what引导宾语从句。

句16 She explained that Rastus was very dear to her.

解构：that引导的宾语从句，作explained的宾语；be dear to意为"对……很珍贵"。

句17 Considering the amount she paid, he was dear in more ways than one!

解构：considering可理解为连词或介词，意为"考虑到"，该短语作原因状语；in more ways than one意为"在更多方面，从多方面看"；dear一语双关，既体现Rastus对Mrs. Ramsay的"宝贵"，也体现金钱方面的"昂贵"。

参考译文

绑架者很少对动物感兴趣。最近，绑架者却盯上了埃莉诺·拉姆齐太太的猫。埃莉诺·拉姆齐太太是一个非常富有的老妇人，多年来，一直同她养的猫拉斯特斯一起住在一所公寓里。拉斯特斯生活很有规律，傍晚常常出去溜达一会儿，并且总是在7点钟以前回来。可是，有一天晚上，它出去后再也没回来。拉姆齐太太急坏了，四处寻找，但没找着。

拉斯特斯失踪3天后，拉姆齐太太收到一封匿名信。写信人声称拉斯特斯安然无恙，只要拉姆齐太太愿意支付1000英镑赎金，便可以立即将猫送还。他让拉姆齐太太把钱放在一个纸盒里，然后将纸盒放在门口。一开始拉姆齐太太打算报警，但又害怕再也见不到拉斯特斯了——这点，信上说得十分明白——于是便改变了主意。她从银行取出1000英镑，并照绑架者的要求做了。第二天早晨，放钱的盒子不见了。但拉姆齐太太确信绑架者是会履行诺言的。果然，当天晚上7点整，拉斯特斯准时回来了。它看上去一切正常，只是口渴得很，喝了半瓶牛奶。拉姆齐太太把她所做的事告诉了警察，警察听后大为吃惊。拉姆齐太太解释说她心疼她的猫拉斯特斯。想到她所花的那笔钱，她的心疼就具有双重意义了。

语篇进阶 *5*

One man's meat is another man's poison
各有所爱

People become quite illogical when they try to decide what can be eaten and what cannot be eaten. If you lived in the Mediterranean, for instance, you would consider octopus a great delicacy. You would not be able to understand why some people find it repulsive. On the other hand, your stomach would turn at the idea of frying potatoes in animal fat—the normally accepted practice in many northern countries. The sad truth is that most of us have been brought up to eat certain foods and we stick to them all our lives.

No creature has received more praise and abuse than the common garden snail. Cooked in wine, snails are a great luxury in various parts of the world. There are countless people who, ever since their early years, have learned to associate snails with food. My friend, Robert, lives in a country where snails are despised. As his flat is in a large town, he has no garden of his own. For years he has been asking me to collect snails from my garden and take them to him. The idea never appealed to me very much, but one day, after a heavy shower, I happened to be walking in my garden when I noticed a huge number of snails taking a stroll on some of my prize plants. Acting on a sudden impulse, I collected several dozen, put them in a paper bag, and took them to Robert. Robert was delighted to see me and equally pleased with my little gift. I left the bag in the hall and Robert and I went into the living room where we talked for a couple of hours. I had forgotten all about the snails when Robert suddenly said that I must stay to dinner. Snails would, of course, be the main dish. I did not fancy the idea and I reluctantly followed Robert out of the room. To our dismay, we saw that there were snails everywhere: they had escaped from the paper bag and had taken complete possession of the hall! I have never been able to look at a snail since then.

句型解构

句 1 People become quite illogical when they try to decide what can be eaten and what cannot be eaten.

解构:become illogical 是系表结构,其中 illogical 为形容词,意为"不合逻辑的,不合常理的"；when引导时间状语从句，作全句的时间背景；连接代词what引导的两个宾语从句并列，均作decide的宾语。

句2 If you lived in the Mediterranean, for instance, you would consider octopus a great delicacy.

解构：if从句为第二类条件状语从句，用虚拟语气，表示对现在的一种假设；the Mediterranean是指"地中海"，海洋名称前须用定冠词the；for instance是插入语，意为"例如"；a great delicacy作宾语octopus的补足语，构成主谓宾补句型；octopus，名词，意为"章鱼"；delicacy，名词，意为"美味，佳肴"。

句3 You would not be able to understand why some people find it repulsive.

解构：虚拟语气，与上句中的主句并列；连接副词why引导的宾语从句，作understand的宾语；repulsive，形容词，意为"令人厌恶的，排斥的"，作宾语补足语。

句4 On the other hand, your stomach would turn at the idea of frying potatoes in animal fat—the normally accepted practice in many northern countries.

解构：on the other hand意为"另一方面"，表示与前文内容的比较；与前文一样，would也使用虚拟语气；turn，动词，意为"反胃，恶心"；at the idea of意为"一想起……就，一想到"；animal fat意为"动物脂肪"；破折号后面的内容是对frying potatoes in animal fat的进一步说明；accepted是过去分词，作形容词，意为"被接受的，被认可的"；practice，名词，意为"做法，惯例"。

句5 The sad truth is that most of us have been brought up to eat certain foods and we stick to them all our lives.

解构：that引导表语从句，作主语补足语；to eat certain foods为动词不定式作most of us的补足语；bring up意为"养育，抚养"；stick to意为"坚持，坚守"，all one's life是副词短语，作时间状语，意为"一辈子，一生"。

句6 No creature has received more praise and abuse than the common garden snail.

解构：creature，名词，意为"生物"；praise，名词，意为"赞扬，称赞"；abuse，名词，意为"辱骂，谩骂"；has received为现在完成时，表结果；该比较级表示的是最高级的含义。

句7 Cooked in wine, snails are a great luxury in various parts of the world.

解构：cooked in wine为过去分词短语，作条件状语；luxury，名词，意为"奢侈品，珍品"。

句8 There are countless people who, ever since their early years, have learned to associate snails with food.

解构：countless/numerous，形容词，意为"许多的，无数的"；关系代词who引导定语从句，修饰限定先行词people；ever since their early years作定语从句的时间状语，句中置于谓语动词之前，表示对该时间状语的强调；associate ... with...意为"把……和……相联系"。

句 9 My friend, Robert, lives in a country where snails are despised.

解构:关系副词 where 引导定语从句,修饰限定 country;despise,动词,意为"鄙视,轻视"。

句 10 As his flat is in a large town, he has no garden of his own.

解构:从属连词 as 引导原因状语从句,通常表示人们已知的原因;of one's own 意为"属于某人自己的,自己的"

句 11 For years he has been asking me to collect snails from my garden and take them to him.

解构:has been asking 为现在完成进行时,表示动作的持续进行。

句 12 The idea never appealed to me very much, but one day, after a heavy shower, I happened to be walking in my garden when I noticed a huge number of snails taking a stroll on some of my prize plants.

解构:appeal to 意为"对……有吸引力,合……的心意";happen to 意为"碰巧,偶然";when 在句中含有突然、意外之意;a huge number of 意为"数量巨大的,大量的";taking a stroll on some of my prize plants 为现在分词短语,作宾语补足语;take a stroll 意为"散步,溜达";prize,形容词,意为"心爱的,珍视的"。

句 13 Acting on a sudden impulse, I collected several dozen, put them in a paper bag, and took them to Robert.

解构:acting on a sudden impulse 为现在分词短语,作原因状语;act on 意为"按照……行事";impulse,名词,意为"冲动",a sudden impulse 意为"一时的冲动";dozen 意为"一打",several dozen 后省略 of snails。

句 14 Robert was delighted to see me and equally pleased with my little gift.

解构:to see me 为动词不定式作原因状语;be pleased with 意为"对……感到满意/高兴";equally,副词,意为"同样地,平等地"。

句 15 I left the bag in the hall and Robert and I went into the living room where we talked for a couple of hours.

解构:关系副词 where 引导定语从句,修饰限定 the living room;a couple of,意为"几个,若干"。

句 16 I had forgotten all about the snails when Robert suddenly said that I must stay to dinner.

解构:had forgotten 为过去完成时,表结果;when 在句中含有突然、意外之意;that 引导的宾语从句,作 said 的宾语;stay to dinner 意为"留下来吃饭"。

句 17 Snails would, of course, be the main dish.

解构：main dish意为"主食，主菜"。

句 18 I did not fancy the idea and I reluctantly followed Robert out of the room.

解构：fancy，名词，意为"喜爱"；reluctantly，副词，意为"不情愿地"。

句 19 To our dismay, we saw that there were snails everywhere: they had escaped from the paper bag and had taken complete possession of the hall!

解构：插入语to our dismay，意为"令我们惊愕的是，令我们沮丧的是"；that引导的宾语从句，作saw的宾语；take possession of意为"占领，占据"。

参考译文

在决定什么能吃而什么不能吃的时候，人们往往变得不合情理。比如，如果你住在地中海地区，你会把章鱼视作美味佳肴，同时不能理解为什么有人一见章鱼就恶心。再比如，你一想到用动物油炸土豆就会反胃，但这在北方许多国家是一种普通的烹饪方法。不无遗憾的是，我们中的大部分人，生来就只吃某几种食品，而且一辈子都这样。

没有一种生物所受到的赞美和厌恶会超过花园里常见的蜗牛了。蜗牛加酒烧煮后，便成了世界上许多地方的一道珍奇的名菜。有不计其数的人们从小就知道蜗牛可做菜。但我的朋友罗伯特住在一个厌恶蜗牛的国家中。他住在大城市里的一所公寓里，没有自己的花园。多年来，他一直让我把我园子里的蜗牛收集起来给他捎去。一开始，他的这一想法没有引起我多大兴趣。后来有一天，一场大雨后，我在花园里漫无目的地散步，突然注意到许许多多蜗牛在我的一些心爱的花木上慢悠悠地蠕动着。我一时冲动，逮了几十只，装进一只纸袋里，带着去找罗伯特。罗伯特见到我很高兴，对我的薄礼也感到满意。我把纸袋放在门厅里，与罗伯特一起进了起居室，在那里聊了好几个钟头。我把蜗牛的事已忘得一干二净，罗伯特突然提出一定要我留下来吃晚饭，这才提醒了我。蜗牛当然是道主菜。我并不喜欢这个主意，所以我勉强跟着罗伯特走出了起居室。使我们惊愕的是，门厅里到处爬满了蜗牛：它们从纸袋里逃了出来，爬得满厅都是！从那以后，我再也不能看蜗牛一眼了。

语篇进阶 6

Five pounds too dear
五镑也太贵

Small boats loaded with wares sped to the great liner as she was entering the harbour. Before she had anchored, the men from the boats had climbed on board and the decks were soon covered with colourful rugs from Persia, silks from India, copper coffee pots, and beautiful handmade silverware. It was difficult not to be tempted. Many of the tourists on board had begun bargaining with the tradesmen, but I decided not to buy anything until I had disembarked.

I had no sooner got off the ship than I was assailed by a man who wanted to sell me a diamond ring. I had no intention of buying one, but I could not conceal the fact that I was impressed by the size of the diamonds. Some of them were as big as marbles. The man went to great lengths to prove that the diamonds were real. As we were walking past a shop, he held a diamond firmly against the window and made a deep impression in the glass. It took me over half an hour to get rid of him.

The next man to approach me was selling expensive pens and watches. I examined one of the pens closely. It certainly looked genuine. At the base of the gold cap, the words "made in the U.S.A." had been neatly inscribed. The man said that the pen was worth ￡50, but as a special favour, he would let me have it for ￡30. I shook my head and held up five fingers indicating that I was willing to pay ￡5. Gesticulating wildly, the man acted as if he found my offer outrageous, but he eventually reduced the price to ￡10. Shrugging my shoulders, I began to walk away when, a moment later, he ran after me and thrust the pen into my hands. Though he kept throwing up his arms in despair, he readily accepted the ￡5 I gave him. I felt especially pleased with my wonderful bargain—until I got back to the ship. No matter how hard I tried, it was impossible to fill this beautiful pen with ink and to this day it has never written a single word!

句型解构

句 1 Small boats loaded with wares sped to the great liner as she was entering the harbour.

解构：loaded with wares为过去分词短语，作定语；load，动词，意为"装载"，ware，名词，意为"货物,制品";speed,动词,意为"飞驰,疾驶";liner,名词,意为"班轮,班机";从属连词 as引导时间状语从句;she指liner,拟人用法。

句2 Before she had anchored, the men from the boats had climbed on board and the decks were soon covered with colourful rugs from Persia, silks from India, copper coffee pots, and beautiful handmade silverware.

解构:本句为before引导的时间状语从句;anchor,动词,意为"抛锚,使固定";on board 意为"在船上";deck,名词,意为"甲板";be covered with意为"充满着,被……盖满"; silverware,名词,意为"银器"。

句3 It was difficult not to be tempted.

解构:it作形式主语,not to be tempted为动词不定式的否定形式,作句子的逻辑主语; tempt,动词,意为"诱惑,吸引"。

句4 Many of the tourists on board had begun bargaining with the tradesmen, but I decided not to buy anything until I had disembarked.

解构:many,代词,意为"许多,许多人";on board为介词短语,作定语;bargain with意为 "与……讨价还价";tradesman,名词,意为"商人";not to buy anything为动词不定式的否定 形式,作decided的宾语;until引导时间状语从句;disembark,动词,意为"登陆,下船,上岸"。

句5 I had no sooner got off the ship than I was assailed by a man who wanted to sell me a diamond ring.

解构:no sooner ... than... 意为"一……就……",no sooner引导的动词表示的动作在 先,故用过去完成时,than引导的动词表示的动作在后,故用一般过去时;assail,动词,意为 "纠缠,缠住";关系代词who引导定语从句,who在从句中作主语。

句6 I had no intention of buying one, but I could not conceal the fact that I was impressed by the size of the diamonds.

解构:have no intention of意为"无意……,没有……的打算";conceal,动词,意为"隐 藏,隐瞒";that引导同位语从句,补充说明the fact的内容。

句7 Some of them were as big as marbles.

解构:some,代词,意为"一些,部分";as ... as...同级比较,意为"和……一样";marble, 名词,意为"弹珠,玻璃球"。

句8 The man went to great lengths to prove that the diamonds were real.

解构:go to great lengths to意为"不遗余力……,竭尽全力……"。

句9 As we were walking past a shop, he held a diamond firmly against the window and made a deep impression in the glass.

解构:as 引导时间状语从句,作时间背景;hold ... against...意为"把……按在……",

impression,名词,意为"压痕,印记"。

句 10 It took me over half an hour to get rid of him.

解构:it作形式主语,to get rid of him为动词不定式短语,作逻辑主语;get rid of意为"摆脱"。

句 11 The next man to approach me was selling expensive pens and watches.

解构:to approach me为动词不定式作定语,其中approach是动词,意为"走进,接近"。

句 12 I examined one of the pens closely.

解构:examine,动词,意为"检查,检测";closely,副词,意为"仔细地,严密地"。

句 13 It certainly looked genuine.

解构:looked genuine为系表结构;genuine,形容词,意为"真的"。

句 14 At the base of the gold cap, the words "made in the U.S.A." had been neatly inscribed.

解构:at the base of意为"在······底部";made in the U.S.A.意为"美国制造",作the words的同位语,补充说明字的内容;had been neatly inscribed为被动语态用于过去完成时,其中neatly为副词,意为"整齐地,工整地",inscribe为动词,意为"雕刻,题写"。

句 15 The man said that the pen was worth ￡50, but as a special favour, he would let me have it for ￡30.

解构:be worth意为"值······";as a special favour意为"作为一种特殊优惠";favour,名词,意为"好处,恩惠";for,介词,意为"换取,以······为价格"。

句 16 I shook my head and held up five fingers indicating that I was willing to pay ￡5.

解构:shake one's head意为"摇头(表示拒绝、不赞成)";hold up意为"举起,伸出";indicating that I was willing to pay ￡5为现在分词短语,作目的状语;that引导的宾语从句,作indicating的宾语。

句 17 Gesticulating wildly, the man acted as if he found my offer outrageous, but he eventually reduced the price to ￡10.

解构:gesticulating wildly为现在分词短语,作方式状语,gesticulate,动词,意为"做手势,用姿势示意";wildly,副词,意为"失控地,抓狂地";as if引导表语从句,作主语the man的补足语;he found my offer outrageous为主谓宾补句型,其中outrageous是形容词,意为"无法容忍的,离谱的";eventually,副词,意为"最终";reduce ... to... 意为"减少······到······,降至"。

句 18 Shrugging my shoulders, I began to walk away when, a moment later, he ran after me and thrust the pen into my hands.

解构：shrugging my shoulders 为现在分词短语，作方式状语；shrug，动词，意为"耸肩"；when 在句中表示突然、意外之意；thrust，动词，意为"硬塞"。

句19 Though he kept throwing up his arms in despair, he readily accepted the ￡5 I gave him.

解构：though 引导让步状语从句；keep doing sth. 意为"一直/不断做某事"；in despair，为介词短语，作状语，意为"绝望地，失望地"；readily，副词，意为"乐意地，欣然地"；I gave him 是定语从句，修饰限定 ￡5。

句20 I felt especially pleased with my wonderful bargain—until I got back to the ship.

解构：especially，副词，意为"特别，尤其"；bargain，名词，意为"还价"。

句21 No matter how hard I tried, it was impossible to fill this beautiful pen with ink and to this day it has never written a single word!

解构：no matter how 引导让步状语从句；it 作形式主语，to fill this beautiful pen with ink 为动词不定式短语，作逻辑主语，其中 fill ... with... 意为"把……装满……"；to this day，时间状语，意为"至今"。

参考译文

当一艘大型客轮进港的时候，许多小船载着各种杂货快速向它驶来。大船还未下锚，小船上的人就纷纷爬上客轮。一会儿工夫，甲板上就摆满了色彩斑斓的波斯地毯、印度丝绸、铜咖啡壶以及手工制作的漂亮的银器。要想不对这些东西动心是很困难的。船上的许多游客开始同商贩讨价还价起来，但我打定主意上岸之前什么也不买。

我刚下船，就被一个人缠住了，他向我兜售一枚钻石戒指。我根本不想买，但我不能掩饰这样一个事实：其钻石之大给我留下了深刻的印象。有的钻石像玻璃球那么大。那人竭力想证明那钻石是真货。我们路过一家商店时，他将一颗钻石使劲地往橱窗上一按，在玻璃上留下一道深痕。我花了半个多小时才摆脱了他的纠缠。

第二个向我兜售的人是卖名贵钢笔和手表的。我仔细察看了一支钢笔，那看上去确实不假，金笔帽下方整齐地刻有"美国制造"字样。那人说那支笔值50英镑，作为特别优惠，他愿意让我出30英镑成交。我摇摇头，伸出5根手指表示我只愿出5英镑。那人激动地打着手势，仿佛我的出价使他不能容忍。但他终于把价钱降到了10英镑。我耸耸肩膀掉头走开了。一会儿，他突然从后面追了上来，把笔塞到我手里。虽然他绝望地举起双手，但他毫不迟疑地收下了我付给他的5英镑。在回到船上之前，我一直为我绝妙的讨价还价而洋洋得意。然而不管我如何摆弄，那支漂亮的钢笔就是吸不进墨水。直到今天，那支笔连一个字也没写过！

语篇进阶 7

The death of a ghost
幽灵之死

For years, villagers believed that Endley Farm was haunted. The farm was owned by two brothers, Joe and Bob Cox. They employed a few farmhands, but no one was willing to work there long. Every time a worker gave up his job, he told the same story. Farm labourers said that they always woke up to find that work had been done overnight. Hay had been cut and cowsheds had been cleaned. A farm worker, who stayed up all night, claimed to have seen a figure cutting corn in the moonlight. In time, it became an accepted fact that the Cox brothers employed a conscientious ghost that did most of their work for them.

No one suspected that there might be someone else on the farm who had never been seen. This was indeed the case. A short time ago, villagers were astonished to learn that the ghost of Endley had died. Everyone went to the funeral, for the "ghost" was none other than Eric Cox, a third brother who was supposed to have died as a young man. After the funeral, Joe and Bob revealed a secret which they had kept for over fifty years.

Eric had been the eldest son of the family, very much older than his two brothers. He had been obliged to join the army during the Second World War. As he hated army life, he decided to desert his regiment. When he learnt that he would be sent abroad, he returned to the farm and his father hid him until the end of the war. Fearing the authorities, Eric remained in hiding after the war as well. His father told everybody that Eric had been killed in action. The only other people who knew the secret were Joe and Bob. They did not even tell their wives. When their father died, they thought it their duty to keep Eric in hiding. All these years, Eric had lived as a recluse. He used to sleep during the day and work at night, quite unaware of the fact that he had become the ghost of Endley. When he died, however, his brothers found it impossible to keep the secret any longer.

句型解构

句 1 For years, villagers believed that Endley Farm was haunted.

解构：for years 提前，表示对时间状语的强调，意为"多年来"；that 引导宾语从句，作

believed 的宾语；be haunted 意为"闹鬼的"。

句2 The farm was owned by two brothers, Joe and Bob Cox.

解构：was owned 是被动语态，意为"被……拥有"；Joe and Bob Cox 作 two brothers 的同位语。

句3 They employed a few farmhands, but no one was willing to work there long.

解构：farmhand，名词，意为"农场工人"；long，副词，意为"长期地，久地"。

句4 Every time a worker gave up his job, he told the same story.

解构：every time 意为"每次，每当"，引导时间状语从句。

句5 Farm labourers said that they always woke up to find that work had been done overnight.

解构：labourer，名词，意为"劳动者，劳工"；that 引导的宾语从句，作 said 的宾语；to find that work had been done overnight 为动词不定式短语，作结果状语，had been done 为被动语态用于过去完成时，其中 overnight 为副词，意为"在夜间，一夜之间"。

句6 Hay had been cut and cowsheds had been cleaned.

解构：and 连接两个主谓结构的简单句，构成并列句；hay，名词，意为"干草"；cowshed，名词，意为"牛棚，牛舍"。

句7 A farm worker, who stayed up all night, claimed to have seen a figure cutting corn in the moonlight.

解构：关系代词 who 引导非限制性定语从句，对 a farm worker 进行补充说明，stayed up 意为"熬夜，不睡觉"；to 引导的动词不定式作 claimed 的宾语；have seen 用于动词不定式中，表示该动作发生在谓语动词 claimed 之前；cutting corn in the moonlight 为现在分词短语，作 a figure 的补足语。

句8 In time, it became an accepted fact that the Cox brothers employed a conscientious ghost that did most of their work for them.

解构：in time 意为"最终，久而久之"；第一个 that 为从属连词，引导同位语从句，补充说明 fact 的具体内容；第二个 that 为关系代词，引导定语从句，修饰限定先行词 ghost；conscientious，形容词，意为"认真的，尽责的"。

句9 No one suspected that there might be someone else on the farm who had never been seen.

解构：suspect，动词，意为"怀疑，猜想"；从属连词 that 引导的宾语从句，作 suspected 的宾语；关系代词 who 引导的定语从句，修饰限定先行词 someone else。

句 10 This was indeed the case.

解构:indeed,副词,意为"的确,事实上",用以加强语气;case,名词,意为"情况"。

句 11 A short time ago, villagers were astonished to learn that the ghost of Endley had died.

解构:to引导的动词不定式短语,作原因状语,说明惊讶的原因。

句 12 Everyone went to the funeral, for the "ghost" was none other than Eric Cox, a third brother who was supposed to have died as a young man.

解构:for引导原因状语从句;none other than意为"不是别人而正是……";a third brother作Eric Cox的同位语;关系代词who引导的定语从句,修饰限定a third brother;as (he was) a young man为省略形式的时间状语从句。

句 13 After the funeral, Joe and Bob revealed a secret which they had kept for over fifty years.

解构:reveal,动词,意为"揭露";关系代词which引导的定语从句,修饰限定a secret;had kept过去完成时,表示动作的持续,同时表示该动作在谓语动词revealed之前。

句 14 Eric had been the eldest son of the family, very much older than his two brothers.

解构:逗号后的形容词短语very much older than his two brothers可理解为省略who was的非限制性定语从句,对Eric进行补充说明;very much为程度副词,修饰比较级older。

句 15 He had been obliged to join the army during the Second World War.

解构:be obliged to意为"不得不……,有义务……";join the army意为"参军"。

句 16 As he hated army life, he decided to desert his regiment.

解构:从属连词as引导原因状语从句;desert,动词,意为"逃走,擅离(部队)";regiment,名词,意为"团,部队"。

句 17 When he learnt that he would be sent abroad, he returned to the farm and his father hid him until the end of the war.

解构:learn,动词,意为"得知,获悉";hide的过去式为hid,过去分词形式为hidden,意为"隐藏"。

句 18 Fearing the authorities, Eric remained in hiding after the war as well.

解构:fearing the authorities为现在分词短语,作原因状语;in hiding为介词短语,作表语,意为"隐藏的,在隐藏中"。

句 19 His father told everybody that Eric had been killed in action.

解构:had been killed为被动语态用于过去完成时;in action意为"在战斗中"。

句 20 The only other people who knew the secret were Joe and Bob. They did not even tell their wives.

解构:关系代词who引导的定语从句,修饰限定people;even,副词,意为"甚至",加强语气。

句 21 When their father died, they thought it their duty to keep Eric in hiding.

解构:it作形式宾语,their duty作宾语补足语,to keep Eric in hiding作逻辑宾语。

句 22 All these years, Eric had lived as a recluse.

解构:had lived为过去完成时,表持续;as,介词,此处意为"如同,像";recluse,名词,意为"隐士,隐居者"。

句 23 He used to sleep during the day and work at night, quite unaware of the fact that he had become the ghost of Endley.

解构:used to意为"过去经常……";quite unaware为形容词短语,作结果状语;that引导的同位语从句,补充说明fact的具体内容。

句 24 When he died, however, his brothers found it impossible to keep the secret any longer.

解构:it作形式宾语,impossible作宾语补足语,to keep the secret any longer作逻辑宾语。

参考译文

多年来,村民们一直认为恩得利农场在闹鬼。恩得利农场属于乔·考科斯和鲍勃·考科斯兄弟俩所有。他们雇了几个农工,但谁也不愿意在那儿长期工作下去。每次雇工辞职后都叙述着同样的故事。雇工们说,常常一早起来发现有人在夜里把活干了,干草已切好,牛棚也打扫干净了。有一个彻夜未眠的雇工还声称他看见一个人影在月光下收割庄稼。随着时间的流逝,考科斯兄弟雇了一个尽心尽责的鬼,他们家的活大部分都让鬼给干了,这件事成了公认的事实。

谁也没想到农场里竟会有一个从未露面的人。但事实上确有此人。不久之前,村民们惊悉恩得利农场的鬼死了。大家都去参加了葬礼,因为那"鬼"不是别人,正是农场主的兄弟埃里克·考科斯。人们以为埃里克年轻时就死了。葬礼之后,乔和鲍勃透露了他们保守了长达50多年的秘密。

埃里克是这家的长子,年龄比他两个弟弟大很多。他在第二次世界大战期间被迫参军。他讨厌军旅生活,决定逃离所在部队。当他了解到自己将被派遣出国时,他逃回农场,父亲把他藏了起来,直到战争结束。由于害怕当局,埃里克战后继续深藏不露。他的父亲告诉大家,埃里克在战争中被打死了。除他父亲之外,只有乔与鲍勃知道这个秘密,但他俩连自己的妻子都没告诉。父亲死后,他们兄弟俩认为有责任继续把埃里克藏起来。这些年来,埃里克过着隐士生活,白天睡觉,夜里出来干活,一点不知道自己已成了恩得利农场的活鬼。他死后,他的弟弟们才觉得无法再保守这个秘密了。

语篇进阶 *8*

Modern cavemen
现代洞穴人

Cave exploration, or pot-holing, as it has come to be known, is a relatively new sport. Perhaps it is the desire for solitude or the chance of making an unexpected discovery that lures people down to the depths of the earth. It is impossible to give a satisfactory explanation for a pot-holer's motives. For him, caves have the same peculiar fascination which high mountains have for the climber. They arouse instincts which can only be dimly understood.

Exploring really deep caves is not a task for the Sunday afternoon rambler. Such undertakings require the precise planning and foresight of military operations. It can take as long as eight days to rig up rope ladders and to establish supply bases before a descent can be made into a very deep cave. Precautions of this sort are necessary, for it is impossible to foretell the exact nature of the difficulties which will confront the pot-holer. The deepest known cave in the world is the Gouffre Berger near Grenoble. It extends to a depth of 3,723 feet. This immense chasm has been formed by an underground stream which has tunnelled a course through a flaw in the rocks. The entrance to the cave is on a plateau in the Dauphine Alps. As it is only six feet across, it is barely noticeable. The cave might never have been discovered had not the entrance been spotted by the distinguished French pot-holer, Berger. Since its discovery, it has become a sort of potholers' Everest. Though a number of descents have been made, much of it still remains to be explored.

A team of pot-holers recently went down the Gouffre Berger. After entering the narrow gap on the plateau, they climbed down the steep sides of the cave until they came to a narrow corridor. They had to edge their way along this, sometimes wading across shallow streams, or swimming across deep pools. Suddenly they came to a waterfall which dropped into an underground lake at the bottom of the cave. They plunged into the lake, and after loading their gear on an inflatable rubber dinghy, let the current carry them to the other side. To protect themselves from the icy water, they had to wear special rubber suits. At the far end of the lake, they came to huge piles of rubble which had been washed up by the water. In this part of the cave, they could hear an insistent booming sound which they found was caused by a small waterspout shooting down into a pool from the roof of the cave. Squeezing through a cleft in the rocks, the pot-holers arrived at an enormous cavern, the size of a huge concert hall. After switching on powerful arc lights, they saw great stalagmites—some of them over forty feet high—rising up like tree-trunks to meet the stalactites suspended from the roof. Round about, piles of limestone glistened in all the colours of the rainbow. In the eerie silence of the cavern, the only sound that could be heard was made by water which dripped continuously from the high dome above them.

句型解构

句 1 Cave exploration, or pot-holing, as it has come to be known, is a relatively new sport.

解构：pot-holing，名词，意为"洞穴探险"；从属连词as引导方式状语从句，在文中作插入语。

句 2 Perhaps it is the desire for solitude or the chance of making an unexpected discovery that lures people down to the depths of the earth.

解构：文中的it is ... that...结构为强调句型，强调主语；solitude，名词，意为"孤独，隐居"；lure，动词，意为"诱惑，引诱"。

句 3 It is impossible to give a satisfactory explanation for a pot-holer's motives.

解构：it作形式主语，to引导的动词不定式短语作逻辑主语；pot-holer，名词，意为"洞穴探险者"；motive，名词，意为"动机，目的"。

句 4 For him, caves have the same peculiar fascination which high mountains have for the climber.

解构：him指pot-holer；peculiar，形容词，意为"特殊的，独特的"；fascination，名词，意为"魅力，魔力"；关系代词which引导的定语从句，修饰限定先行词fascination。

句 5 They arouse instincts which can only be dimly understood.

解构：arouse，动词，意为"引起，激发"；instinct，名词，意为"本能，天性，直觉"；dimly，副词，意为"朦胧地，模糊地"。

句 6 Exploring really deep caves is not a task for the Sunday afternoon rambler.

解构：exploring really deep caves为动名词短语，作主语；rambler，名词，意为"漫步者"。

句 7 Such undertakings require the precise planning and foresight of military operations.

解构：undertaking，名词，意为"（重大或艰巨的）任务，项目"；foresight，名词，意为"预见，远见"；operation，名词，意为"（有组织的）活动，行动"。

句8 It can take as long as eight days to rig up rope ladders and to establish supply bases before a descent can be made into a very deep cave.

解构：it作形式主语，to rig up ... and to establish... 为两个动词不定式短语，是句子的逻辑主语；rig up 意为"装配，搭建"；descent，名词，意为"下降，降落"。

句9 Precautions of this sort are necessary, for it is impossible to foretell the exact nature of the difficulties which will confront the pot-holer.

解构：precaution，名词，意为"预防措施"；for引导原因状语从句，it作形式主语，to foretell为动词不定式短语，作逻辑主语；foretell，动词，意为"预测，预言"；nature，名词，意为"性质，本质"；confront，动词，意为"降临于，使……面对"。

句10 The deepest known cave in the world is the Gouffre Berger near Grenoble.

解构：known为过去分词作形容词定语，意为"已知的，知名的"。

句11 It extends to a depth of 3,723 feet.

解构：extend to意为"延伸至，扩展到"。

句12 This immense chasm has been formed by an underground stream which has tunnelled a course through a flaw in the rocks.

解构：chasm，名词，意为"裂口，深坑，峡谷"；tunnel，动词，意为"开凿，挖掘"；flaw，名词，意为"裂缝，裂纹"。

句13 The entrance to the cave is on a plateau in the Dauphine Alps.

解构：to the cave为介词短语，作定语；plateau，名词，意为"高原"。

句14 As it is only six feet across, it is barely noticeable.

解构：从属连词as引导原因状语从句；across，副词，意为"宽地"；barely，副词，意为"勉强，几乎不"；noticeable，形容词，意为"显而易见的，明显的"。

句15 The cave might never have been discovered had not the entrance been spotted by the distinguished French pot-holer, Berger.

解构：might+完成时，表示原本可能发生而实际却未发生的事情；had not... 为省略if的非真实条件状语从句，使用倒装语序，该条件句为第三类if条件句，表示与过去的事实相反；distinguished，形容词，意为"著名的，卓越的，杰出的"。

句16 Since its discovery, it has become a sort of potholers' Everest.

解构：it指the Gouffre Berger；a sort of意为"一种，有点"；Everest，名词，意为"珠穆朗玛峰"。

句 17 Though a number of descents have been made, much of it still remains to be explored.

解构:though引导让步状语从句;much of it意为"它的大部分"。

句 18 A team of pot-holers recently went down the Gouffre Berger.

解构:a team of意为"一组,一队";go down意为"下降"。

句 19 After entering the narrow gap on the plateau, they climbed down the steep sides of the cave until they came to a narrow corridor.

解构:after entering为分词短语,作时间状语;gap,名词,意为"间隙,裂口";until引导时间状语从句;corridor,名词,意为"走廊"。

句 20 They had to edge their way along this, sometimes wading across shallow streams, or swimming across deep pools.

解构:edge one's way意为"挤过去,侧身而过";sometimes wading ... or swimming across...为两个现在分词短语,作方式状语,修饰edge;wade across意为"蹚过,涉过"。

句 21 Suddenly they came to a waterfall which dropped into an underground lake at the bottom of the cave.

解构:waterfall,名词,意为"瀑布";drop in意为"落进,坠入";underground lake意为"地下湖"。

句 22 They plunged into the lake, and after loading their gear on an inflatable rubber dinghy, let the current carry them to the other side.

解构:plunged与let为并列谓语;插入语and after loading...作时间状语,说明let的时间;plunge,动词,意为"跳进";load,动词,意为"装载";gear,名词,意为"设备";inflatable,形容词,意为"充气的";rubber dinghy意为"橡皮艇";current,名词,意为"水流"。

句 23 To protect themselves from the icy water, they had to wear special rubber suits.

解构:to protect为动词不定式短语,作目的状语;had to体现时态,不能用must。

句 24 At the far end of the lake, they came to huge piles of rubble which had been washed up by the water.

解构:at the far end of意为"在……的远端,在……的那头";a huge pile of意为"一大堆";rubble,名词,意为"碎石,瓦砾";wash up意为"冲刷"。

句 25 In this part of the cave, they could hear an insistent booming sound which they found was caused by a small waterspout shooting down into a pool from the roof of the cave.

解构:insistent,形容词,意为"连续的";booming sound"隆隆声";which ... of the cave定语从句,修饰限定先行词sound;插入语they found进行补充说明;shooting down into为

现在分词短语作定语，修饰 waterspout；waterspout，名词，意为"水柱"。

句 26 Squeezing through a cleft in the rocks, the pot-holers arrived at an enormous cavern, the size of a huge concert hall.

解构：squeezing through 为现在分词短语，作时间状语；squeeze，动词，意为"挤进"；cleft，名词，意为"裂缝"；cavern，名词，意为"大洞穴，大山洞"；the size of a huge concert hall 作 cavern 的同位语，进行补充说明。

句 27 After switching on powerful arc lights, they saw great stalagmites—some of them over forty feet high—rising up like tree-trunks to meet the stalactites suspended from the roof.

解构：switch on 意为"打开，开启"；arc light 意为"弧光灯"；stalagmite，名词，意为"石笋"；插入语 some of them...进一步说明 stalagmites；rising up ... from the roof 为现在分词短语，作宾语 stalagmites 的补足语；to meet the... 为动词不定式短语，作结果状语；suspended from the roof 为过去分词短语，作 stalactites 的定语；tree-trunk 意为"树干"；stalactite，名词，意为"钟乳石"；suspend，动词，意为"悬挂，悬浮"。

句 28 Round about, piles of limestone glistened in all the colours of the rainbow.

解构：round about 意为"周围"，作地点状语；piles of 意为"成堆的"；limestone，名词，意为"石灰岩"；glisten，动词，意为"闪光，闪烁"；in all the colours of the rainbow 为介词短语，作方式状语。

句 29 In the eerie silence of the cavern, the only sound that could be heard was made by water which dripped continuously from the high dome above them.

解构：地点状语 in the eerie silence of the cavern 提至句首表示对其进行强调，并使句子整体更为均衡；that could be heard 定语从句，修饰限定先行词 sound；which dripped ... above them 定语从句，修饰限定先行词 water；eerie，形容词，意为"可怕的，怪异的"；drip，动词，意为"滴下"；dome，名词，意为"圆顶"。

参考译文

洞穴勘探——或洞穴探险——是一项比较新的体育活动，已逐渐被人们了解。寻求独居独处的愿望或寻求意外发现机会的欲望吸引着人们来到地下深处。要想对洞穴探险者的动机做出满意的解释是不可能的。对洞穴探险者来说，洞穴有一种特殊的魅力，就像高山对于登山者有特殊的魅力一样。为什么洞穴能引发人的那种探险本能，人们对此只能有一种模模糊糊的认识。

探测非常深的洞穴不是那些在星期日下午漫步的人所能胜任的。这种活动需要有军事行动般的周密部署和预见能力。有时需要花费整整 8 天时间来搭起绳梯，建立供应基地，然后才能下到一个很深的洞穴里。做出这样的准备是必要的，因为人们无法预见到洞穴探险者究竟会遇到什么性质的困难。世界上最深的洞穴是格里诺布尔附近的高弗·伯杰洞，深达3723英尺。这个深邃的洞穴是由一条地下暗泉冲刷岩石中的缝隙并使之慢慢变大而形成的。此洞的洞口在丹芬阿尔卑斯山的高原上，仅6英尺宽，很难被人发现。若不是法国著名洞穴探险家伯杰由于偶然的机会发现了这个洞口的话，这个洞也许永远不会为人所知。自从被发现以后，这个洞成了洞穴探险者心中的"珠穆朗玛峰"，人们多次进入洞内探险，但至今尚有不少东西有待勘探。

最近，一个洞穴探险队下到了高弗·伯杰洞里。他们从高原上的窄缝进去，顺着笔直陡峭的洞壁往下爬，来到了一条狭窄的走廊上。他们不得不侧着身子往前走，有时蹚过浅溪，有时游过深潭。突然，他们来到一道瀑布前，那瀑布奔泻而下，注入洞底一处地下湖里。他们跳入湖中，把各种器具装上一只充气橡皮艇，听任水流将他们带往对岸。湖水冰冷刺骨，他们必须穿上一种特制的橡皮服以保护自己。在湖的尽头，他们见到一大堆一大堆由湖水冲刷上岸的碎石。在这儿，他们可以听见一种连续不断的轰鸣声。后来他们发现这是由山洞顶部的一个小孔里喷出的水柱跌落到水潭中时发出的声音。洞穴探险者从岩石缝里挤过去，来到一个巨大的洞里，其大小相当于一个音乐厅。他们打开强力弧光灯，看见一株株巨大的石笋，有的高达40英尺，像树干似的向上长着，与洞顶悬挂下来的钟乳石相接。周围是一堆堆石灰石，像彩虹一样闪闪发光。洞里有一种可怕的寂静，唯一可以听见的声响是高高的圆顶上不间断地滴水的滴答声。

语篇进阶 **9**

Do it yourself
自己动手

So great is our passion for doing things for ourselves, that we are becoming increasingly less dependent on specialized labour. No one can plead ignorance of a subject any longer, for there are countless do-it-yourself publications. Armed with the right tools and materials, newlyweds gaily embark on the task of decorating their own homes. Men, particularly, spend hours of their leisure time installing their own fireplaces, laying out their own gardens; building garages and making furniture. Some really keen enthusiasts go so far as to build their own computers. Shops cater for the do-it-yourself craze not only by running special advisory services for novices, but by offering consumers bits and pieces which they can assemble at home. Such things provide an excellent outlet for pent up creative energy, but unfortunately not all of us are born handymen.

Some wives tend to believe that their husbands are infinitely resourceful and can fix anything. Even men who can hardly drive a nail in straight are supposed to be born electricians, carpenters, plumbers and mechanics. When lights fuse, furniture gets rickety, pipes get clogged, or vacuum cleaners fail to operate, some women assume that their husbands will somehow put things right. The worst thing about the do-it-yourself game is that sometimes even men live under the delusion that they can do anything, even when they have repeatedly been proved wrong. It is a question of pride as much as anything else.

Last spring my wife suggested that I call in a man to look at our lawn mower. It had broken down the previous summer, and though I promised to repair it, I had never got round to it. I would not hear of the suggestion and said that I would fix it myself. One Saturday afternoon, I hauled the machine into the garden and had a close look at it. As far as I could see, it needed only a minor adjustment: a turn of a screw here, a little tightening up there, a drop of oil and it would be as good as new. Inevitably the repair job was not quite so simple. The mower firmly refused to mow, so I decided to dismantle it. The garden was soon littered with chunks of metal which had once made up a lawn mower. But I was extremely pleased with myself. I had traced the cause of the trouble. One of the links in the chain that drives the wheels had snapped. After buying a new chain I was faced with the insurmountable task of putting the confusing jigsaw puzzle together again. I was not surprised to find that the machine still refused to work after I had reassembled it, for the simple reason that I was left with several curiously shaped bits of metal which did not seem to fit anywhere. I gave up in despair. The weeks passed and the grass grew. When my wife nagged me to do something about it, I told her that either I would have to buy a new mower or let the grass grow. Needless to say our house is now surrounded by a jungle. Buried somewhere in deep grass there is a rusting lawn mower which I have promised to repair one day.

句型解构

句 1 So great is our passion for doing things for ourselves, that we are becoming increasingly less dependent on specialized labour.

解构:副词 so 置于句首时,通常采用倒装结构,句中对 great 进行强调,正常语序为 Our passion for doing things for ourselves is so great that we...;so ... that... 引导结果状语从句;be/become dependent on 意为"依赖,依靠";specialized labour 意为"专业化劳动力,专业化分工"。

句 2 No one can plead ignorance of a subject any longer, for there are countless do-it-yourself publications.

解构:plead ignorance of 意为"以不知道……而辩解";for 引导原因状语从句;do-it-yourself 作定语,意为"自己动手的";publication,名词,意为"出版物"。

句 3 Armed with the right tools and materials, newlyweds gaily embark on the task of decorating their own homes.

解构:armed with 为过去分词短语,作方式状语,修饰 embark;newlywed,名词,意为"新婚夫妇";gaily,副词,意为"快乐地,轻松地";embark on 意为"开始,着手,从事"。

句 4 Men, particularly, spend hours of their leisure time installing their own fireplaces, laying out their own gardens; building garages and making furniture.

解构:install,动词,意为"安装";fireplace,名词,意为"壁炉";lay out 意为"布置";动名词 installing/laying out/building/making 均作 spend 的宾语。

句 5 Some really keen enthusiasts go so far as to build their own computers.

解构:keen,形容词,意为"热心的,热衷的";enthusiast,名词,意为"爱好者,狂热者";go so far as to 意为"甚至,竟然"。

句 6 Shops cater for the do-it-yourself craze not only by running special advisory services for novices, but by offering consumers bits and pieces which they can assemble at home.

解构：cater for意为"迎合，满足"；craze，名词，意为"狂热"；by running special advisory与by offering consumers均作方式状语，修饰cater for；run，动词，意为"提供，开设（服务、课程）"；advisory，形容词，意为"咨询的"；novice，名词，意为"初学者，新手"；which引导定语从句，修饰限定先行词bits and pieces；bits and pieces意为"零零碎碎，零件"；assemble，动词，意为"组装，装配"。

句 7 Such things provide an excellent outlet for pent up creative energy, but unfortunately not all of us are born handymen.

解构：outlet，名词，意为"出路，表现机会"；pent up意为"被压抑的，被抑制的"；handyman，名词，意为"手巧的人"。

句 8 Some wives tend to believe that their husbands are infinitely resourceful and can fix anything.

解构：tend to意为"趋向，易于"；that引导的宾语从句，作believe的宾语；infinitely，副词，意为"极其，无比"，resourceful，形容词，意为"足智多谋的，机智的"。

句 9 Even men who can hardly drive a nail in straight are supposed to be born electricians, carpenters, plumbers and mechanics.

解构：who引导定语从句，修饰限定men；drive in意为"钉入"；straight，副词，意为"笔直地，径直地"；electrician，名词，意为"电工"；carpenter，名词，意为"木匠"；plumber，名词，意为"水管工"；mechanic，名词，意为"机械师"。

句 10 When lights fuse, furniture gets rickety, pipes get clogged, or vacuum cleaners fail to operate, some women assume that their husbands will somehow put things right.

解构：fuse，动词，意为"（保险丝）熔断"；rickety，形容词，意为"摇晃的，要散架的"；clogged，形容词，意为"阻塞的，堵住的"；vacuum cleaner意为"吸尘器"；assume，动词，意为"认为，设想"。

句 11 The worst thing about the do-it-yourself game is that sometimes even men live under the delusion that they can do anything, even when they have repeatedly been proved wrong.

解构："...is that sometimes..."中的that引导表语从句；live under a/the delusion意为"存有幻想，抱有错误想法"；"...under the delusion that..."中的that引导同位语从句，补充说明delusion的内容。

句12 It is a question of pride as much as anything else.

解构：as much as anything else意为"跟别的一样重要,非常重要的",作定语,修饰pride。

句13 Last spring my wife suggested that I call in a man to look at our lawn mower.

解构：suggested后的宾语从句中应使用虚拟语气,call前面省略了should;call in意为"请……来,召来";look at意为"检查";lawn mower意为"割草机"。

句14 It had broken down the previous summer, and though I promised to repair it, I had never got round to it.

解构：though I promised to repair it为让步状语从句;get round to意为"抽出时间来做……,找时间做……"。

句15 I would not hear of the suggestion and said that I would fix it myself.

解构：情态动词would表意愿,would not意为"不愿意";hear of意为"听从";连词and表示结果,意为"于是……"。

句16 One Saturday afternoon, I hauled the machine into the garden and had a close look at it.

解构：haul意为"(用力)拖,拉";have a close look at意为"仔细检查"。

句17 As far as I could see, it needed only a minor adjustment: a turn of a screw here, a little tightening up there, a drop of oil and it would be as good as new.

解构：minor,形容词,意为"较小的,轻微的";adjustment,名词,意为"调整";a turn of.../a little tightening.../a drop of...均作adjustment的同位语,解释说明adjustment所包含的具体内容;as good as可理解为副词性质的固定短语,相当于almost/actually。

句18 Inevitably the repair job was not quite so simple.

解构：inevitably,副词,意为"不可避免地,必然地";repair意为"修理,修复",名词作定语。

句19 The mower firmly refused to mow, so I decided to dismantle it.

解构：the mower firmly refused为拟人用法,更显生动;dismantle,动词,意为"拆开,拆卸"。

句20 The garden was soon littered with chunks of metal which had once made up a lawn mower.

解构：be littered with意为"布满,被……盖满";chunk,名词,意为"大块"。

句21 But I was extremely pleased with myself. I had traced the cause of the trouble.

解构：be pleased with意为"对……感到高兴/满意";trace,动词,意为"找到,追溯"。

句22 One of the links in the chain that drives the wheels had snapped.

解构:link,名词,意为"节,环节";chain,名词,意为"链条";that drives the wheels为定语从句,其中that作从句的主语;drive,动词,意为"驱动";snap,动词,意为"断裂"。

句23 After buying a new chain I was faced with the insurmountable task of putting the confusing jigsaw puzzle together again.

解构:be faced with意为"面临,面对";insurmountable,形容词,意为"无法克服的,不可逾越的";jigsaw puzzle,意为"拼图游戏"。

句24 I was not surprised to find that the machine still refused to work after I had reassembled it, for the simple reason that I was left with several curiously shaped bits of metal which did not seem to fit anywhere.

解构:to find that ... work为动词不定式短语,作原因状语,解释说明not surprised的原因;从属连词after引导时间状语从句,说明I was not surprised的时间;从属连词for引导原因状语从句;从属连词that引导同位语从句,补充说明reason的内容;关系代词which引导定语从句,修饰限定bits of metal;leave with意为"留给……"。

句25 I gave up in despair. The weeks passed and the grass grew.

解构:in despair为介词短语,作状语,意为"失望地,绝望地";and并列两个主谓结构的简单句。

句26 When my wife nagged me to do something about it, I told her that either I would have to buy a new mower or let the grass grow.

解构:nag,动词,意为"不断唠叨";either ... or...意为"要么……要么……"。

句27 Needless to say our house is now surrounded by a jungle.

解构:needless to say意为"不用说"。

句28 Buried somewhere in deep grass there is a rusting lawn mower which I have promised to repair one day.

解构:buried somewhere in deep grass为过去分词短语,作定语,修饰限定先行词lawn mower,提至句首一可起到强调作用,二可避免与句末which引导的定语从句相连而造成歧义,三可对句子结构起到平衡作用。

参考译文

现在我们对自己动手做事的热情很高,结果对专业工人的依赖越来越少了。由于教人自己动手做事的书报杂志不计其数,所以没有人能再说对某事一无所知。新婚夫妇找来合适的工具和材料,喜气洋洋地开始布置新房。特别是男人,常利用空闲时间安装壁炉、布置花园、建造车库、制作家具。有些热衷于自己动手的人甚至自己组装电脑。为了满足"自己动手热"的需要，商店不仅为初学者提供专门的咨询服务，而且为顾客准备了各种零件，供他们买回家去安装。这些东西为人们潜在的创造力提供了一个绝妙的用武之地。但遗憾的是，我们并非人人都是天生的能工巧匠。

妻子常常认为她们的丈夫无比聪明能干，甚至那些连一枚钉子都钉不直的男人都被认为是天生的电工、木匠、水管工和机械师。每当电灯保险丝被烧断、家具榫头松动、管道堵塞、吸尘器出故障时，有些妻子认为丈夫总有办法。自己动手的例子中最糟糕的是，有时甚至于男人尽管接连失败却还误以为自己什么都行，原因就是要面子。

去年春天，妻子让我请人检查一下我家的割草机。那台割草机去年夏天就坏了，尽管我答应修，但一直没抽出时间，我不愿听妻子的建议，说我自己会修。一个星期六的下午，我把割草机拉到了花园里，仔细检查了一番。在我看来，只需稍加调整即可。这儿紧紧螺丝，那儿固定一下，再加几滴油，就会像新的一样了。事实上，修理工作远不是那么简单。修完后割草机还是纹丝不动。于是，我决定把它拆开。一会儿工夫，割草机便被拆成一个个金属零件，乱七八糟地堆在花园里。但我非常高兴，因为我找到了毛病所在。驱动轮子的链条断了一节。我买来一根新链条后，面临的就是如何把这些令人眼花缭乱的拼板重新组装起来。等我装完后，那台割草机仍然一动不动，对此我倒并不感到吃惊，原因很简单，因为还剩下几个形状奇特的零件似乎哪里也装不上去。我无可奈何，只好罢休。几个星期过去了，草长了起来。妻子喋喋不休地让我想点办法。我告诉她，要么买一台新割草机，要么让草长下去。不用说，我家现在已被丛林包围。深草丛中的某个地方有一台正在生锈的割草机，那就是我曾答应某日要修理的割草机。

语篇进阶 *10*

New Year resolutions
新年的决心

The New Year is a time for resolutions. Mentally, at least, most of us could compile formidable lists of "dos" and "don'ts". The same old favorites recur year in year out with monotonous regularity. We resolve to get up earlier each morning, eat less, find more time to play with the children, do a thousand and one jobs about the house, be nice to people we don't like, drive carefully, and take the dog for a walk every day. Past experience has taught us that certain accomplishments are beyond attainment. Most of us fail in our efforts at self-improvement because our schemes are too ambitious and we never have time to carry them out. We also make the fundamental error of announcing our resolutions to everybody so that we look even more foolish when we slip back into our bad old ways. Aware of these pitfalls, this year I attempted to keep my resolutions to myself. I limited myself to two modest ambitions: to do physical exercises every morning and to read more of an evening. An all-night party on New Year's Eve provided me with a good excuse for not carrying out either of these new resolutions on the first day of the year, but on the second, I applied myself assiduously to the task.

The daily exercises lasted only eleven minutes and I proposed to do them early in the morning before anyone had got up. The self-discipline required to drag myself out of bed eleven minutes earlier than usual was considerable. Nevertheless, I managed to creep down into the living room for two days before anyone found me out. After jumping about on the carpet and twisting the human frame into uncomfortable positions, I sat down at the breakfast table in an exhausted condition. It was this that betrayed me. The next morning the whole family trooped in to watch the performance. That was really unsettling, but I fended off the taunts and jibes of the family good-humouredly and soon everybody got used to the idea. However, my enthusiasm waned. The time I spent at exercises gradually diminished. Little by little the eleven minutes fell to zero. By January 10th, I was back to where I had started from. I argued that if I spent less time exhausting myself at exercises in the morning, I would keep my mind fresh for reading when I got home form work. Resisting the hypnotizing effect of television, I sat in my room for a few evenings with my eyes glued to a book. One night, however, feeling cold and lonely, I went downstairs and sat in front of the television pretending to read. That proved to be my undoing, for I soon got back to my old bad habit of dozing off in front of the screen. I still haven't given up my resolution to do more reading. In fact, I have just bought a book entitled *How to Read a Thousand Words a Minute*. Perhaps it will solve my problem, but I just haven't had time to read it!

句型解构

句1 The New Year is a time for resolutions.

解构：resolution，名词，意为"决心，决定"。

句2 Mentally, at least, most of us could compile formidable lists of "dos" and "don'ts".

解构：mentally，副词，意为"精神上，心理上，思想上"；compile，动词，意为"编制，编辑"；formidable，形容词，意为"令人敬畏的，艰难的"；"dos" and "don'ts"意为"行为准则，守则"，表示应做的事情和不应做的事情。

句3 The same old favorites recur year in year out with monotonous regularity.

解构：favorite，名词，意为"喜爱的事"；recur，动词，意为"循环，反复"；year in year out意为"年复一年地，不断地"，作时间状语，修饰recur；with monotonous regularity作方式状语，其中monotonous为形容词，意为"单调的，千篇一律的"，regularity为名词，意为"规律性"。

句4 We resolve to get up earlier each morning, eat less, find more time to play with the children, do a thousand and one jobs about the house, be nice to people we don't like, drive carefully, and take the dog for a walk every day.

解构：resolve to意为"决心……"；a thousand and one意为"许许多多，无数的"。

句5 Past experience has taught us that certain accomplishments are beyond attainment.

解构：that引导的宾语从句，作双宾语动词taught的直接宾语；certain，形容词，意为"某些，某种"；accomplishment，名词，意为"成就"；beyond attainment意为"做不到的，无法实现的"。

句6 Most of us fail in our efforts at self-improvement because our schemes are too ambitious and we never have time to carry them out.

解构：fail in意为"在……上失败"；self-improvement，名词，意为"自我完善，自我提升"；because引导原因状语从句；scheme，名词，意为"计划，方案"；ambitious，形容词，意为"雄心勃勃的，有野心的"；carry out意为"执行，实行，贯彻"。

句7 We also make the fundamental error of announcing our resolutions to everybody so that we look even more foolish when we slip back into our bad old ways.

解构：fundamental，形容词，意为"基本的，根本的"；announce ... to... 意为"向……宣布，通知某人"；so that引导结果状语从句；slip back into意为"重新陷入，滑回到"。

句 8 Aware of these pitfalls, this year I attempted to keep my resolutions to myself.

解构：aware of 为形容词短语，一作结果状语，即"So I'm aware of these pitfalls..."，二作原因状语，即"As I'm aware of these pitfalls..."；pitfall，名词，意为"陷阱，隐患"；attempt to意为"尝试，试图"；keep ... to oneself意为"保守秘密"。

句 9 I limited myself to two modest ambitions: to do physical exercises every morning and to read more of an evening.

解构：limit ... to... 意为"把……限制在……"；modest，形容词，意为"适度的"；of an evening/in the evenings意为"每逢晚上，往往在晚上"。

句 10 An all-night party on New Year's Eve provided me with a good excuse for not carrying out either of these new resolutions on the first day of the year, but on the second, I applied myself assiduously to the task.

解构：provide with意为"提供，供给"；an excuse for... 意为"……的理由/借口"；but on the second后面省略day of the year；apply oneself to意为"致力于，专心从事"；assiduously，副词，意为"刻苦地，认真地"。

句 11 The daily exercises lasted only eleven minutes and I proposed to do them early in the morning before anyone had got up.

解构：daily exercises意为"日常锻炼，日常练习"；propose to意为"打算"。

句 12 The self-discipline required to drag myself out of bed eleven minutes earlier than usual was considerable.

解构：required to ... than usual为过去分词短语，作定语；considerable，形容词，意为"相当大的"。

句 13 Nevertheless, I managed to creep down into the living room for two days before anyone found me out.

解构：nevertheless，副词，意为"不过，然而"；creep，动词，意为"缓慢移动，爬行"。

句 14 After jumping about on the carpet and twisting the human frame into uncomfortable positions, I sat down at the breakfast table in an exhausted condition.

解构：jump about意为"跳来跳去"，twist ... into... 意为"把……扭曲成……"；human frame意为"身躯"。

句 15 It was this that betrayed me.

解构：强调句，强调代词this，this指上句中的I sat down at ... in an exhausted condition。

句 16 The next morning the whole family trooped in to watch the performance.

解构:troop in 意为"结队而入";to watch the performance 为动词不定式短语,作目的状语。

句 17 That was really unsettling, but I fended off the taunts and jibes of the family good-humouredly and soon everybody got used to the idea.

解构:unsettling,形容词,意为"令人不安的";fend off 意为"避开";taunt,名词,意为"嘲笑,讥讽";jibe,名词,意为"嘲讽,挖苦";good-humouredly,副词,意为"脾气好地,和气地",作方式状语;get used to+名词/动名词,意为"习惯于……"。

句 18 However, my enthusiasm waned.

解构:enthusiasm,名词,意为"热情,热忱";wane,动词,意为"衰弱,变小,消逝"。

句 19 The time I spent at exercises gradually diminished.

解构:I spent at exercises 为定语从句,修饰 time;diminish,动词,意为"减少,缩减"。

句 20 Little by little the eleven minutes fell to zero.

解构:Little by little 意为"渐渐地,逐步地";fall to 意为"降至,成为"。

句 21 By January 10th, I was back to where I had started from.

解构:where I had started from 从句作 to 的宾语。

句 22 I argued that if I spent less time exhausting myself at exercises in the morning, I would keep my mind fresh for reading when I got home form work.

解构:that ... from work 为宾语从句,作 argued 的宾语;keep one's mind fresh 意为"保持头脑清醒"。

句 23 Resisting the hypnotizing effect of television, I sat in my room for a few evenings with my eyes glued to a book.

解构:resisting the... 为现在分词短语,作目的状语;with my eyes glued to a book 为独立主格结构,作方式状语,my eyes 作逻辑主语,glued to a book 为过去分词短语,作逻辑谓语;hypnotize,动词,意为"催眠,使恍惚";glue,动词,意为"注视,专注于"。

句 24 One night, however, feeling cold and lonely, I went downstairs and sat in front of the television pretending to read.

解构:feeling cold and lonely 为现在分词短语,作原因状语;pretending to read 为现在分词短语,作状语,表示伴随状态。

句 25 That proved to be my undoing, for I soon got back to my old bad habit of dozing off in front of the screen.

解构:undoing,名词,意为"祸根,毁灭的原因";for 引导原因状语从句;get back to 意为

"回到，重返"；doze off意为"打瞌睡，困倦"。

句26 I still haven't given up my resolution to do more reading.

解构：to do more reading为介词短语，作resolution的定语。

句27 In fact, I have just bought a book entitled *How to Read a Thousand Words a Minute*.

解构：entitled为过去分词短语，作定语，修饰a book；entitle，动词，意为"给……提名，称呼"。

句28 Perhaps it will solve my problem, but I just haven't had time to read it!

解构：haven't had为现在完成时，强调结果；have time to...意为"有时间去……"。

参考译文

新年是下决心的时候，至少在大多数人的心里会编排出一份"应做什么"和"不应做什么"的令人生畏的单子。相同的决心以单调的规律年复一年地出现。我们决心每天早晨起得早些；吃得少些；多花点时间与孩子们一起做游戏；做大量的家务；对不喜欢的人友善一些；小心驾车；每天都要带着狗散步；等等。以往的经验告诉我们有些事是办不到的。我们大多数人想自我完善却遭到失败，这是因为我们的规划过于宏大，而又根本没有时间去实施。我们还犯有一个根本性的错误，即把我们的决心向大家宣布。这样一旦滑回到那些坏的老习惯上去，我们在别人的眼里会显得更加难堪。我深知这些问题，于是，今年我对自己的计划要严加保密，只给自己定下两项适中的任务：每天早上锻炼身体，每天晚上多看点书。新年前夕举办的一次通宵晚会，使我理直气壮地在新年头一天免去了这两项任务。不过，新年第二天，我全力以赴地照着去做了。

早锻炼一共只有11分钟，我打算在别人起床之前进行。这就要求我比平日早11分钟把自己从床上拽起来，这种自我约束是很艰苦的。不过开头两天我还是成功地蹑手蹑脚地来到楼下起居室，没被人发现。我在地毯上跳过来蹦过去，扭曲身子，摆出各种姿势，弄得浑身不舒服，然后坐到桌边吃早饭，一副筋疲力尽的样子。正是这副模样泄露了我的秘密。第二天早晨全家人结队来到起居室看我表演。这真叫人不好意思，但我心平气和地顶住了全家人的嘲笑和奚落。不久，大家对我习以为常了，而这时我的热情却减退了。我花在锻炼上的时间逐渐减少，慢慢地从11分钟减到了零。到了1月10日，我恢复了原来的作息时间。我辩解说，早晨少耗费精力锻炼，晚上下班回家看书时头脑更清醒些。有几天晚上，我极力摆脱了电视的诱惑，坐在自己房间里，两眼盯在书上。可是，有一天夜里，我感到又冷又孤单，便来到楼下坐在电视机前假装看书。这下我可完了，因为不一会儿，我就恢复了以前的坏习惯，在屏幕前打起瞌睡来。但我还没有放弃多看些书的决心。事实上，我刚买来一本叫《一分钟读一千字的诀窍》的书。也许这本书能解决我的问题，但我一直还没时间去看这本书！